Transmission of Financial Crises and Contagion

Finance and the Economy

A CERF Series edited by John Eatwell

The Cambridge Endowment for Research in Finance (CERF) was founded in 2001 as an independent resource at the University of Cambridge. It is dedicated to developing an enhanced understanding of the evolution and behaviour of financial markets and institutions, notably in their role as major determinants of economic behaviour and performance. CERF promotes theoretical, quantitative and historical studies, crossing conventional disciplinary boundaries to bring together research groups of economists, mathematicians, lawyers, historians, computer scientists and market practitioners. Particular attention is paid to the analysis of the impact of financial market activity on the formulation of public policy. As well as individual research projects, CERF funds *Cambridge Finance*, the organisation that brings together researchers in finance from all departments of Cambridge University. The CERF series of publications on *Finance and the Economy* embodies new research in these areas.

Global Governance of Financial Systems: The International Regulation of Systemic Risk
Edited by Kern Alexander, Rahul Dhumale, and John Eatwell

Identifying International Financial Contagion: Progress and Challenges
Edited by Mardi Dungey and Demosthenes N. Tambakis

Transmission of Financial Crises and Contagion: A Latent Factor Approach
Coauthored by Mardi Dungey, Renée A. Fry,
Brenda González-Hermosillo, and Vance L. Martin

Transmission of Financial Crises and Contagion

A Latent Factor Approach

Mardi Dungey, Renée A. Fry,
Brenda González-Hermosillo, and
Vance L. Martin

OXFORD
UNIVERSITY PRESS

OXFORD
UNIVERSITY PRESS

Oxford University Press, Inc., publishes works that further
Oxford University's objective of excellence
in research, scholarship, and education.

Oxford   New York
Auckland   Cape Town   Dar es Salaam   Hong Kong   Karachi
Kuala Lumpur   Madrid   Melbourne   Mexico City   Nairobi
New Delhi   Shanghai   Taipei   Toronto

With offices in
Argentina   Austria   Brazil   Chile   Czech Republic   France   Greece
Guatemala   Hungary   Italy   Japan   Poland   Portugal   Singapore
South Korea   Switzerland   Thailand   Turkey   Ukraine   Vietnam

Copyright © 2011 by Oxford University Press

Published by Oxford University Press, Inc.
198 Madison Avenue, New York, New York 10016
www.oup.com

Library of Congress Cataloging-in-Publication Data

Transmission of financial crises and contagion : a latent factor approach/
Mardi Dungey . . . [et al.].
    p. cm.
Includes bibliographical references and index.
ISBN 978-0-19-973983-7 (cloth : alk. paper) 1. Financial crises—Mathematical
models. 2. International finance—Mathematical models. 3. Transmission
mechanism (Monetary policy) I. Dungey, Mardi.
HB3722.T73 2010
332'.042015915—dc22

112009051238

9 8 7 6 5 4 3 2 1

Printed in the United States of America
on acid-free paper

Contents

Preface

Contagion in financial markets is a general term that is widely used in academic research, policy debates, and the media to represent the spread of shocks through asset markets within countries and across national borders during times of financial crises. Contagion as a description of financial crises, was first introduced during the Asian financial crisis of 1997–98, beginning with the large depreciation of the Thai bhat on July 2, 1997. The term was subsequently used to explain the spread of shocks during other financial crises such as the Russian bond default in 1998, the collapse of Long Term Capital Management (LTCM) in September 1998, the crisis in Brazilian asset markets in early 1999, the dot-com bust/correction in 2000, the Argentinian crisis from 2001 to 2005, and more recently the global financial crisis that began with the U.S. subprime mortgage and credit crisis stemming from mid-2007.

Despite the widespread use of contagion to describe the transmission of shocks, much of the earlier empirical work lacked a coherent framework in which to estimate and test the presence of contagion. Part of the problem stemmed from the difficulty in measuring contagion per se, as the presence of contagion in contributing to increases in asset market volatility during financial crises was always inferred and never directly measured. The approach adopted by the authors in this collection of papers is to use a modelling framework to identify and to test for contagion for various markets and episodes in times of stress. A common underlying theme of the modelling framework is the use of latent factors to capture many of the linkages that connect asset markets both nationally and internationally during financial crises.

The use of latent factors provides a useful and flexible way to quantify both the size and the significance of contagion in affecting volatility in times of financial crises. The flexibility of the approach is highlighted in Chapter 2 where the modelling framework is used to summarize many of the existing empirical modelling techniques commonly adopted to study contagion. The importance of the framework is demonstrated in Chapter 3, where it is used to understand the role of contagion in transmitting shocks in international bond markets during the Russian and LTCM crises of 1998, and in Chapter 4, where the focus is on studying the effects of the Russian bond default on international equity markets. A broader range of financial crises is considered in Chapter 5, where various crises are compared and identified for potential common linkages, beginning with the Russian crisis and ending with the recent U.S. subprime crisis. This chapter is cowritten with Chrismin Tang, and sample Gauss code and data for the chapter are available at http://www.dungey.bigpondhosting.com. Having established that contagion exists but varies in importance across crises and financial markets, in Chapter 6 the emphasis turns to modelling the time-varying contribution of contagion effects in emerging markets via a model of global risk. This shows that most of the time contagion effects are dominated by other components of risk in markets. The overall policy conclusions outlined in Chapter 7 include the result that while there is definite evidence for significant and sometimes substantial contagion effects in crises, the variation in its relative contribution means that it would be a mistake to base financial market reforms solely on evidence of the existence of contagion channels.

Acknowledgments

A number of people have been important at various stages in providing comments on the chapters, including Monica Billio, Hans Blommestein, Andrea Cipollini, David Cook, Roger Craine, John Creedy, Jon Danielsson, Amil Dasgupta, Jakob de Haan, Jurgen Doornik, Jerry Dwyer, Barry Eichengreen, Sylvester Eijssinger, Robert Eisenbeis, Carlo Favero, Thomas Flavin, Prasanna Gai, Charles Goodhart, Don Harding, Lex Hoogduin, Harry Huizinga, Leslie Hull, Takatoshi Ito, Jose Lopez, Graciela Kaminsky, Laura Kodres, Jenny Ligthart, Paul Masson, Minhael McAleet, Marcus Miller, Adrian Pagan, Hashem Pesaran, Andreas Pick, Olwen Renowden, Roberto Rigobon, Hyun Shin, Demosthenes Tambakis, Susan Thorp, Reza Vaez-Zadeh, David Vines, and Mike Wickens. Special thanks go to the International Monetary Fund where much of the work was initiated and written. The authors have also benefitted from the suggestions of anonymous referees and comments received at various seminars where earlier versions of the chapters were presented.

Dungey and Martin also acknowledge funding from ARC Large Grant A00001350, while Fry acknowledges funding from ARC grant DP0556371. We are grateful to the editors and publishers for permission to reprint the material in Chapters 2 to 4. Chapter 2 is reprinted from *Quantitative Finance*, Volume 5, Edition 1, pp. 9–24, 2005, as "Empirical Modelling of Contagion: A Review of Methodologies" with permission from Taylor & Francis Group, http://www.informaworld.com. Chapter 3 is reprinted from the *Journal of Financial Stability*, Volume 2(1), pp. 1–27, 2006, "Contagion in International Bond Markets During the Russian and LTCM crises" with permission from Elsevier. Chapter 4 is reprinted from *Journal of North American Economics and Finance*, 18 (2), pp. 155–174, 2007, as "Shocks and Systemic Influences: Contagion in Global Equity Markets In 1998" with permission from Elsevier. Finally, Chapters 5 and 6 have been available in previous versions as working papers from the Centre for Applied Macroeconomic Analysis and the International Monetary Fund, respectively.

Contributors

Mardi Dungey is professor of economics and finance at the University of Tasmania senior research associate at the Centre for Financial Analysis and Policy, University of Cambridge, and adjunct professor at the Centre for Macroeconomic Analysis at the Australian National University. Her research encompasses open economy macroeconomics, financial crises, and high-frequency financial econometrics.

Renée Fry is a fellow at the Centre for Applied Macroeconomic Analysis at the Australian National University, where she is also the co-director of the Finance and Macroeconomy program. She is a research associate at the Centre for Financial Analysis and Policy, University of Cambridge, and has worked extensively on models of financial market contagion.

Brenda González-Hermosillo is deputy division chief of the Global Financial Stability Division at the International Monetary Fund and visiting professor at the Massachusetts Institute of Technology Sloan School of Management. She has presented research and directed several analytical chapters of the IMF *Global Financial Stability Report*, and has contributed to several G20 initiatives on global financial stability. She has also published on areas related to global financial market risks, financial crises and early warning indicators, contagion, interbank markets, and investors' risk appetite.

Vance Martin is a professor of econometrics at the University of Melbourne, whose research interests include contagion and financial econometrics.

Chrismin Tang is a lecturer at the La Trobe University and a research associate of the Centre for Applied Macroeconomic Analysis at the Australian National University. She previously worked as an economist in the Financial Surveillance Division at the Monetary Authority of Singapore. Her research interests are in areas relating to financial market contagion, risk assessment, and systemic stability.

1

Introduction

Linkages between asset markets both internationally and domestically never receive as much attention as during a financial market crisis. As regulators, investors, and policy-makers attempt to piece together the likely path of a crisis to determine optimal policy, investment and financial responses, understanding the nature of links between markets is fundamental. Of course, asset markets are linked in non-crisis times too. Linkages may be economic and based on trade and finance, or institutional, such as banking networks. These linkages mean that if one country or market is affected by a crisis, then others will be affected also, potentially adversely. These effects are expected, based on historical knowledge of existing relationships between asset markets.

In a crisis period, it often appears that linkages between markets arise that are not present during periods of tranquility, or in terms of networks, linkages that exist in periods of tranquility are broken or magnified. It is these changes in the linkages, or commensurately changes in the transmission of shocks across markets during a crisis period compared with a non-crisis period, that are known as contagion. The recent use of the term contagion is represented as "pure" contagion in the earlier literature, as distinct from the effects of linkages present in all periods, denoted as spillovers or sometimes "fundamentals-based" contagion.

This book draws together a series of papers examining the role of contagion during financial market crises, with applications to various crises of the last decade. The motivation for the book is a desire to understand how contagion can be measured and how those measures may be usefully applied to inform policy makers and investors. The global financial crisis, originating in the U.S. subprime mortgage market and subsequently spreading throughout the world, illustrates the importance of better understanding contagion. The crises of the last decade have raised many issues that need to be addressed including: (i) forming policies on the architecture of the international financial system; (ii) understanding the role of institutions in transmitting crises; (iii) developing country specific policies to mitigate crisis transmission by determining how previously unrelated asset markets are suddenly related; and (iv) determining globally coordinated policy to mitigate crisis transmission. Analyzing the linkages existing in a crisis period is important in informing these issues.

To facilitate research in the area of contagion modelling and its application to studying the transmission mechanisms of financial crises, some of the data and computer codes used to generate the empirical results in the book are available from the following website:

http://www.dungey.bigpondhosting.com

Chapter 2 begins by examining the development of empirical tests of contagion that focus on the detection of contagion compared with linkages during a non-crisis period. The chapter reviews a number of alternative methods proposed to test for the presence of contagion, and shows how they are related to each other in a unified framework based on the latent factor class of models (Dungey and Martin 2007, Corsetti, Pericoli, and Sbracia 2001, 2005, and Bekaert, Harvey, and Ng 2005). The latent factor approach has the advantage of quantifying the effects of contagion, as well as providing a test for its existence, unlike many alternatively available tests. The chapter compares the latent factor approach with the correlation analysis approach of Forbes and Rigobon (2002), the VAR approach of Favero and Giavazzi (2002), the probability model of Eichengreen, Rose, and Wyplosz (1995, 1996) and the co-exceedance approach of Bae, Karolyi, and Stulz (2003).

The results of Chapter 2 show that the differences in the empirical definitions used to test for contagion are minor and under certain conditions are even equivalent. The differences arise from the amount of information in the data used to detect contagion. Interpreting the approaches in this way provides a natural ordering of models across the information spectrum with some models representing full information methods and others representing partial information methods. Chapter 2 also presents a number of extensions to the suite of tests of contagion that are able to accommodate multivariate testing, endogeneity issues and structural breaks. The empirical results of the alternative tests are compared using data for the Asian equity markets during the speculative attack on the Hong Kong currency in October 1997. The results show that the Forbes and Rigobon (2002) adjusted correlation test is a conservative test, whereas the contagion test of Favero and Giavazzi (2002) tends to reject the null hypothesis of no contagion too easily. The remaining tests investigated fall between these two extremes. The latent factor model framework underlying the tests examined in Chapter 2 forms the basis of the models examined in Chapters 3 to 5.

Chapters 3 and 4 analyze linkages across single asset markets during the crisis surrounding the suspension of payment on debt of the Russian government and the near collapse of the U.S.-based hedge fund Long Term Capital Management (LTCM) in August–September 1998. The Russian crisis began on August 17, 1998, with the widening of the trading band around the rouble, and a 90-day moratorium on the repayment of private external debt. The Russian government's announced plan to restructure official debt obligations due to the end of 1999 resulted in a substantial widening of spreads for emerging market debt over that of developed markets, as risks were reassessed by financial market participants internationally. The subsequent LTCM crisis is seen to be related to these wider spreads and resulted in what was then an extraordinary intervention by the Federal Reserve to coordinate an agreement between private investors to stave off the crisis. Bond markets, which had been relatively stable in historical memory, as well as the traditionally more volatile equity markets were both affected during this time. Prior to the recent period, the Russian/LTCM crisis had the greatest systemic implications for the global financial system, and hence provides an important point of comparison for the development of strategies potentially to be employed in the latest crisis.

Chapter 3 focuses on the role of contagion in transmitting crises across international bond markets during the Russian and LTCM crises. The debt payment suspension means that the bond market acts as the source of the shock in this period. Using the latent factor model first presented in Chapter 2 and a data set spanning bond markets across advanced and emerging countries in Asia, Europe, and the Americas, several propositions regarding contagion are assessed. In particular, the chapter examines evidence for the existence of contagion, for the role of the banking system in transmitting contagion, the evidence for regional proximity as an indicator of vulnerability to contagion, and whether or not strong economic fundamentals insulate a country from a crisis. Compared with other methods, the latent factor approach has the advantage that the strength of contagion in terms of the contribution of contagion to volatility can be quantified. The results show that the maximum amount of contagion that any of the countries investigated experience is about 17% of total volatility in bond spreads, with the main effects due to the Russian crisis. The effects of the LTCM crisis on international bond markets are much less characterized by contagion. The results also show that both emerging and developed markets experience contagion during the period, with strong evidence that contagion operates in Europe in particular. The proposition is that linkages via cross border financial institutions provide a conduit for contagion across countries. This seems to be evident in transmitting the crisis from Russia to other bond markets.

In a companion to Chapter 3, Chapter 4 focuses on a similar latent factor model for equity markets during the same crises. The model is applied to ten equity markets consisting of 4 developed and 6 emerging markets from three regions (Latin America, Asia, and Eastern Europe), and uses daily equity returns over 1998. In contrast to the results of Chapter 3, it is during the LTCM crisis that contagion is most widespread in equity markets, particularly for the industrial countries and the regional Latin American markets. Evidence of contagion in equity markets exists during the Russian crisis, but it was more selective in terms of the countries affected, including some advanced countries.

Chapters 3 and 4 indicate that the bond and equity asset markets operate differently during the Russian and LTCM crises. This suggests the construction of a more general model of asset markets, combining both bond and equity returns, in testing for contagion. This is the subject of Chapter 5. The focus of the chapter is to consider whether a single modelling framework fits multiple distinct crises in which contagion effects link markets across national borders and asset classes. The model is applied to a sample containing emerging and developed markets from 1998 to 2007. The application uses data for six countries across five distinct crises: Russia and LTCM in the second half of 1998, Brazil in early 1999, the dot-com correction in 2000, Argentina in 2001–2005, and the U.S. subprime mortgage and credit crisis in 2007. The modelling framework is related to the theoretical model of Kodres and Pritsker (2002), which is reworked to express their results in terms of asset returns rather than prices.

The model of Chapter 5 examines a number of potential channels for contagion effects, via market effects, country effects, and individual asset idiosyncratic effects. The empirical results show that financial crises can be captured by this single modelling framework, and are alike, as all forms of contagion linkages specified are statistically important across all crises. However, the strength of these linkages varies across crises. The combined contribution of the channels of contagion are widespread during the Russian/LTCM crisis, but are less important during the subsequent crises of Brazil, dot-com and Argentina, until in the recent subprime crisis, where again the transmission of the crisis through contagion is rampant.

Chapter 6 revisits the Russian and LTCM crises along with the Brazilian crisis, and builds on the work of previous chapters by relating asset market volatility to observable rather than latent variables. In particular, movements in the bond risk premia of nine emerging markets during the Russian, LTCM, and Brazilian financial crises, are explained in terms of the risk preferences of investors. A theoretical framework to price risk using the stochastic discount factor model is used to motivate the approach, with restrictions derived from this model providing identification for the estimation of a structural vector autoregression (SVAR) model. The restrictions of interest are those on the long run dynamics of the system.

Three broad characteristics of risk are considered in Chapter 6: Global risk factors which comprise credit, liquidity, and volatility risks; country risk arising from idiosyncratic shocks originating in individual countries; and contagion risk caused by the presence of additional cross-border linkages arising during financial crises as in the previous chapters. In the empirical application, liquidity and volatility risks are measured using indices compiled by JP Morgan, while credit risk is measured as the spread between U.S. industrial BBB1 10-year yields and the 10-year U.S. Treasury bond. In line with the previous chapters, the country and contagion factors are treated as latent. Country risk is measured as the idiosyncratic shocks from the SVAR. The empirical results show that all risk components are generally important in explaining the widening of spreads during the Russian and LTCM crises, whereas the Brazilian crisis is better characterized in terms of changes in global credit risk and country risk. The model is used to decompose the bond risk premia into the quantity and price of risk.

The conclusions of Chapters 2 to 6 are drawn together in Chapter 7. Several insights are gleaned from the body of work. These include that contagion is a significant feature of all financial crises considered in the empirical applications of the various chapters. However, the channels through which contagion spreads differ across the crises in terms of the weighting of each channel. Despite the role for contagion, it is still the common factors that usually dominate the new channels of contagion, and market risk factors facing investors are usually larger than risk from contagion. The evidence also suggests that a country with strong market fundamentals is likely to weather a crisis better than those without. However, there is evidence that the contagion effects can be transmitted via institutional linkages such as banking and financial networks.

The implications of the result that the channels through which contagion spread differ across the crises in terms of the weighting of each channel suggest that the dominance of one form of contagion in a particular crisis can mask the dangers inherent in other crises. For example, the role of the banking sector in transmitting the Russian crisis is documented, but that did not alert the financial system to the fragility of banking networks in advance of the sub-prime crisis sufficiently to promote policy action to correct it. The implication is that policy makers and regulators require a number of contingency plans to cover a great number of potential scenarios in crises. However, it is unlikely that all types of crisis events have been realized, and so policymakers also require discretion over their actions as a crisis unfolds and reveals its particular nature. The conclusions that can be garnered thus far indicated that policies and regulation promoting sound economic fundamentals and sound financial networks will help to reduce the risk of common shocks, which dominate contagion effects in the risks facing the financial system.

2

Review of the Empirical Literature

2.1 Introduction

There is now a reasonably large body of empirical work testing for the existence of contagion during financial crises. A range of different methodologies are in use, making it difficult to assess the evidence for and against contagion, and particularly its significance in transmitting crises between countries. The origins of current empirical studies of contagion stem from Sharpe (1964) and Grubel and Fadner (1971), and more recently from King and Wadhwani (1990), Engle, Ito, and Lin (1990), and Bekaert and Hodrick (1992).[1]

The aim of the present chapter is to provide a unifying framework to highlight the key similarities and differences between the various approaches. For an overview of the literature see Pericoli and Sbracia (2003) and Dornbusch, Park, and Claessens (2000). The proposed framework is based on a

---

1. As this chapter focuses on empirical models of contagion it does not discuss the corresponding theoretical literature and more generally the literature on financial crises. For examples of theoretical models of contagion see Allen and Gale (2000), Calvo and Mendoza (2000), Kyle and Xiong (2001), Chue (2002), Kiyotaki and Moore (2002), and Kodres and Pritsker (2002).The literature on financial crises is overviewed in Flood and Marion (1999).

latent factor structure, which forms the basis of the models of Dungey and Martin (2007), Corsetti, Pericoli, and Sbracia (2001; 2005), and Bekaert, Harvey, and Ng (2005). This framework is used to compare directly the correlation analysis approach popularized in this literature by Forbes and Rigobon (2002), the VAR approach of Favero and Giavazzi (2002), the probability model of Eichengreen, Rose, and Wyplosz (1995; 1996) and the co-exceedance approach of Bae, Karolyi, and Stulz (2003).

An important outcome of this chapter is that differences in the definitions used to test for contagion are minor and under certain conditions are even equivalent. In particular, all definitions are interpreted as arising from the same model, with the differences stemming from the amount of information used in the data to detect contagion. Interpreting the approaches in this way provides a natural ordering of models across the information spectrum with some models representing full information methods and others representing partial information methods.

The chapter proceeds as follows. The definition of contagion is formalized in Section 2.2 and compared with existing definitions currently adopted in the empirical literature. In Section 2.3 a framework is developed to model the interdependence between asset returns in a non-crisis environment. This framework is augmented in Section 2.4 to give a model that includes an avenue for contagion during a crisis. The relationship between this model and the bivariate correlation tests for contagion of Forbes and Rigobon is discussed in Section 2.5. This section also includes a number of extensions of the original Forbes and Rigobon approach, as well as its relationship with the approaches of Favero and Giavazzi (2002), Eichengreen, Rose, and Wyplosz (1995; 1996), and Bae, Karolyi, and Stulz (2003). An empirical example comparing the various contagion tests is contained in Section 2.6. The results show that the Forbes and Rigobon adjusted correlation test is a conservative test, whereas the contagion test of Favero and Giavazzi tends to reject the null of no contagion too easily. The remaining tests investigated yield results falling within these two extremes. Concluding comments are given in Section 2.7 together with a number of suggestions for future research that encompass both theoretical and empirical issues.

2.2 Defining Contagion

The concept of contagion from both a theoretical and empirical viewpoint is controversial in the literature. Recent overviews of the issues are provided by Sachs, Tornell, and Velasco (1996), Masson (1999a,b,c), Dornbusch, Park, and Claessens (2000), Pericoli and Sbracia (2003) and Dungey, Fry, González-Hermosillo, and Martin (2005b). The definition of contagion adopted in this book is that contagion represents the effects of contemporaneous movements in asset returns across countries having conditioned on a range of factors as represented by the common factors, regional and idiosyncratic factors.

In this book, contagion is explicitly modeled as the difference between the observed movements in asset returns and the set of conditioning factors. For example, in modeling currency returns during the Asian crisis of 1997–98, Masson decomposes exchange rate changes into four components. These are "monsoonal shocks," or global shocks affecting all countries simultaneously; linkages that occur through normal trade and economic relationships; country-specific shocks; and a residual, which is the component unexplained by these systematic relationships. It is this last component that represents contagion.

Masson (1999a,b,c) attributes part of the residual process to multiple equilibria, or sunspots, where there is a role for self-fulfilling expectations leading to contagion if opinions are coordinated across countries, an approach also taken by Loisel and Martin (2001). Multiple equilibria models are also consistent with other channels for contagion, such as wake-up calls due to Goldstein (1998) or heightened awareness due to Lowell, Neu, and Tong (1998). In these cases a reappraisal of one country's fundamentals leads to a reappraisal of the fundamentals in other countries, thereby resulting in the transmission of crises. Kyle and Xiong (2001) explain contagion in the LTCM and Russian crises as a wealth effect, as traders operating in risky markets encounter shocks and liquidate their portfolios. Thus, a shock in one market can reverberate in seemingly unconnected markets. The wake-up call, wealth effect model, and Masson's definition of contagion are consistent with the class of factor models developed in this book.

The transmission of expectations in both the multiple equilibrium and wake-up call models can lead to herd behavior as in work by Kaminsky and Schmukler (1999) and Calvo and Mendoza (2000). Herd behavior leads to a concept distinguished as unwarranted contagion by Kruger, Osakwe, and Page (1998), which occurs when a crisis spreads to another country that otherwise would not have experienced a speculative attack. This also corresponds with contagion defined as a residual. A further potential channel of contagion is through asset bubbles created by self-fulfilling expectations, moral hazard, or government guarantees, either implied or explicit. Krugman (1998) shows how herd behavior may burst these bubbles.

An important outcome of the development of the factor model, and its relationship to much of the existing empirical work on contagion, is that the definitions of contagion commonly adopted naturally fit into the current framework. Examples discussed above include, Forbes and Rigobon (2002) who test for changes in the correlation structure between asset returns, and Favero and Giavazzi (2002) who concentrate on testing for the transmission of large shocks across markets. The effect of news announcements in transmitting crises is investigated by Baig and Goldfajn (1999) and Ellis and Lewis (2000) for a range of countries. Kaminsky and Schmukler (1999) also analyze the effects of news, where contagion is defined as the spread of investors' moods across national borders. Their key result is that some of the largest swings in the stock market occurred on days of no news. However, Baig and Goldfajn (1999) and Kaminsky and Schmukler (1999) make no distinction between anticipated or unanticipated news.

Alternative definitions of contagion that lie outside the framework adopted in this book tend to be based on market fundamental linkages. In the framework of latent factor model developed here, these channels are captured by the global and regional factors of the model contained in the variable w_t. For example, Reside and Gochoco-Bautista (1999) define contagion as the spillover effects of domestic disturbances on nearby or related economies, using lagged changes in the exchange rates as their contagion variable. Goldstein, Kaminsky, and Reinhart (2000) construct a contagion vulnerability index based on correlations between stock markets, trade linkages, presence of common markets and inter-linkages between banking systems. Van Rijckeghem and Weder (2001) construct a subjective binary variable to examine contagion effects due to financial and trade linkages. Eichengreen, Rose, and Wyplosz (1996), Wirjanto (1999), and Kruger, Osakwe, and Page (1998) condition their models on the existence of a crisis elsewhere.

2.3 A Model of Interdependence

Before developing a model of contagion, a model of interdependence of asset markets during non-crisis periods is specified as a latent factor model of asset returns. The model has its origins in the factor models in finance based on Arbitrage Pricing Theory for example, where asset returns are determined by a set of common factors representing non-diversifiable risk and a set of idiosyncratic factors representing diversifiable risk (Sharpe 1964, Solnik 1974). Similar latent factor models of contagion are used by Corsetti, Pericoli, and Sbracia (2001; 2005), Dungey and Martin (2007), Dungey, Fry, González-Hermosillo, and Martin (2006), Forbes and Rigobon (2002), and Bekaert, Harvey, and Ng (2005).

To simplify the analysis, the number of assets considered is three. Extending the model to N assets or asset classes is straightforward. Let the returns of three assets during a non-crisis period be defined as

$$\{x_{1,t}, x_{2,t}, x_{3,t}\}. \tag{2.1}$$

All returns are assumed to have zero means. The returns could be on currencies, national equity markets, or a combination of currency and equity returns in a particular country or across countries.[2] The following trivariate factor model is assumed to summarize the dynamics of the three processes during a period of tranquility

$$x_{i,t} = \lambda_i w_t + \phi_i u_{i,t}, \quad i = 1, 2, 3. \tag{2.2}$$

The variable w_t represents common shocks that impact upon all asset returns with loadings λ_i. These shocks could represent

2. See, for example, Hartmann, Stratemans, and de Vries (2004), Bekaert, Harvey, and Ng (2005), and Granger, Huang, and Yang (2000), who model the interactions between asset classes.

financial shocks arising from changes to the risk aversion of international investors, or changes in world endowments (Mahieu and Schotman 1994, Rigobon 2003b, Cizeau, Potters, Bouchard 2001). In general, w_t represents market fundamentals that determine the average level of asset returns across international markets during normal, that is, tranquil, times. This variable is commonly referred to as a world factor, which may or may not be observed.[3] For expositional purposes, the world factor is assumed to be a latent stochastic process with zero mean and unit variance

$$w_t \sim (0, 1).$$ (2.3)

The properties of this factor are extended below to capture richer dynamics including both autocorrelation and time-varying volatility. The terms $u_{i,t}$ in equation (2.2) are idiosyncratic factors that are unique to a specific asset market. The contribution of idiosyncratic shocks to the volatility of asset returns is determined by the loadings $\phi_i > 0$. These factors are also assumed to be stochastic processes with zero mean and unit variance

$$u_{i,t} \sim (0, 1).$$ (2.4)

To complete the specification of the model, all factors are assumed to be independent

$$E\left[u_{i,t}u_{j,t}\right] = 0, \qquad \forall i \neq j$$ (2.5)

$$E\left[u_{i,t}w_t\right] = 0, \qquad \forall i.$$ (2.6)

To highlight the interrelationships amongst the three asset returns in (2.2) during a non-crisis period, the covariances are given by

$$E\left[x_{i,t}x_{j,t}\right] = \lambda_i\lambda_j, \qquad \forall i \neq j,$$ (2.7)

3. The model outlined here can be extended to allow for a richer set of factors, including observed fundamentals (Eichengreen, Rose, and Wyplosz 1995; 1996), trade linkages (Glick and Rose 1999 and Pesaran and Pick 2007), financial flows (Van Rijckeghem and Weder 2001), geographical distance (Bayoumi, Fazio, Kumar, and MacDonald 2003), and Fama-French factors (Flood and Rose 2005).

whilst the variances are

$$E\left[x_{i,t}^2\right] = \lambda_i^2 + \phi_i^2, \qquad \forall i. \tag{2.8}$$

Expression (2.7) shows that any dependence between asset returns is solely the result of the influence of common shocks arising from w_t, that simultaneously impact upon all markets. Setting

$$\lambda_1 = \lambda_2 = \lambda_3 = 0, \tag{2.9}$$

results in independent asset markets with all movements determined by the idiosyncratic shocks, $u_{i,t}$.[4] The identifying assumption used by Mahieu and Schotman (1994) in a similar problem is to set $\lambda_i \lambda_j$ to a constant value, L, for all $i \neq j$.

2.4 An Empirical Model of Contagion

In this chapter contagion is represented by the contemporaneous transmission of local shocks to another country or market after conditioning on common factors that exist over a non-crisis period, given by w_t in equation (2.2). This definition is consistent with Sachs, Tornell, and Velasco (1996), Masson (1999a,b,c), Dornbusch, Park, and Claessens (2000), and Pericoli and Sbracia (2003), who decompose shocks to asset markets into common, spillovers that result from some identifiable channel, and contagion. As shown below this definition is also consistent with that of other approaches, such as Forbes and Rigobon (2002), where contagion is represented by an increase in correlation during periods of crisis. For a recent survey, also see Dungey, Fry, González-Hermosillo, and Martin (2005b).

The first model discussed is based on the factor structure developed by Dungey, Fry, González-Hermosillo, and Martin (2006; 2007). Consider the case of contagion from country 1 to country 2. The factor model in (2.2) is now augmented as follows

$$\begin{aligned}
y_{1,t} &= \lambda_1 w_t + \phi_1 u_{1,t} \\
y_{2,t} &= \lambda_2 w_t + \phi_2 u_{2,t} + \kappa u_{1,t} \\
y_{3,t} &= \lambda_3 w_t + \phi_3 u_{3,t},
\end{aligned} \tag{2.10}$$

---

4. Of course, just two of the restrictions in (2.7) are sufficient for independence of asset markets.

where the $x_{i,t}$ in (2.2) are replaced by $y_{i,t}$ to signify demeaned asset returns during the crisis period. The expression for $y_{2,t}$ now contains a contagious transmission channel as represented by local shocks from the asset market in country 1, with its impact measured by the parameter κ. The fundamental aim of all empirical models of contagion is to test the statistical significance of the parameter κ.[5]

2.4.1 Bivariate Testing

Bivariate tests of contagion focus on changes in the volatility of pairs of asset returns. From (2.10), the covariance between the asset returns of countries 1 and 2 during the crisis is

$$E\left[y_{1,t}y_{2,t}\right] = \lambda_1\lambda_2 + \kappa\phi_1. \tag{2.11}$$

Comparing this expression with the covariance for the non-crisis period in (2.7) shows that the change in the covariance between the two periods is

$$E\left[y_{1,t}y_{2,t}\right] - E\left[x_{1,t}x_{2,t}\right] = \kappa\phi_1. \tag{2.12}$$

If $\kappa > 0$, there is an increase in the covariance of asset returns during the crisis period as $\phi_1 > 0$ by assumption. This is usually the situation observed in crisis data. However, it is possible for $\kappa < 0$, in which case there is a reduction in the covariance. Both situations are valid as both represent evidence of contagion via the impact of shocks in (2.10). Hence a test of contagion is given by testing the restriction

$$\kappa = 0, \tag{2.13}$$

in the factor model in equation (2.10). This is the approach adopted by Dungey, Fry, González-Hermosillo, and Martin (2002a; 2006; 2007) and Dungey and Martin (2004).[6]

---

5. An important assumption underlying (2.10) is that the common shock (w_t) and idiosyncratic shocks $(u_{i,t})$ have the same impact during the crisis period as they have during the non-crisis period. This assumption of no structural break is discussed in Section 2.4.3.
6. Most concern seems to center on the case where $\kappa > 0$, that is where contagion is associated with a rise in volatility. The existing tests can be characterized as testing the null hypothesis of $\kappa = 0$ against either a two-sided alternative or a one-sided alternative.

An alternative way to construct a test of contagion is to use the volatility expression for $y_{2,t}$, which is given by

$$E\left[y_{2,t}^2\right] = \lambda_2^2 + \phi_2^2 + \kappa^2. \tag{2.14}$$

Comparing this expression with (2.8) shows that the change in volatility over the two periods is solely attributed to the presence of contagion

$$E\left[y_{2,t}^2\right] - E\left[x_{2,t}^2\right] = \kappa^2. \tag{2.15}$$

Thus, the contagion test based on (2.13) can be interpreted as a test of whether there is an increase in volatility. Expression (2.14) suggests that a useful description of the volatility of $y_{2,t}$ is to decompose the effects of shocks into common, idiosyncratic, and contagion respectively as follows

$$\frac{\lambda_2^2}{\lambda_2^2 + \phi_2^2 + \kappa^2}, \frac{\phi_2^2}{\lambda_2^2 + \phi_2^2 + \kappa^2}, \frac{\kappa^2}{\lambda_2^2 + \phi_2^2 + \kappa^2}. \tag{2.16}$$

This decomposition provides a descriptive measure of the relative strength of contagion in contributing to the volatility of returns during a crisis period. As before, the strength of contagion is determined by the parameter κ, which can be tested formally.

2.4.2 Multivariate Testing

The test for contagion presented so far is a test for contagion from country 1 to country 2. However, it is possible to test for contagion in many directions provided that there are sufficient moment conditions to identify the unknown parameters. For example, (2.10) can be extended as

$$y_{1,t} = \lambda_1 w_t + \phi_1 u_{1,t} + \kappa_{1,2} u_{2,t} + \kappa_{1,3} u_{3,t}$$
$$y_{2,t} = \lambda_2 w_t + \phi_2 u_{2,t} + \kappa_{2,1} u_{1,t} + \kappa_{2,3} u_{3,t} \tag{2.17}$$
$$y_{3,t} = \lambda_3 w_t + \phi_3 u_{3,t} + \kappa_{3,1} u_{1,t} + \kappa_{3,2} u_{2,t},$$

or more succinctly

$$y_{i,t} = \lambda_i w_t + \phi_i u_{i,t} + \sum_{j=1, j \neq i}^{3} \kappa_{i,j} u_{j,t}, \quad i = 1, 2, 3. \tag{2.18}$$

The theoretical variances and covariances are an extension of the expressions given in (2.14) and (2.11) respectively. For example, the variance of the returns of country 1 is

$$E\left[y_{1,t}^2\right] = \lambda_1^2 + \phi_1^2 + \kappa_{1,2}^2 + \kappa_{1,3}^2, \tag{2.19}$$

whereas the covariance of asset returns between countries 1 and 2 is

$$E\left[y_{1,t}y_{2,t}\right] = \lambda_1\lambda_2 + \phi_1\kappa_{2,1} + \phi_2\kappa_{1,2} + \kappa_{1,3}\kappa_{2,3}. \tag{2.20}$$

In this case there are 6 parameters, $\kappa_{i,j}$, controlling the strength of contagion across all asset markets. This model, by itself, is unidentified as there are 12 unknown parameters. However, by combining the empirical moments of the variance-covariance matrix during the crisis period, 6 moments, with the empirical moments from the variance-covariance matrix of the non-crisis period, another 6 moments, gives 12 empirical moments in total that can be used to estimate the 12 unknown parameters by Generalized Method of Moments (GMM).

A joint test of contagion using the factor models in (2.2) and (2.17), can be achieved by comparing the objective function from the unconstrained model, q_u, with the value obtained from estimating the constrained model, q_c, where the contagion parameters are set to zero. As the unconstrained model is just identified in this case, $q_u = 0$, the test is simply a test that under the null hypothesis of no contagion

$$H_0 : q_c = 0, \tag{2.21}$$

which is distributed asymptotically as χ^2 with 6 degrees of freedom under the null. As before, the test of contagion can be interpreted as testing for changes in both variances and covariances.

2.4.3 Structural Breaks

The model given by equations (2.2) and (2.18) is based on the assumption that the increase in volatility during the crisis period is solely generated by contagion, that is, $\kappa_{i,j} \neq 0, \forall i, j$. However, another scenario is that there is a general increase in volatility without any contagion; denoted as increased interdependence by Forbes and Rigobon (2002). This would arise if either the world loadings (λ_i) change, or idiosyncratic loadings (ϕ_i) change, or a combination of the two. The former would be representative of a general increase in volatility across all asset markets brought about, for example, by an increase in the risk aversion of international investors. The latter would arise from increases in the shocks of (some) individual asset markets that are entirely specific to those markets and thus independent of other asset markets.

To allow for structural breaks in the underlying relation-ships, the number of contagious linkages that can be entertained needs to be restricted. In the case where changes in the idiosyncratic shocks are allowed across the sample periods in all $N = 3$ asset markets, equation (2.18) becomes

$$y_{i,t} = \lambda_i w_t + \phi_{y,i} u_{i,t} + \sum_{j=1, j \neq i}^{3} \kappa_{i,j} u_{j,t}, \qquad (2.22)$$

where $\phi_{j,i} \neq \phi_i$, are the idiosyncratic parameters during the crisis period. Bekaert, Harvey, and Ng (2005) adopt a different strategy for modeling structural breaks by specifying time varying factor loadings.

The number of world and idiosyncratic parameters now increases to $3N$. Because the model is still block-recursive, there are just $N(N+1)/2$ empirical moments from the crisis period available to identify the contagion parameters ($\kappa_{i,j}$) and the structural break parameters ($\phi_{y,i}$). This means that there are $N(N+1)/2 - N = N(N-1)/2$, excess moments to identify contagion channels.

Extending the model to allow for structural breaks in both common and idiosyncratic factors in all N asset markets increases the number of world and idiosyncratic parameters to $4N$, now yielding $N(N+1)/2 - 2N = N(N-3)/2$, excess moments to identify contagion channels in the crisis period. For a trivariate model ($N = 3$) that allows for all potential structural breaks in common and idiosyncratic factors, no contagion channels can be tested as the model is just identified. Extending the model to $N = 4$ assets allows for $N(N-3)/2 = 2$ potential contagion channels. Further extending the model to $N = 6$ assets means that the number of contagion channels that can be tested increases to $N(N-3)/2 = 9$.

2.4.4 Using Just Crisis Data

Identification of the unknown parameters in the factor model framework discussed above is based on using information from both non-crisis and crisis periods. For certain asset markets it may be problematic to use non-crisis data to obtain empirical moments to identify unknown parameters. An example being the move from fixed to floating exchange rate regimes during the East Asian currency crisis. However, it is nonetheless possible to identify the model using just crisis period data, provided that the number of asset returns exceeds 3 and a limited number of contagious links are entertained. For example, for $N = 4$ asset returns, there are 10 unique empirical moments from the variance-covariance matrix using crisis data. Specifying the factor model in (2.2) for $N = 4$ assets, means that there are 4 world parameters and 4 idiosyncratic parameters. This implies that 2 contagious links can be specified and identified.

2.4.5 Autoregressive and Heteroskedastic Dynamics

Given that an important feature of financial returns during crises is that they exhibit high volatility, models that do not incorporate this feature are potentially misspecified. This suggests that the framework developed so far be extended to allow for a range of dynamics.[7] Four broad avenues are possible. The first consists of including lagged values of the returns in the system. When the number of assets being studied is large, this approach can give rise to a large number of unknown parameters, thereby making estimation difficult. The second approach is to capture the dynamics through lags in the common factor, w_t. This provides a more parsimonious representation of the system's dynamics as a result of a set of cross equation restrictions arising naturally from the factor structure. A third approach is to specify autoregressive representations for the idiosyncratic factors, $u_{i,t}$. The specification of dynamics on all of the factors yields a state-space representation that can

---

7. This implies that methods based on principal components, such as Kaminsky and Reinhart (2004), which assume constant covariance matrices are inappropriate to model financial crises.

be estimated using a Kalman filter, see for example Mody and Taylor (2003).

A fourth approach for specifying dynamics, which is potentially more important for models of asset returns than dynamics in the mean, is the specification of dynamics in the variance. This is especially true in models of contagion as increases in volatility are symptomatic of crises.[8] A common way to capture this phenomenon is to include a *GARCH* structure on the factors.[9] This approach is adopted by Dungey, Fry, González-Hermosillo, and Martin (2006; 2007), Bekaert, Harvey, and Ng (2005), Dungey and Martin (2004), as well as Chernov, Gallant, Ghysels, and Tauchen (2003). In the case where there is a single factor a suitable specification is

$$w_t = e_t,$$ (2.23)

where

$$e_t \sim (0, h_t),$$ (2.24)

with conditional volatility h_t, given by the following *GARCH* factor structure (Diebold and Nerlove 1989, Dungey, Martin, and Pagan 2000)

$$h_t = (1 - \alpha - \beta) + \alpha e_{t-1}^2 + \beta h_{t-1}.$$ (2.25)

The choice of the normalization $(1 - \alpha - \beta)$, constrains the unconditional volatility to equal unity and is adopted for identification.

Using (2.10) augmented by (2.23) to (2.25) gives the total (conditional) volatility of $y_{2,t}$, the asset return in the crisis period, as

$$E_{t-1}\left[y_{2,t}^2\right] = E_{t-1}\left[\left(\lambda_2 w_t + \phi_2 u_{2,t} + \kappa u_{1,t}\right)^2\right]$$

$$= \lambda_2^2 h_t + \phi_2^2 + \kappa^2.$$

8. A further approach is by Jeanne and Masson (2000) who allow for a Markovian switching structure to incorporate the multiple equilibria features of theoretical contagion models.

9. For reviews of GARCH models, see Bollerslev, Chou, and Kroner (1992) and Bollerslev, Engle, and Nelson (1994). Also see Engle (2009) for recent multivariate GARCH models and their applications to modeling time-varying correlations.

where the assumption of independent factors in (2.5) and (2.6), is utilized. The conditional covariance between $y_{1,t}$ and $y_{2,t}$, during the crisis period for example, is

$$E_{t-1}\left[y_{1,t}y_{2,t}\right] = E_{t-1}\left[\left(\lambda_1 w_t + \phi_1 u_{1,t}\right)\left(\lambda_2 w_t + \phi_2 u_{2,t} + \kappa u_{1,t}\right)\right]$$
$$= \lambda_1\lambda_2 h_t + \kappa\phi_1.$$

Both the conditional variance and covariance during the crisis period are affected by the presence of contagion ($\kappa \neq 0$). In particular, contagion has the effect of causing a structural shift during the crisis period in the conditional covariance by $\kappa\phi_1$, and the conditional variance by κ^2.

An important advantage of adopting a *GARCH* factor model of asset returns is that it provides a parsimonious multivariate *GARCH* model. This model, when combined with a model of contagion, can capture changes in the variance and covariance structures of asset returns during financial crises.[10] The parsimony of the factor *GARCH* model specification contrasts with multivariate *GARCH* models based on the *BEKK* specification (Engle and Kroner 1995), which require a large number of parameters for even moderate size models.[11]

2.5 Correlation and Covariance Analysis

Forbes and Rigobon (2002) define contagion as the increase in correlation between two variables during a crisis period. In performing their test, the correlation between the two asset returns during the crisis period is adjusted to overcome the problem that correlations are a positive function of volatility. As crisis periods are typically characterized by an increase in volatility, a test based on the (conditional) correlation is biased upwards resulting in evidence of spurious contagion (Forbes and Rigobon 2002, Boyer, Gibson, and Loretan 1999, Loretan and English 2000, Corsetti, Pericoli, and Sbracia 2005).[12]

---

10. Further extensions to allow for asymmetric shocks are by Dungey, Fry, and Martin (2003) and asymmetric volatility by Bekaert, Harvey, and Ng (2005).
11. Problems in estimating multivariate *GARCH* models are noted by Malliaroupulos (1997).
12. Butler and Joaquin (2002) conduct the same test across bull and bear markets, although they do not specifically use the terminology of contagion.

2.5.1 Bivariate Testing

To demonstrate the Forbes and Rigobon (2002) approach, consider testing for contagion from country 1 to country 2 where the returns volatilities are $\sigma_{x,i}^2$ and $\sigma_{y,i}^2$ in the non-crisis and crisis periods respectively. The correlation between the two asset returns is ρ_y during the crisis period (high-volatility period) and ρ_x in the non-crisis (low-volatility period).[13] If there is an increase in the volatility of the asset return of country 1, $\sigma_{y,1}^2 > \sigma_{x,1}^2$, without there being any change to the fundamental relationship between the asset returns in the two markets, then $\rho_y > \rho_x$ giving the false appearance of contagion. To adjust for this bias, Forbes and Rigobon show that the adjusted (unconditional) correlation is given by; see also Boyer, Gibson, and Loretan (1999), Loretan and English (2000) and Corsetti, Pericoli and Sbracia (2001; 2005)[14]

$$v_y = \frac{\rho_y}{\sqrt{1 + \left(\dfrac{\sigma_{y,1}^2 - \sigma_{x,1}^2}{\sigma_{x,1}^2}\right)\left(1 - \rho_y^2\right)}}. \tag{2.26}$$

This is the unconditional correlation $\left(v_y\right)$, which is the conditional correlation $\left(\rho_y\right)$ scaled by a nonlinear function of the percentage change in volatility in the asset return of the source country $\left(\left(\sigma_{y,1}^2 - \sigma_{x,1}^2\right)/\sigma_{x,1}^2\right)$, country 1 in this case, over the high-and low-volatility periods. If there is no fundamental change in the relationship between the two asset markets then $v_y = \rho_x$.

To test that there is a significant increase in correlation in the crisis period, the null hypothesis is for no contagion

$$H_0 : v_y = \rho_x, \tag{2.27}$$

13. Forbes and Rigobon (2002), in their empirical application, compare the crisis period correlation with the correlation calculated over the total sample period (low-volatility period). That is, x is replaced by $z = (x; y)$. This alternative formulation is also discussed below.
14. Other approaches using correlation analysis are Karolyi and Stulz (1996) and Longin and Solnik (1995).

against the alternative hypothesis of

$$H_1 : v_y > \rho_x. \tag{2.28}$$

A t-statistic for testing these hypothesis is given by

$$FR_1 = \frac{\widehat{v}_y - \widehat{\rho}_x}{\sqrt{\dfrac{1}{T_y} + \dfrac{1}{T_x}}}, \tag{2.29}$$

where the $\widehat{}$ signifies the sample estimator, and T_y and T_x are the respective sample sizes of the high-volatility and low-volatility periods. The standard error in (2.29) derives from assuming that the two samples are drawn from independent normal distributions. That is

$$
\begin{aligned}
Var\left(\widehat{v}_y - \widehat{\rho}_x\right) &= Var\left(\widehat{v}_y\right) + Var\left(\widehat{\rho}_x\right) - 2Cov\left(\widehat{v}_y, \widehat{\rho}_x\right) \\
&= Var\left(\widehat{v}_y\right) + Var\left(\widehat{\rho}_x\right) \\
&\simeq \frac{1}{T_y} + \frac{1}{T_x},
\end{aligned} \tag{2.30}
$$

where the second step follows from the independence assumption, and the last step follows from the assumption of normality and the use of an asymptotic approximation (Kendall and Stuart 1973; p.307). To improve the finite sample properties of the test statistic, Forbes and Rigobon (2002) suggest using the Fisher transformation[15]

$$FR_2 = \frac{\frac{1}{2}\ln\left(\dfrac{1+\widehat{v}_y}{1-\widehat{v}_y}\right) - \frac{1}{2}\ln\left(\dfrac{1+\widehat{\rho}_x}{1-\widehat{\rho}_x}\right)}{\sqrt{\dfrac{1}{T_y - 3} + \dfrac{1}{T_x - 3}}}. \tag{2.31}$$

In the adjusted correlation test adopted by Forbes and Rigobon (2002) in their empirical work, the non-crisis period is

---

15. This tranformation is valid for small values of the correlation coefficients, ρ_x and v_y. Further refinements are discussed in Kendall and Stuart (1969, p.391). For the case of independence, $\rho_x = v_y = 0$, an exact expression for the variance of the transformed correlation coefficient is available. An illustration of these problems for the Forbes and Rigobon method is given in Dungey and Zhumabekova (2001).

defined as the total sample period. For this case, the test statistic in equation (2.29) becomes

$$FR_3 = \frac{\widehat{v}'_y - \widehat{\rho}_z}{\sqrt{\frac{1}{T_y} + \frac{1}{T_z}}},$$

(2.32)

where x is replaced by z and

$$\widehat{v}'_y = \frac{\rho_y}{\sqrt{1 + \left(\frac{\sigma^2_{y,1} - \sigma^2_{z,1}}{\sigma^2_{z,1}}\right)\left(1 - \rho^2_y\right)}},$$

(2.33)

which is (2.26) with $\sigma^2_{x,1}$ replaced by $\sigma^2_{z,1}$. From (2.31), the Fisher adjusted version of the test statistic is

$$FR_4 = \frac{\frac{1}{2}\ln\left(\frac{1 + \widehat{v}_y}{1 - \widehat{v}_y}\right) - \frac{1}{2}\ln\left(\frac{1 + \widehat{\rho}_z}{1 - \widehat{\rho}_z}\right)}{\sqrt{\frac{1}{T_y - 3} + \frac{1}{T_z - 3}}}.$$

(2.34)

Underlying (2.32) and (2.34) is the assumption that the variances of $\widehat{v}'_y$ and $\widehat{\rho}_z$ are independent. Clearly this cannot be correct in the case of overlapping data. One implication of this result is that the standard error in (2.30) is too large as it neglects the (negative) covariance term arising from the use of overlapping data. This biases the t-statistic to zero resulting in a failure to reject the null of contagion.

2.5.2 Alternative Formulation

In implementing the correlation test in (2.29) or (2.31), equation (2.26) shows that the conditional correlation needs to be scaled initially by a nonlinear function of the change in volatility in the asset return of the source country, country 1 in this case, over the pertinent sample periods. Another way to implement the Forbes and Rigobon test of contagion is to scale the asset returns and perform the contagion test within a regression framework.[16] Continuing with the example of testing

---

16. Corsetti, Pericoli, and Sbracia (2001) extend the Forbes and Rigobon framework to a model equivalent to the factor structure given in (2.10).

for contagion from the asset market of country 1 to the asset market of country 2, consider scaling the asset returns during the non-crisis period by their respective standard deviations. First, define the following regression equation during the non-crisis period where the returns are scaled by their respective standard errors

$$\left(\frac{x_{2,t}}{\sigma_{x,2}}\right) = \alpha_0 + \alpha_1 \left(\frac{x_{1,t}}{\sigma_{x,1}}\right) + \eta_{x,t}, \tag{2.35}$$

where $\eta_{x,t}$ is a disturbance term and α_0 and α_1 are regression parameters. The non-crisis slope regression parameter equals the non-crisis correlation coefficient, $\alpha_1 = \rho_x$. Second, for the crisis returns the regression equation is given as follows, where the scaling of asset returns is still by the respective standard deviations from the non-crisis periods

$$\left(\frac{y_{2,t}}{\sigma_{x,2}}\right) = \beta_0 + \beta_1 \left(\frac{y_{1,t}}{\sigma_{x,1}}\right) + \eta_{y,t}, \tag{2.36}$$

where $\eta_{y,t}$ is a disturbance term and β_0 and β_1 are regression parameters. The crisis regression slope parameter $\beta_1 = \nu_y$, which is the Forbes-Rigobon adjusted correlation coefficient given in (2.26).

This alternative formulation suggests that another way to implement the Forbes-Rigobon adjusted correlation is to estimate (2.35) and (2.36) by OLS and test the equality of the regression slope parameters. This test is equivalent to a Chow test for a structural break of the regression slope. Implementation of the test can be based on the following pooled regression equation over the entire sample

$$\left(\frac{z_{2,t}}{\sigma_{x,2}}\right) = \gamma_0 + \gamma_1 d_t + \gamma_2 \left(\frac{z_{1,t}}{\sigma_{x,1}}\right) + \kappa \left(\frac{z_{1,t}}{\sigma_{x,1}}\right) d_t + \eta_t, \tag{2.37}$$

where

$$z_i = \left(x_{i,1}, x_{i,2}, \ldots, x_{i,T_x}, y_{i,1}, y_{i,2}, \ldots, y_{i,T_y}\right)', \qquad i = 1, 2, \tag{2.38}$$

Their approach requires evaluating quantities given by the ratio of the contribution of idiosyncratic and common factors to volatility, ϕ_i^2/λ_i^2 for example. These quantities can be estimated directly using GMM as discussed in Section 3.2.

represents the $\left(T_x + T_y\right) \times 1$ pooled data set by stacking the non-crisis and crisis data and η_t is a disturbance term. The slope dummy, d_t, is defined as

$$d_t = \begin{cases} 1: & t > T_x \\ 0: & \text{otherwise} \end{cases}. \tag{2.39}$$

The parameter $\kappa = \beta_1 - \alpha_1$ in (2.37) captures the effect of contagion. It represents the additional contribution of information on asset returns in country 2 to the non-crisis regression: If there is no change in the relationship the dummy variable provides no new additional information during the crisis period, resulting in $\kappa = 0$. Thus the Forbes and Rigobon contagion test can be implemented by estimating (2.37) by OLS and performing a one-sided t-test of

$$H_0 : \kappa = 0, \tag{2.40}$$

in (2.37), which is equivalent to testing

$$H_0 : \alpha_1 = \beta_1, \tag{2.41}$$

in (2.35) and (2.36).[17] Of course, the test statistic to perform the contagion test is invariant to scaling transformations of the regressors, such as the use of $\sigma_{x,1}$ and $\sigma_{x,2}$ to standardize z_t. This suggests that an even more direct way to test for contagion is to implement a standard test of parameter constancy in a regression framework simply based on z_t, the unscaled data.[18]

There is one difference between the regression approach to correlation testing for contagion based on (2.37) and the approach implemented by Forbes and Rigobon, and that is

---

17. Interestingly, Caporale, Cipollini, and Spagnolo (2002) conduct a test of contagion based on a slope dummy, but do not identify the connection of the test with the Forbes and Rigobon (2002) correlation approach.

18. To implement the form of the Forbes and Rigobon (2002) version of the correlation test within the regression framework in (2.37), the pre-crisis data is now replaced by the total sample data. That is, the low-volatility period is defined as the total sample period and not the pre-crisis period. This requires redefining the pertinent variables as $z = (x, y, y)$ and the slope dummy as $d = \left(0_{T_x}, 0_{T_y}, 1_{T_y}\right)$, and scaling the variables using the total sample period.

the standard errors used in the test statistics are different in small samples. The latter approach is based on the asymptotic adjustment given in (2.31) or (2.34), whilst the former are based in general on the usual least squares standard errors or some robust estimator.

2.5.3 Multivariate Testing

The regression framework developed above for implementing the Forbes and Rigobon test suggests that a multivariate analogue can be easily constructed as follows. Given that there is no need to scale the data to perform the contagion test, in the case of three asset returns the non-crisis period equations are

$$
\begin{aligned}
x_{1,t} &= \alpha_{1,2}x_{2,t} + \alpha_{1,3}x_{3,t} + \eta_{x,1,t} \\
x_{2,t} &= \alpha_{2,1}x_{1,t} + \alpha_{2,3}x_{3,t} + \eta_{x,2,t} \\
x_{3,t} &= \alpha_{3,1}x_{1,t} + \alpha_{3,2}x_{2,t} + \eta_{x,3,t}
\end{aligned}
\tag{2.42}
$$

whilst the crisis equations are specified as

$$
\begin{aligned}
y_{1,t} &= \beta_{1,2}y_{2,t} + \beta_{1,3}y_{3,t} + \eta_{y,1,t} \\
y_{2,t} &= \beta_{2,1}y_{1,t} + \beta_{2,3}y_{3,t} + \eta_{y,2,t} \\
y_{3,t} &= \beta_{3,1}y_{1,t} + \beta_{3,2}y_{2,t} + \eta_{y,3,t},
\end{aligned}
\tag{2.43}
$$

where $\eta_{x,i,t}$ and $\eta_{y,i,t}$ are error terms. A joint test of contagion is given by

$$
\alpha_{i,j} = \beta_{i,j}, \qquad \forall i \neq j,
\tag{2.44}
$$

which represents 6 restrictions. A convenient way to implement the multivariate version of the Forbes and Rigobon test is to adopt the strategy of (2.37) and write the model as a *three-equation* system augmented by a set of slope dummy variables to capture the impact of contagion on asset returns

$$
\begin{aligned}
z_{1,t} &= \alpha_{1,2}z_{2,t} + \alpha_{1,3}z_{3,t} + \kappa_{1,2}z_{2,t}d_t + \kappa_{1,3}z_{3,t}d_t + \eta_{1,t} \\
z_{2,t} &= \alpha_{2,1}z_{1,t} + \alpha_{2,3}z_{3,t} + \kappa_{2,1}z_{1,t}d_t + \kappa_{2,3}z_{3,t}d_t + \eta_{2,t} \\
z_{3,t} &= \alpha_{3,1}z_{1,t} + \alpha_{3,2}z_{2,t} + \kappa_{3,1}z_{1,t}d_t + \kappa_{3,2}z_{2,t}d_t + \eta_{3,t},
\end{aligned}
\tag{2.45}
$$

where the $z_{i,t}$ pooled asset returns are as defined in (2.38), $\eta_{i,t}$ are disturbance terms, d_t is the dummy variable defined in (2.39), and $\kappa_{i,j} = \beta_{i,j} - \alpha_{i,j}$ are the parameters that control the strength of contagion.

The multivariate contagion test is based on testing the null hypothesis

$$H_0 : \kappa_{i,j} = 0, \qquad \forall i \neq j. \tag{2.46}$$

Implementation of the test can be performed by using standard multivariate test statistics, including likelihood ratio, Wald and Lagrange multiplier statistics.

Rigobon (2003b) suggests an alternative multivariate test of contagion. This test is referred to as the determinant of the change in the covariance matrix (DCC) as it is based on comparing the covariance matrices across two samples (non-crisis and crisis) and taking the determinant to express the statistic as a scalar. The DCC statistic is formally defined as

$$DCC = \frac{\left|\widehat{\Omega}_y - \widehat{\Omega}_x\right|}{\widehat{\sigma}_{DCC}}, \tag{2.47}$$

where $\widehat{\Omega}_y$ and $\widehat{\Omega}_x$ are the estimated covariance matrices of asset returns in the crisis and non-crisis periods respectively, and $\widehat{\sigma}_{DCC}$ is an estimate of the pertinent standard error of the statistic. Under the null hypothesis there is no change in the covariance structure of asset returns across sample periods, resulting in a value of $DCC = 0$. If contagion increases volatility during the crisis period, then $DCC > 0$, resulting in a rejection of the null hypothesis of no contagion.

The DCC test represents a test of parameter stability and thus provides an alternative test to a Chow test. However, given the relationship between Chow and contagion tests discussed previously, this implies that potentially the DCC test is also a test of contagion. To highlight this point, consider the following bivariate factor model based on the first two equations in (2.2) and (2.10). The non-crisis and crisis covariance matrices are respectively

$$\Omega_x = \begin{bmatrix} \lambda_1^2 + \phi_1^2 & \lambda_1 \lambda_2 \\ \lambda_1 \lambda_2 & \lambda_2^2 + \phi_2^2 \end{bmatrix}, \quad \Omega_y = \begin{bmatrix} \lambda_1^2 + \phi_1^2 & \lambda_1 \lambda_2 + \kappa \phi_1 \\ \lambda_1 \lambda_2 + \kappa \phi_1 & \lambda_2^2 + \phi_2^2 + \kappa^2 \end{bmatrix}.$$

The numerator of the DCC statistic is this case is

$$\left| \widehat{\Omega}_y - \widehat{\Omega}_x \right| = \begin{vmatrix} 0 & \widehat{\kappa \phi_1} \\ \widehat{\kappa \phi_1} & \widehat{\kappa^2} \end{vmatrix} = -\widehat{\kappa}^2 \widehat{\phi_1^2},$$

where the $\hat{}$ signifies a parameter estimator. Under the null hypothesis $DCC = 0$, which is achieved when $\kappa = 0$, a result that is equivalent to the tests of contagion already discussed.

In implementing the DCC test, the covariance matrices employed tend to be conditional covariance matrices if dynamics arising from lagged variables and other exogenous variables are controlled for. One approach is to estimate a VAR for the total period, $T_x + T_y$, and base the covariances on the VAR residuals. This is the approach adopted in the empirical application of Rigobon (2003b). The advantage of working with VAR residuals, as compared to structural residuals, is that the VAR represents an unconstrained reduced form, thereby circumventing problems of simultaneity bias. Endogeneity issues are now discussed.

2.5.4 Endogeneity Issues

The potential simultaneity biases arising from the presence of endogenous variables are more evident when the Forbes and Rigobon test is cast in a linear regression framework. Forbes and Rigobon perform the correlation test on pairs of countries under the assumption that contagion spreads from one country to another with the source country being exogenous. The test can then be performed in the reverse direction with the implicit assumption of exogeneity on the two asset returns reversed. Performing the two tests in this way is inappropriate as it clearly ignores the simultaneity bias problem.[19]

Forbes and Rigobon (2002) show using a Monte Carlo analysis that the size of the simultaneity bias is unlikely to be severe if the size of the correlations between asset returns are relatively small. Interestingly, Rigobon (2003b) notes that the volatility adjustment in performing the test in (2.26) is incorrect in the presence of simultaneity bias. However, as noted above, the Forbes and Rigobon adjustment acts as a scaling parameter

---

19. Forbes and Rigobon recognize this problem and do not test for contagion in both directions being very clear about their exogeneity assumptions.

that has no affect on the properties of the test statistic in a linear regression framework. The problem of simultaneity bias is the same whether the endogenous explanatory variables are scaled or not.

To perform the Forbes and Rigobon contagion test while correcting for simultaneity bias, equations (2.42) and (2.43) need to be estimated initially using a simultaneous equations estimator and the tests of contagion based on the simultaneous equation estimates of $\kappa_{i,j}$ in (2.45). To demonstrate some of the issues, the bivariate model is expanded to allow for structural breaks in the idiosyncratic loadings. The bivariate versions of the model without intercepts during the non-crisis and crisis periods are respectively

$$x_{1,t} = \alpha_1 x_{2,t} + \eta_{x,1,t}$$
$$x_{2,t} = \alpha_2 x_{1,t} + \eta_{x,2,t}$$
(2.48)

where $\eta_{x,i,t}$ are *iid* with zero means and variances $E\left[\eta_{x,i}^2\right] = \omega_{x,i}^2$, and

$$y_{1,t} = \beta_1 y_{2,t} + \eta_{y,1,t}$$
$$y_{2,t} = \beta_2 y_{1,t} + \eta_{y,2,t}$$
(2.49)

where $\eta_{y,i,t}$ are *iid* with zero means and variances $E\left[\eta_{y,i}^2\right] = \omega_{y,i}^2$. The respective reduced forms are

$$x_{1,t} = \frac{1}{1 - \alpha_1 \alpha_2} \left(\eta_{x,1,t} + \alpha_1 \eta_{x,2,t}\right)$$
$$x_{2,t} = \frac{1}{1 - \alpha_1 \alpha_2} \left(\eta_{x,2,t} + \alpha_2 \eta_{x,1,t}\right)$$
(2.50)

for the non-crisis period and

$$y_{1,t} = \frac{1}{1 - \beta_1 \beta_2} \left(\eta_{y,1,t} + \beta_1 \eta_{y,2,t}\right)$$
$$y_{2,t} = \frac{1}{1 - \beta_1 \beta_2} \left(\eta_{y,2,t} + \beta_2 \eta_{y,1,t}\right)$$
(2.51)

for the crisis period. For the two sub-periods the variance-covariance matrices are respectively

$$
\Omega_x = \frac{1}{(1 - \alpha_1\alpha_2)^2} \begin{bmatrix} \omega_{x,1}^2 + \alpha_1^2\omega_{x,2}^2 & \alpha_1^2\omega_{x,2}^2 \\ \alpha_1\omega_{x,2}^2 & \omega_{x,2}^2 + \alpha_2^2\omega_{x,1}^2 \end{bmatrix} \tag{2.52}
$$

$$
\Omega_y = \frac{1}{(1 - \beta_1\beta_2)^2} \begin{bmatrix} \omega_{y,1}^2 + \beta_1^2\omega_{y,2}^2 & \beta_1\omega_{y,2}^2 \\ \beta_1\omega_{y,2}^2 & \omega_{y,2}^2 + \beta_2^2\omega_{y,1}^2 \end{bmatrix}. \tag{2.53}
$$

The model at present is underidentified as there is a total of just six unique moments across the two samples, to identify the eight unknown parameters

$$
\left\{ \alpha_1, \alpha_2, \beta_1, \beta_2, \omega_{x,1}^2, \omega_{x,2}^2, \omega_{y,1}^2, \omega_{y,2}^2 \right\}.
$$

In a study of the relationship between Mexican and Argentinian bonds, Rigobon (2003a) identifies the model by setting $\alpha_1 = \beta_1$ and $\alpha_2 = \beta_2$. However, from (2.41), this implies that there is no contagion, just a structural break in the idiosyncratic variances. An alternative approach to identification, which is more informative in the context of testing for contagion, is not to allow for a structural break and set $\omega_{x,1}^2 = \omega_{y,1}^2$, and $\omega_{x,2}^2 = \omega_{y,2}^2$. Now there are six equations to identify the six unknowns. A test of contagion is given by a test of the over-identifying restrictions under the null hypothesis of no contagion. The observational equivalence between the two identification strategies has already been noted earlier in the discussion of the factor model. However, if the idiosyncratic variances are changing over the sample, the contagion test is undersized (Toyoda and Ohtani 1986). Another alternative solution is to expand the number of asset markets investigated. For example, increasing the number of assets to $N = 3$ results in a just identified model as there are 12 unknown parameters,

$$
\left\{ \alpha_1, \alpha_2, \alpha_3, \beta_1, \beta_2, \beta_3, \omega_{x,1}^2, \omega_{x,2}^2, \omega_{x,3}^2, \omega_{y,1}^2, \omega_{y,2}^2, \omega_{y,3}^2 \right\},
$$

and 12 moments, as there are six unique moments from each of the variance-covariance matrices from the two sub-periods.

Rigobon (2002) also suggests using instrumental variables to obtain consistent parameter estimates with the instruments defined as

$$s_i = \left(-x_{i,1}, -x_{i,2}, ..., -x_{i,T_x} \quad y_{i,1}, y_{i,2}, ..., y_{i,T_y} \right)', \qquad i = 1, 2.$$

This choice of instruments is an extension of the early suggestions of Wald (1940) and Durbin (1954). For example, Wald
defined the instrument set as a dummy variable with a 1 signi-
fying observations above the median and a -1 for observations
below the median. In the case of contagion and modeling
financial crises, observations above (below) the median can
be expected to correspond to crisis (non-crisis) observations.
This suggests that the Rigobon instrument is likely to be
more efficient than the instrument chosen by Wald as it uses
more information. Rigobon then proceeds to estimate pooled
equations as in (2.45), but with $\kappa_{i,j} = 0$. But this is not a
test of contagion as $\alpha_i = \beta_i$ is imposed and not tested. Not
surprisingly, the IV estimator of the structural parameters
in this case is equivalent to the matching moment estimator
using (2.52) and (2.53), subject to the restrictions $\alpha_1 = \beta_1$ and
$\alpha_2 = \beta_2$.

2.5.5 Relationship with Other Models

Interpreting the Forbes and Rigobon contagion test as a Chow
test provides an important link connecting this approach with
the contagion modeling framework of Dungey, Fry, González-
Hermosillo, and Martin (2006; 2007) discussed in the previous
section. To highlight this link, let the dynamics of the processes
be represented by the first two expressions of the contagion
model in (2.10)

$$y_{1,t} = \lambda_1 w_t + \phi_1 u_{1,t} \tag{2.54}$$

$$y_{2,t} = \lambda_2 w_t + \phi_2 u_{2,t} + \kappa u_{1,t}, \tag{2.55}$$

where as before contagion from the asset market in country
1 to country 2 is controlled by the parameter κ. Combining
these expressions to substitute out $u_{1,t}$ from the equation for $y_{2,t}$
gives

$$y_{2,t} = \left(\frac{\lambda_2 \phi_1 - \lambda_1 \kappa}{\phi_1} \right) w_t + \frac{\kappa}{\phi_1} y_{1,t} + \phi_2 u_{2,t}. \tag{2.56}$$

The corresponding asset equation in the non-crisis period is given by setting $\kappa = 0$, and changing $y_{i,t}$ to $x_{i,t}$

$$x_{2,t} = \left(\frac{\lambda_2 \phi_1 - \lambda_1 \kappa}{\phi_1} \right) w_t + \phi_2 u_{2,t}. \tag{2.57}$$

Stacking equations (2.57) and (2.56) yields an equation of the same form as (2.37), provided that the common factor is taken as $w_t = z_{1,t}$, the stacked vector of asset returns in country 1 across non-crisis and crisis periods. In this scenario the Forbes and Rigobon and Dungey, Fry, González-Hermosillo, and Martin approaches are equivalent with the test of contagion still being based on $\kappa = 0$. This amounts to testing the additional explanatory power of the asset returns in country 1 to explain movements in the asset returns in country 2 over and above the factors that govern movements in asset markets during non-crisis periods.

In practice, Forbes and Rigobon (2002) identify the common factor w_t using a number of observed variables including U.S. interest rates. These variables are initially extracted from the asset returns data by regressing the returns on the chosen set of common factors and using the residuals from these regressions in the contagion tests given in (2.26) to (2.31). In conducting the contagion tests, the analysis is performed in pairs with the source country changing depending on the hypothesis being tested. This testing strategy is highlighted in (2.56) and (2.57), where the source country is country 1.

Testing for contagion based on the dummy variable version of the Forbes and Rigobon contagion test in equation (2.37) also introduces the links to a range of other tests for contagion. For example, the approach of Favero and Giavazzi (2002) consists of defining the dummy variable in (2.39) as

$$d_{i,t} = \begin{cases} 1 : & |v_{i,t}| > 3SD_i \\ 0 : & \text{otherwise,} \end{cases} \tag{2.58}$$

where SD_i is computed as the standard deviation of the residuals $v_{i,t}$, in a VAR(p) associated with the variable $y_{i,t}$.[20] A structural model is then specified where each return is

---

20. In a related approach, Pesaran and Pick (2007) also identify outliers by constructing dummy variables that are used in a structural model to test

expressed as a function of all other returns, own lagged returns and the full set of dummy variables. The system of equations is estimated by FIML and the contagion test is based on a joint test of the parameters on the dummy variables of the other returns. The test will identify contagion if extreme returns in the dependent variable are matched with extreme returns in the other variables. The dummy variables define the period of the crisis. This contrasts with the approach of Forbes and Rigobon and DFGM where the crisis period is determined a priori. One implication of the Favero and Giavazzi test is that the results can potentially be driven by a small number of observations thereby making the test rather fragile. A further implication of this approach concerns the use of lag variables to identify the simultaneous equations model. In the case where it is asset returns that are being modeled, the autocorrelation structure of asset returns is expected to be low.[21] This results in a weak instrument problem where the bias of a simultaneous estimator can exceed the bias of the OLS estimator, which, in turn, can yield spurious results (Nelson and Startz 1990, Stock, Wright, and Yogo 2002).

Eichengreen, Rose, and Wyplosz (1995; 1996) choose dummy variables for both $y_{1,t}$ and $y_{2,t}$, respectively, as

$$d_{1,t} = \begin{cases} 1: & y_{1,t} > f(EMP_{1,t}) \\ 0: & \text{otherwise} \end{cases}$$

$$d_{2,t} = \begin{cases} 1: & y_{2,t} > f(EMP_{2,t}) \\ 0: & \text{otherwise,} \end{cases} \tag{2.59}$$

where $EMP_{i,t}$ is the exchange market pressure index.[22] As a result of the binary dependent variable, the model is estimated as a probit model. Bae, Karolyi, and Stulz (2003) extend this

for contagion. One important difference is that Pesaran and Pick do not define the dummy variables for each outlier, but combine the outliers associated with each dummy variable.

21. This is less of a problem in the application considered by Favero and Giavazzi (2002), who used interest rates that have strong autocorrelation structures.

22. The threshold indicator $EMP_{i,t}$ represents the Exchange Market Pressure Index corresponding to the *ith* asset return at time *t*, which is computed as a linear combination of the change in exchange rates, interest differentials, and

model to provide for polychotomous variables, where the dummy variables, $d_{i,t}$, are defined as exceedances

$$d_{1,t} = \begin{cases} 1: & |y_{1,t}| > THRESH \\ 0: & \text{otherwise} \end{cases}$$

$$d_{2,t} = \begin{cases} 1: & |y_{2,t}| > THRESH \\ 0: & \text{otherwise.} \end{cases} \tag{2.61}$$

In their application *THRESH* is chosen to identify the 5% of extreme observations in the sample. A co-exceedance occurs when $d_{1,t} = d_{2,t} = 1$. The number of exceedances and co-exceedances at time t yields a polychotomous variable that is then used in a multinominal logit model to test for contagion.[23]

An important part of the Eichengreen et al. (1995; 1996) approach is that it requires choosing the threshold value of the EMP index for classifying asset returns into crisis and non-crisis periods. As with the threshold values adopted by Favero and Giavazzi (2002) and Bae, Karolyi, and Stulz (2003), the empirical results are contingent on the choice of the threshold value. In each of these approaches, this choice is based on sample estimates of the data, resulting in potentially non-unique classifications of the data for different sample periods.[24]

---

changes in levels of reserve assets for country i with respect to some numeraire country, 0,

$$EMP_{i,t} = a\Delta e_{i,t} + b(r_{i,t} - r_{0,t}) + c(\Delta R_{i,t} - \Delta R_{0,t}), \tag{2.60}$$

where e_i is the log of the bilateral exchange rate, r_i is the short-term interest rate, and R_i is the stock of reserve assets. The weights, a, b, and c, are given by the inverse of the standard deviation of the individual component series over the sample period. Kaminsky and Reinhart (2000) adopt a different weighting scheme whereby the weight on interest rates is zero.

23. In the application of Bae, Karolyi, and Stulz (2003) the cases of negative and positive returns are considered separately. They also combined all exceedances into a single category. However, by separating the exceedances of each variable it is possible to test for contagion from the host country to the remaining countries separately, see Dungey, Fry, González-Hermosillo, and Martin (2005a). This is done in the application in Section 2.6.

24. Both Eichengreen et al. and Kaminsky and Reinhart (2000) use some matching of their crisis index constructed using these thresholds to market events to validate the threshold choice.

The construction of binary dummies in (2.58) to (2.61) in general amounts to a loss of sample information resulting in inefficient parameter estimates and a loss of power in testing for contagion. A more direct approach that does not result in any loss of sample information is to estimate (2.56) by least squares and perform a test of contagion by undertaking a t-test of κ. In fact, the probit model delivers consistent estimates of the same unknown parameters given in (2.56), but these estimates suffer a loss of efficiency as a result of the loss of sample information in constructing the dummy variables.[25]

2.6 Application

To illustrate the application of the alternative empirical methodologies discussed above, this section explores the turmoil in equity markets resulting from the speculative attack on the Hong Kong currency in October 1997.[26] This attack was successfully defended by the Hong Kong Monetary Authority, but resulted in a substantial decline in Hong Kong equity markets. A number of Asian markets were also affected. This application considers the potential contagion from this crisis to the equity markets of Korea and Malaysia, with the United States equity markets used as a control for common shocks, as per Forbes and Rigobon (2002).

The non-crisis period covers from January 1, 1997, to October 17, 1997. The Hong Kong equity markets declined rapidly beginning October 20-23, 1997. The Hang Seng Index fell by almost a quarter and was associated with large falls in other international markets including Japan, the United States, and local Asian indices. The crisis period here covers from October 20, 1997, to August 31, 1998, a period often associated with the end of the Asian financial crisis, marked by the repegging of the Malaysian ringgit.

The example presented here is not intended as a definitive analysis of this crisis, but serves rather as an example of the

25. The dummy variable framework can be extended further by allowing for asymmetric shocks (Dungey, Fry, and Martin 2003, Butler and Joaquin 2002, Baig and Goldfajn 2001, Ellis and Lewis 2000 and Kaminsky and Schmukler 1999).
26. This application is based on Dungey, Fry, González-Hermosillo, and Martin (2005a)

application of the contagion testing procedures outlined in the first part of the chapter. Further analysis of this particular data set and crisis are presented in Dungey, Fry, González-Hermosillo, and Martin (2005a) and other analyses of the Asian crisis episode include Forbes and Rigobon (2002), Bae, Karolyi, and Stulz (2003) and Dungey, Fry, and Martin (2003).

2.6.1 Stylized Facts

Table 2.1 contains some descriptive statistics as well as variance-covariances of equity returns during the non-crisis and crisis sample periods for the three countries. The increase in volatility experienced during the crisis period is evident by the large increase in the variances in each country. In the case of Hong Kong the variance in equities rises over three fold, while for both Korea and Malaysia there is more than a five-fold increase. All countries experience a fall in their average returns during the crisis period. In addition, for each country the extreme minimum and maximum daily return occurs during the crisis period.

2.6.2 Implementation Issues

There are a number of practical issues in implementing the contagion tests outlined in the previous sections. These include

Table 2.1
Descriptive statistics and variance-covariances of daily percentage equity returns for selected sample periods. Non-crisis period (January 1, 1997 to October 17, 1997), Crisis period (October 20, 1997 to August 31, 1998).

	Non-crisis period			Crisis period		
	Hong Kong	Korea	Malay.	Hong Kong	Korea	Malay.
Descriptive Statistics						
Mean	0.05	−0.06	−0.21	−0.30	−0.30	−0.47
Max	6.88	4.02	1.67	17.25	10.02	20.82
Min	−5.15	−4.31	−5.82	−14.74	−11.60	−11.74
Covariance Matrix						
Hong Kong	2.24	−	−	10.79	−	−
Korea	0.26	2.05	−	1.61	13.11	−
Malay.	0.63	0.06	2.78	4.72	3.35	10.29

identifying the crisis period from the non-crisis period, the use of proxy variables to identify common factors, choice of frequency of data and the treatment of missing observations and time zones. Each of these issues is dealt with in more detail in Dungey, Fry, González-Hermosillo, and Martin (2005a), but are briefly outlined in what follows.

There are two broad approaches to identifying the timing of crises. The first approach is based on ex post observation of events in the existing literature as in Forbes and Rigobon (2002) (the FR test) and Dungey, Fry, González-Hermosillo, and Martin (2006) (the DFGM test). The second approach is based on the identification of some threshold value, such as in Favero and Giavazzi (2002) (the FG test), Bae, Karolyi, and Stulz (2003) (the BKS test), and Eichengreen, Rose, and Wyplosz (1996).

The choice of proxy variables for the common factors is often related to the choice of data frequency. One group of researchers recognizes contagion in its effects on relatively low-frequency data where appropriate macroeconomic controls can be taken into account, for example Eichengreen, Rose, and Wyplosz (1995; 1996). Then there are those who would presumably prefer to test at higher frequency, but are constrained by the availability of control data, such as Glick and Rose (1999) who consider trade flows. And finally the majority of studies consider contagion in relatively high-frequency data, at either daily or weekly frequency, where contagion is viewed as a relatively short-lived phenomenon. This is the case with all of the correlation analysis studies, most of the extreme value studies, threshold models and the latent factor models. Some studies also utilize observed high-frequency data as common variable controls, such as in Forbes and Rigobon (2002), who use U.S. interest rates. This is the approach adopted in the empirical application whereby a VAR containing one lag and U.S. returns is estimated, with the residuals representing the filtered returns. This prefiltering of the data is used in the calculations of the DFGM, FR and BKS tests, but not the FG test so as to be commensurate with their methodology.

To allow for differences in the time zones between the U.S. and the three Asian equity markets, the U.S. interest rates are dated at time $t-1$. In general, time zone alignment problems arise because markets may be open on nominally the same date, but there may be no actual trading time overlap. Kaminsky and Reinhart (2003) find significant time zone effects in equity markets. One approach to this problem is to control for differences in time zones by using moving averages of returns (Forbes and Rigobon 2002, Ellis and Lewis 2000). However, this may mask movements in asset prices and hence introduce biases into the tests of contagion. Bae, Karolyi, and Stulz (2003) choose different lags depending on the time zone under investigation, which works because two distinct time zones are involved. Dungey, Fry, González-Hermosillo, and Martin (2007) suggest using simulation methods by treating time zone problems as a missing observation issue.

Finally, missing observations cause problems in tracking volatility across markets in a single period, and are usually dealt with by either replacing the missing observation with the previous market observation or removing that data point from the investigation. In practice, most researchers seem to use a strategy of excluding days corresponding to missing observations, which is the approach adopted here.

2.6.3 Contagion Testing

To gain some insight into the relative size of contagion amongst equity markets during the crisis, table 2.2 provides the DFGM factor decompositions of the variances and the covariances given in table 2.1. As the model is just identified, these decompositions provide a breakdown of these moments in terms of the underlying factors, including contagion.

The variance decompositions in table 2.2 show that asset return volatility during the crisis is dominated by contagion with much smaller contributions from the world and idiosyncratic factors. The dominant contagion channels are from Hong Kong to both Korea (7.97) and Malaysia (5.97), which are over 50% of the total volatility of the returns in these two countries (13.11 and 10.29 respectively). There are also important reverse contagion channels from Korea and Malaysia to Hong Kong (3.71 and 4.86), and from Malaysia to Korea (3.18).

The covariance decompositions in table 2.2 reveal that contagion from Hong Kong had positive impacts on the covariances between all asset returns. In contrast, contagion from Korea and Malaysia tended to have a negative impact on several of the covariances.

The volatility decompositions discussed above provide a description of the relative magnitude of contagion linking the

Table 2.2
Unconditional volatility decompositions of Asian equity markets
during the crisis period, expressed in squared returns: based on
(2.19) and (2.20).

Components	Country		
	Variance Decomposition		
	Hong Kong	*Korea*	*Malaysia*
World factor	0.06	1.76	0.02
Idiosyncratic factor	2.17	0.28	2.76
Contagion from:			
Hong Kong	–	7.97	5.79
Korea	3.71	–	1.72
Malaysia	4.86	3.18	–
Sub-total	8.56	11.15	7.52
Total	10.79	13.11	10.29
	Covariance Decomposition		
	Hong Kong/ Korea	*Hong Kong/ Malaysia*	*Korea/ Malaysia*
World factor	0.32	0.03	0.18
Idiosyncratic factor	0.00	0.00	0.00
Contagion from:			
Hong Kong	4.16	3.55	6.80
Korea	1.02	−2.53	−0.69
Malaysia	−3.89	3.66	−2.93
Sub-total	1.29	4.69	3.17
Total	1.61	4.72	3.17

three equity markets. To examine the strength of these linkages
more formally, table 2.3 presents the results of seven contagion
tests. The first column gives the direction of contagion. The
remaining seven columns give the results of the contagion tests
based on the DFGM test, the FR test with overlapping data
(FR-0) and with non-overlapping data (FR-N), the multivariate
version of the FR test (FRM), the FG test with an endogeneity
correction (FG-E) and a non-endogeneity corrected version
(FG-N), and the BKS test. The row headed "Both" in each panel
of the table gives the results of a joint test of contagion from the
host country to the two recipient countries. The last panel of the
table gives the results of the joint test of no contagion amongst
all three countries.

Table 2.3

Contagion tests of Asian equity markets: Hong Kong (HK), Korea (K) and Malaysia (M), with p-values in parentheses.

Direction	DFGM	FR-O	FR-N	FRM	FG-E	FG-N	BKS
Hong Kong to Korea							
	158.17	−0.30	−1.00	1.18	117.58	7.59	2.21
	(0.00)	(0.62)	(0.84)	(0.28)	(0.00)	(0.18)	(0.14)
Hong Kong to Malaysia							
	1.57	−0.51	−0.26	1.16	137.67	8.88	6.02
	(0.21)	(0.69)	(0.60)	(0.28)	(0.00)	(0.11)	(0.01)
Hong Kong to Korea and Malaysia							
	182.06	−	−	1.97	217.45	17.85	10.02
	(0.00)			(0.37)	(0.00)	(0.06)	(0.00)
Korea to Hong Kong							
	45.65	−0.32	−1.06	1.52	304.92	11.08	2.15
	(0.00)	(0.62)	(0.86)	(0.22)	(0.00)	(0.09)	(0.14)
Korea to Malaysia							
	12.09	−0.26	0.21	1.03	356.65	17.55	2.37
	(0.00)	(0.60)	(0.42)	(0.31)	(0.00)	(0.01)	(0.12)
Korea to Hong Kong and Malaysia							
	439.76	−	−	1.87	65.40	33.91	8.52
	(0.00)			(0.39)	(0.00)	0.00	(0.00)
Malaysia to Hong Kong							
	53.58	−0.35	0.19	6.58	146.70	23.25	6.86
	(0.00)	(0.64)	(0.43)	(0.01)	(0.00)	(0.00)	(0.01)
Malaysia to Korea							
	0.77	−0.11	0.65	4.96	73.39	24.64	2.18
	(0.38)	(0.54)	(0.26)	(0.03)	(0.00)	(0.00)	(0.14)
Malaysia to Hong Kong and Korea							
	70.01	−	−	10.77	202.75	51.44	11.15
	(0.00)			(0.01)	(0.00)	(0.00)	(0.00)
Joint							
	772.47	−	−	14.36	1085.28	101.97	−
	(0.00)			(0.03)	(0.00)	(0.00)	

The results in table 2.3 show that the Forbes and Rigobon test (FR-O) finds no evidence of contagion in any of the channels tested. This lack of any rejection of the null hypothesis is consistent with the discussion in Section 2.5, where it was concluded that this is a conservative test as it is biased towards zero as a result of the variance of the test statistic being incorrect when the non-crisis period is defined as the total sample period.

To examine the issue concerning the downward bias in the Forbes and Rigobon test further, the results of the Forbes and Rigobon test (FR-N), where the non-crisis period is based on non overlapping data, are also presented in table 2.3. The results show that four of the six bivariate contagion tests do indeed lead to lower p-values. However, at the 5% level, this test still seems to be conservative as it does not identify any significant contagion linkages. Further confirmation of the bias in the Forbes and Rigobon test FR-O, arising from overlapping data, is given by the multivariate version of the Forbes and Rigobon test (FRM). Here the results point to uniformly stronger contagious linkages, that is lower p-values, with significant evidence of contagion detected from Malaysia to both Hong Kong and Korea.

In complete contrast to the FR test results in table 2.3, the FG test (FG-E) finds evidence of contagion in all cases.[27] To control for potential weak instrument problems, the Favero and Giavazzi test is recomputed with no endogeneity correction (FG-N) by simply estimating the pertinent structural model by OLS. The results show a very different story with now just half of the bivariate contagion tests showing significant evidence of contagion at the 5% level. The strong evidence of contagion based on FG-E appear to be spurious and arise from the presence of weak instruments.[28] Comparing the results of the FG-N test and DFGM tests shows that the two methods produce similar qualitative results in four of the six bivariate cases at the 10% level. The two differences are the test of contagion from Hong Kong to Korea where the DFGM test finds evidence of contagion, and the test of contagion from Malaysia to Korea where the FG-N test finds evidence of contagion. The transmission channel from Hong Kong to Korea identified by the DFGM test is consistent with the strong level of contagion identified in the variance decomposition given in table 2.3. In addition, the lack of significant evidence of contagion from Malaysia to Korea identified by the DFGM test is also consistent

27. The Favero and Giavazzi test based on the dummy variable in (2.58) identifies 19 outliers: 1 common outlier, 5 outliers in Hong Kong, 6 in Korea and 7 in Malaysia.
28. Performing the weak instrument test based on the F-test of the regressors in the three reduced form equations yields values of 12.89, 7.62, 15.37. Using the critical values reported in Stock, Wright, and Yogo (2000, Table 1) shows that the null of a weak instrument is not rejected.

with the moderate level of contagion identified in the variance decomposition in table 2.2 as well.

The last test results reported in table 2.3 are for the Bae, Karolyi, and Stultz (BKS) test.[29] Comparing the bivariate DFGM and BKS results shows that the two testing procedures give opposite results where Hong Kong and Korea are the hosts, but the same results where Malaysia is the host. Part of the explanation underlying these results could be the dating of the crisis period, which is determined a priori in the case of the DFGM test, whereas for the BKS test is determined endogenously. An additional issue surrounding the BKS test is that it discards information in constructing the dummy dependent and independent variables, which may in turn lead to a loss of efficiency in the parameter estimates.

In general, these results in table 2.3 provide evidence of the difficulties in obtaining consistent information on the existence of contagion from the different tests. This is not unique to this example, similar outcomes emerge in other applied examples for the 1994 Mexican crisis and the 2001 Argentine crisis provided in Dungey, Fry, González-Hermosillo, and Martin (2005a).

2.7 Conclusions

This chapter has overviewed a number of important tests for the presence and characteristics of contagion in financial markets adopted in the current literature. Using a framework of a latent factor model similar to that proposed in the finance literature, the different testing methodologies are shown to be related. In essence, each method is shown to be a test on a common parameter regarding the transmission of a shock from one country or market to another.

An important result of this chapter is that the main distinguishing feature of alternative empirical models of contagion is the way in which the information is used to identify contagion. Dungey, Fry, González-Hermosillo, and Martin (2006) and Forbes and Rigobon (2002) use the information on all of the

29. The BKS test is based on 22 exceedances, 4 co-exceedances between Hong Kong and Korea, 5 co-exceedances between Hong Kong and Malaysia and 4 co-exceedances between Korea and Malaysia.

shocks in the crisis period to test for contagion. Under certain conditions these two models are the same. Favero and Giavazzi (2002) utilize shift dummies at selected crisis points to represent potentially contagious transmissions. Eichengreen, Rose, and Wyplosz (1995; 1996) also use dummy variables to identify contagion, however they transform both the dependent and independent indicators into binary variables, which results in a further reduction of the information used in estimation. Bae, Karolyi, and Stulz (2003) provide an extension of the Eichengreen, Rose, and Wyplosz approach by allowing for a polychotomous dependent variable, based on the number of co-exceedances in their crisis indicator.

Some of the properties and relationships of the various contagion tests were demonstrated in an empirical application of the Asian crisis of 1997–1998. A number of empirical issues concerning missing observations, time zones, dating of crises and data frequency were also discussed. The results showed that the Forbes and Rigobon contagion test was a conservative test as it failed to find evidence of contagion in any of the linkages tested. The Favero and Giavazzi test was at the other extreme, finding evidence of contagion in all cases investigated. Much of this evidence of linkages was found to be spurious, being the result of weak instruments. Correcting the Favero and Giavazzi test for weak instruments yielded contagion channels similar to the channels identified by the DFGM test. The BKS test results tended to be inconsistent with the results of these last two tests.

The policy relevant outcome of this chapter is to highlight the difficulties for users of econometric methodologies in making an assessment of contagion. If policy is designed to mitigate contagion effects, then knowledge of the existence and extent of contagion effects is vital. This chapter has shown that a number of popular methods for detecting contagion when applied to the same data set give vastly different outcomes. Using the FR test analysts will conclude that there is no contagion, using the BKS test they will conclude it is ever present. Policy responses to contagion from these outcomes differ greatly— from no response at all in the case that contagion does not exist, to invoking a major platform of financial reform if contagion is dominant. Clearly these issues are important.

This chapter has shown that the main tests proposed in the literature can be nested within a single framework that dominates them in terms of information usage. Hence, it makes sense to attempt to use that encompassing framework to make an assessment of the presence of contagion during crises. This is the subject of the next three chapters, which work toward the final model of multiple markets and multiple assets across different crises in a fully specified model of contagion in Chapter 5. As building blocks, and to explore various aspects of the model design, Chapters 3 and 4 begin with applications to single asset markets, bonds and equities respectively, during the Russian and LTCM crises of 1998. The issues considered include: (i) the behavior of different asset returns; (ii) incorporating region-specific factors to explore whether contagion is regional; (iii) examining whether contagion is more truly an emerging market than a developed market issue; (iv) accounting for nested crises and; (v) the potential for structural breaks in the data-generating process. The next chapter turns to the applications of the latent factor framework to emerging and developed market bonds during the Russian and LTCM crises of late 1998.

3

Contagion in Global Bond Markets

3.1 Introduction

This chapter examines evidence for contagion in the period corresponding to the Russian bond default in August 1998, followed by the announcement of a recapitalization package for the hedge fund Long Term Capital Management (LTCM) in September, where bond markets in emerging and industrial countries exhibited widespread volatility. The Bank of International Settlements survey of market participants characterized this period as " the worst crisis"in recent times (Committee of the Global Financial System 1999, p.40). A special feature of this crisis was that the duration was extremely short, possibly as a result of the aggressive easing of monetary policy by the U.S. Federal Reserve in the period following the recapitalization announcement.

This chapter identifies the transmission mechanisms of shocks from both the Russian bond default and the LTCM recapitalization announcement to bond markets in emerging and industrial countries. Most analyses of recent financial crises tend to focus on either currency, banking, or equity markets. In contrast, there is little empirical literature on the spread of crises through international bond markets.[1] This is partly because a consistent and comprehensive historical time series database on bonds for many emerging economies is difficult to obtain. It is also partly the result of bond markets being relatively more stable during other financial crises such as the 1997–1998 Asian crisis, where it was equity and currency markets that exhibited relatively greater volatility; see for example Forbes and Rigobon (2002), Bae, Karolyi and Stulz (2003) and Granger, Huang, and Yang (2000). The results on bond markets during the Russian/LTCM crisis are extended in Chapter 4 to equity markets and in Chapter 5 to cross-market linkages between bond and equity markets.

The empirical analysis is conducted on a panel of daily bond spreads for a broad range of emerging and industrial countries over 1998. The spreads of the emerging economies are the long-term sovereign bonds issued in international markets relative to a comparable risk-free benchmark, whilst the spreads of the industrial countries are the long-term corporate bonds issued in the domestic economy relative to a comparable risk-free benchmark. One advantage of working with bond spreads is that they reflect the risk premium that investors assign to prospective borrowers. These risks include the perceived creditworthiness of borrowers, the willingness of lenders to take on risk, and the liquidity in the market, all of which are entangled during crisis episodes.[2]

The identification of the transmission mechanisms linking international bond markets is based on specifying a latent factor model of bond spreads. Four types of factors are considered. The first three types of factors include a common factor that impacts upon all bond markets, a set of regional factors, which are common to countries within a geographical area, and country-specific factors, which are idiosyncratic to a specific bond market. The fourth type of factor

---

1. The exceptions are Dungey, Fry, González-Hermosillo, and Martin (2006), which this chapter is based on, Jorion (2000), and the Committee on the Global Financial System (1999), who all study the effects of the Russian and LTCM shocks on international bond markets.
2. This interpretation is consistent with the widening of the liquidity premium on otherwise similar assets (e.g. on-the-run 30-year versus off-the-run 29-year U.S. Treasury bonds) following the LTCM recapitalization announcement. The credit risk view of the Russian shock is also consistent with a cash-out of liquid markets with increased credit risks as investors' rebalanced their portfolios.

investigated is the contagion channel as it represents the effects of contemporaneous movements across markets having conditioned on the common, regional, and idiosyncratic factors; see Chapter 2 for a further discussion of this definition. An important feature of this modeling strategy is that it is possible to decompose the observed volatility in bond spreads into various components and thereby identify the contribution of contagion to total volatility in each country's bond market.[3]

The empirical analysis leads to four important findings. First, there is substantial contagion evidence emerging from the Russian shock but relatively little from the LTCM shock. The contribution of contagion to total observed volatility in the change in bond spreads ranged from under 1% (to the United States) to around 17% (to the Netherlands and Brazil). The second result points to the importance of financial exposures to the crisis countries in transmitting the crisis: The countries most affected by contagion from Russia had substantial banking exposures to Russia. The third result provides some evidence supporting the literature that contagion effects are regional in nature: Contagion is consistently present in the Eastern European countries of the sample. The final important result is that contagion effects are not necessarily more apparent in developing financial markets than developed markets. Although the level of volatility experienced in developing markets is generally higher than developed markets, the proportionate effect of contagion does not systematically differ between them.

The remainder of this chapter is organized as follows. Section 3.2 provides a review of the background of events and puts forward a set of four propositions about the transmission of the crises. This is followed by a discussion of the empirical characteristics of the data in Section 3.3. A model of contagion is described in Section 3.4, which extends upon the latent factor structure developed in Chapter 2. The estimation method is discussed in Section 3.5 followed by the empirical results in Section 3.6. Concluding comments are given in Section 3.7.

---

3. Another advantage of the latent factor model is that it circumvents the need to use proxy variables to measure market fundamentals, as they are identified by extracting the common movements in bond spreads. Examples of using proxy variables to measure market fundamentals include Eichengreen, Rose, and Wyplosz (1996), Glick and Rose (1999), and Forbes and Rigobon (2002).

3.2 Background of Events and Propositions

3.2.1 Stylized Facts

During the Asian crisis, the turmoil that began with the devaluation of the Thai baht in July 1997 quickly precipitated declines in currencies and equities in the region and in other emerging markets (Granger, Huang, and Yang 2000). This contrasts with debt markets during this period where the effects on the risk premia of international bonds issued by emerging countries were rather limited. Apart from the relatively short period of turmoil in global financial markets resulting from the speculative attack on Hong Kong on October 27, 1997, bond spreads remained relatively stable in non-Asian countries during the second half of 1997 (see figure 3.1).

Figures 3.1 and 3.2 also show that the stability experienced in international bond markets in the second half of 1997 continued into the first part of 1998. However, on August 17, 1998, when Russia widened the trading band of the ruble, imposed a 90-day moratorium on the repayment of private external debt, and announced its plan to restructure official debt obligations due to the end of 1999, financial turmoil ensued.[4] Following the Russian default, spreads in other bond markets jumped, particularly in emerging markets, as markets reassessed global credit risks (see figures 3.1 and 3.2).

In a matter of weeks after the Russian crisis, on September 23, 1998, financial markets learned of the plan to rescue LTCM, a large U.S. hedge fund that was in danger of collapse. LTCM operated by placing highly leveraged positions on the expectation of falling yield spreads based on historical evidence. Many historical correlations were overturned following the Russian crisis with LTCM losing enormous amounts of money on these positions; see Jorion (2000), who documents the evolution of LTCM's problems. The situation became serious quickly, to the extent that the New York Federal Reserve acted to facilitate a meeting between major banks, which eventually cooperated to provide a bailout package to the troubled hedge fund.

During this period the U.S. Federal Reserve cut interest rates in three steps, on September 29, October 15, and November 17,

---

4. See Kharas, Pinto, and Ulatov (2001) for a discussion of the Russian crisis.

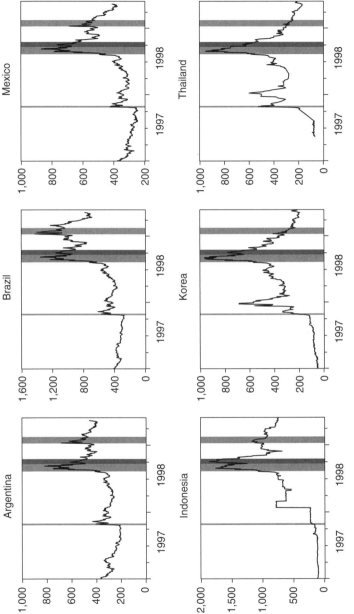

Figure 3.1 Bond spreads, January 1997 to May 1999 (basis points). The shaded areas refer to episodes of crisis in international bond markets: the Hong Kong speculative attack on October 27, 1997; the Russian bond default on August 17, 1998; the LTCM recapitalization announcement on September 23, 1998; the inter-FOMC Fed interest rate cut on October 15, 1998; and the Brazilian effective devaluation on January 13, 1999 followed by several weeks of internal turmoil at the central bank. Data Sources: U.S. Federal Reserve, Bloomberg, Scotia Capital and Credit Swiss First Boston.

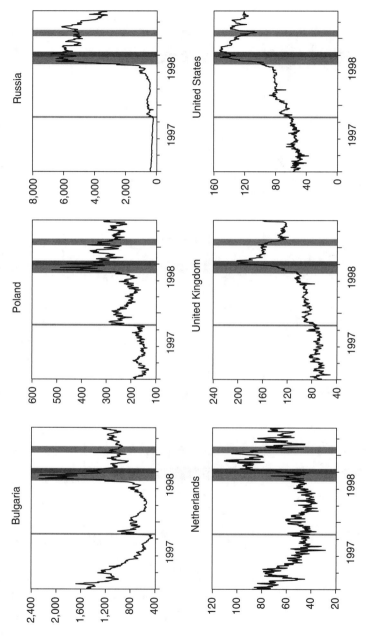

Figure 3.1 (Cont'd)

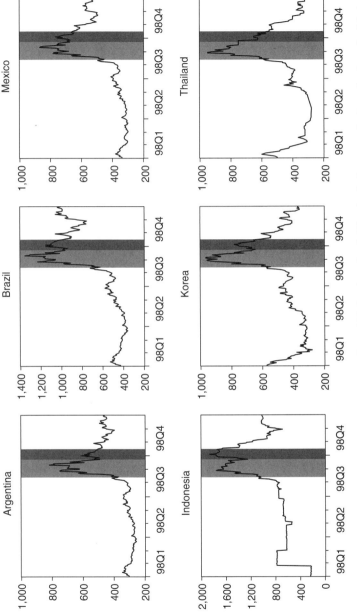

Figure 3.2 Bond spreads, January 1998 to December 1998 (basis points). The shaded areas refer to episodes of crisis in international bond markets during this period: the Russian bond default on August 17, 1998; the LTCM recapitalization announcement on September 23, 1998; and the inter-FOMC Fed interest rate cut on October 15, 1998. Data Sources: U.S. Federal Reserve, Bloomberg, Scotia Capital and Credit Swiss First Boston.

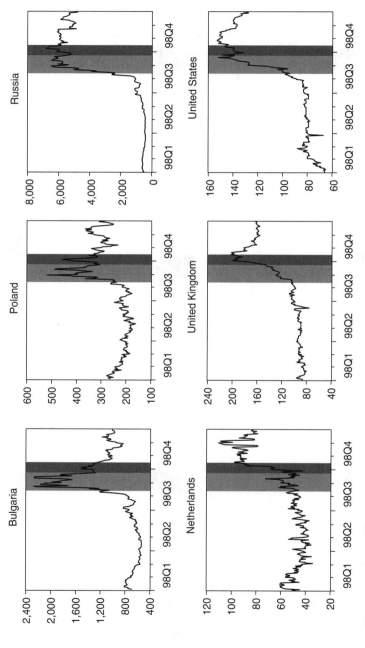

Figure 3.2 (Cont'd)

partly due to concerns that the dramatic rises in bond spreads, particularly for corporate debt, were indicative of a liquidity crisis. The October 15 interest rate cut was considered a surprise, as it occurred between FOMC meetings. This cut was also interpreted as signaling a return to confidence in the markets, according to market participants surveyed in Committee on the Global Financial System (1999, pp. 9,39,45).[5]

Informal examination of the data for the second half of 1998 (figure 3.2) suggests that the Russian crisis had a discernible impact on bond markets in both developed economies and emerging markets. The LTCM recapitalization announcement also appears to have had an impact on all the countries, with a relatively smaller hump experienced by most emerging countries relative to the effect of the Russian shock. The data suggest that the Russian and the LTCM recapitalization announcement shocks were reinforcing in their effects on other financial markets as practically all markets experienced two jumps in their spreads: one following the Russian default (the first band in figure 3.2) and another one following the announcement of the LTCM financial problems (the second band in figure 3.2).

Unlike other recent financial crises, the shocks that occurred during August and September 1998 seem to have been trans-mitted across countries with little in common. This includes countries that do not fit traditional explanations of contagion based on trade links, competitive devaluation, or regional effects as suggested in the taxonomies of contagion by Lowell, Neu, and Tong (1998) and Goldstein (1998). These crises affected countries as diverse as the United Kingdom and Brazil, and spanned emerging and developed markets. Disentangling the crises of 1998 is particularly complex because of its relative brevity and the fact that two distinct shocks occurred within weeks of each other.

---

5. The exact timing of the LTCM crisis is necessarily approximate as pressures began building before the announcement of the recapitalization package for LTCM. Here we date the crisis as beginning with the recapitalization announcement on September 23, 1998, and ending with inter-FOMC Fed interest rate cut on October 15, 1998, which signaled the beginning of the "end" of the LTCM crisis. This otherwise arbitrary "end" to the crisis of 1998, is supported by the findings of Kumar and Persaud (2001).

3.2.2 Propositions

The discussion above suggests that a number of propositions can be formulated around the transmission of contagion across national borders. Four broad propositions are formulated. The first is based on the existence of contagion, whereas the other three propositions are concerned with the conditions that control the strength of contagious transmission mechanisms.

Proposition A: Transmission of the crises through contagion   The empirical evidence for contagion effects is mixed. Some papers find little evidence of contagion while others find significant contagion; see for example Forbes and Rigobon (2002), Bae, Karolyi, and Stulz (2003), and Favero and Giavazzi (2002). Most approaches test the statistical significance of the contagion. Here we consider whether contagion effects exist and measure their relative contribution to volatility in the bond spreads during the crisis. If contagion is not important, then the transmission mechanisms solely arise from trade and other macroeconomic linkages that occur during non-crisis periods as well.

Proposition B: Exposure through the banking system   Countries whose financial institutions have relatively larger exposures to Russia are expected to experience greater contagion. The implications of financial and institutional linkages between countries as a channel of contagion have been investigated by Kaminsky and Reinhart (2000), Van Rijckeghem and Weder (2001; 2003), and Pritsker (2001). Table 3.1 provides information on the relative size of offshore banking exposure for the industrial economies of the United States, United Kingdom, and the Netherlands. These figures show that as a proportion of the total economy, total offshore banking exposure is 23.4% for the Netherlands in 1998, which is nearly twice that of the United States and more than 10 times that of the United Kongdom. In terms of exposure to Russia, the proportion is nearly 10 times more than both the United States and the United Kingdom. These figures suggest that the Netherlands is potentially more vulnerable to contagion arising from the Russian bond default than either the United States or the United Kingdom.

Table 3.1
Industrial Country Offshore Banking Exposure, June 1998 (nominal US$ terms).[a]

Country	Size of Economy (GNI, US$bil.)	Offshore Banking Exposure			
		Total	Russia	Total	Russia
		(US$ million)		(% of GNI)	
	(1)	(2)	(3)	(2) to (1)	(3) to (2)
United States	8447	160784	7781	1.9	0.1
United Kingdom	1327	165815	1834	12.5	0.1
Netherlands	403	94394	3979	23.4	1.0

(a) Sources: Column (1) is drawn from World Bank World Tables provided in dX Data; Columns (2) and (3) are sourced from the historical data from Table 9C in the BIS Quarterly Review.

Proposition C: Regional effects   If contagion impacts within regions, it is expected that the Russian bond default should particularly impact upon the Eastern European countries, Poland and Bulgaria. The importance of testing the regional effects of contagion is emphasized by Eichengreen, Rose, and Wypolz (1996), Glick and Rose (1999), and Kaminsky and Reinhart (2000).

Proposition D: Fundamentals and vulnerabilities   Countries with strong market fundamentals are less susceptible to the effects of contagion (Mody and Taylor 2003, and Sachs, Tornell, and Velasco 1996). This suggests that the emerging market economies investigated here are more likely to be prone to contagion than the developed economies, namely the United States, the United Kingdom, and the Netherlands. In a similar vein, the Committee on the Global Financial System (1999, pp. 7–8) claims that the Russian crisis affected emerging markets, while the LTCM recapitalization announcement affected developed markets. In equity markets, Kaminsky and Reinhart (2002) find that developed markets act as a conduit for financial crises between emerging markets, while Bae, Karolyi, and Stulz (2003) find greater impact of crises on emerging equity markets.

3.3 Data

The dataset comprises daily data for 12 countries collected for February to December 1998 (Argentina, Brazil, Mexico,

Indonesia, Korea, Thailand, Bulgaria, Poland, Russia, the Netherlands, the United Kingdom and the United States). This sample period allows estimation to incorporate a clear pre-crisis period and the two crisis events of the Russian bond default and the LTCM recapitalization announcement. The choice of daily data, over lower frequency data, is made in order to disentangle the effects of the Russian shock and the LTCM recapitalization announcement, which occurred in close proximity to each other.

The data represent the spread of long-term debt over the appropriate risk-free yield for each country (see Appendix 3.A for source descriptions, definitions and details). This spread is labeled as the "premium" while recognizing that it does in fact reflect a myriad of factors, including the liquidity premium and the term structure of the yield curve. The choice of the risk-free rate is specific to each long-term bond. In the case of emerging countries, sovereign bonds are issued in United States dollars and hence the spread is calculated against the comparable maturity-matched U.S. Treasury bond rate. Where possible, the bonds selected for emerging markets are sovereign issues to reflect the true cost of new foreign capital — the exceptions are Poland and Bulgaria, which are represented by Brady bonds. In the case of the developed bond markets, which are able to issue international bonds in domestic currency, BBB investment grade corporate bonds are compared to the corresponding risk-free Treasury bond in each country.[6]

The data for the United States are obtained directly from the Federal Reserve, and not from published sources. The source of the data for countries other than the United States is the authorities of each country. This data set was originally collated for the Committee on the Global Financial System to examine the events surrounding the market stresses in the third quarter of 1998 and is summarized in the Committee on the Global Financial System (1999). In those cases where there are missing observations, the data are obtained from either Bloomberg database or Credit Swiss First Boston directly (see Appendix 3.A for more details).

---

6. Below-investment grade corporate issues experienced even bigger jumps in their spreads and in their volatility. However, data limitations restricted the study to investment grade bonds.

A potential problem with using just price data is that prices may be biased due to lack of active market makers during the crisis periods. This is especially true during the LTCM recapitalization announcement period, which was a crisis of liquidity. To circumvent this problem would require data on trade quantities. However, quantity data are not available at high frequency for the range of countries considered. Using lower frequency data would have the disadvantage of yielding insufficient information to characterize the Russian and LTCM recapitalization announcement crises, which are of a relatively short duration. For this reason, attention is focused on using daily price data.

The statistical characteristics of the data are summarized as follows, with full details given in Appendix 3.B. The rise in spreads over the period is approximated by a unit root, as the corresponding risk free rates remained relatively constant during 1998. Both larger means and absolute movements are evident in the premia of developing markets compared with the industrialized countries. The data display non-normality, and fitting univariate integrated GARCH(1,1) models to the changes in the premia suggests that there is a common time-varying volatility structure underlying the data. This feature of the structure is exploited in the model described in the following section.

3.4 A Factor Model of Bond Spreads

Volatility in the premia of each country is hypothesized to be influenced by events that are country-specific and events that are common to all economies. However, it is difficult to ascertain both the timing and nature of these events. In the existing literature, contagion is tested by conditioning on events chosen by the researcher after the observed financial crises; for example the work of Eichengreen, Rose, and Wyplosz (1995; 1996), Sachs, Tornell, and Velasco (1996), and Glick and Rose (1999) follow this approach. The economic indicators chosen in this way are often statistically insignificant, and it is difficult to know whether they are the correct choice even ex-post. A desirable alternative, noted by authors such as Dooley (2000) and Edwards (2000), is to use a modeling specification that does not require the choice of specific indicators with which to associate the crises, that is to use latent factors.

Latent factor models have been specified for a number of markets. The majority of the existing empirical work has focused on currency and equity markets, such as represented in Diebold and Nerlove (1989), Ng, Engle, and Rothschild (1992), Mahieu and Schotman (1994), and King, Sentana, and Wadhwani (1994). Empirical work on interest rates is rather less extensive. Gregory and Watts (1995) explore long bond yields across countries, while Dungey, Martin and Pagan (2000) apply a latent factor model to the spreads between individual country bonds and the U.S. bond.[7]

The basic model of the bond market adopted in this chapter is similar to that specified by Forbes and Rigobon (2002) and King, Sentana and Wadhwani (1994) for equity markets and builds on the specification outlined in Chapter 2. Letting $r_{i,t}$ be the interest rate on the bond in country i, the interest rate is determined by a risk-free rate of interest, $rf_{i,t}$, a world factor, w_t and a time-varying country-specific factor $u_{i,t}$

$$r_{i,t} = rf_{i,t} + \lambda_i w_t + \phi_i u_{i,t}, \qquad i = 1, \cdots, n, \tag{3.1}$$

where n is the number of bond markets. The loadings on these world and country-specific factors are given by the parameters λ_i and ϕ_i, respectively. The common factor, w_t, affects the premia in all countries, but with a differing parameter in each case.

Regional effects have been posited to be important in the spread of crises, for example in the work of Kaminsky and Reinhart (2002) and Glick and Rose (1999). To incorporate these effects, equation (3.1) is extended as follows

$$r_{i,t} = rf_{i,t} + \lambda_i w_t + \phi_i u_{i,t} + \gamma_i R_{k,t}, \quad i = 1, \cdots, n, \quad k = Lat, As, Eur, \tag{3.2}$$

where $R_{k,t}$ is a time-varying regional factor and $K = 3$ is the number of regions. The first regional factor is common to the Latin American countries (Argentina, Brazil and Mexico) and is denoted $R_{Lat,t}$. The second is a regional factor common to the Asian economies (Indonesia, Korea, and Thailand)

---

7. A similar class of models is adopted by Kose, Otrok, and Whiteman (2003) in studying business cycles.

denoted as $R_{As,t}$, whilst the third regional factor corresponds to Eastern Europe (Bulgaria, Poland, and Russia), which is denoted by $R_{Eur,t}$. No regional factor is included for the industrialized countries comprising the United States, the United Kingdom, and the Netherlands. Defining the premium to be $P_{i,t} = r_{i,t} - rf_{i,t}$, the model without contagion is specified as

$$
\begin{bmatrix} P_{A,t} \\ P_{B,t} \\ P_{M,t} \\ P_{I,t} \\ P_{K,t} \\ P_{T,t} \\ P_{BU,t} \\ P_{P,t} \\ P_{R,t} \\ P_{N,t} \\ P_{UK,t} \\ P_{U,t} \end{bmatrix} = \begin{bmatrix} \lambda_A \\ \lambda_B \\ \lambda_M \\ \lambda_I \\ \lambda_K \\ \lambda_T \\ \lambda_{BU} \\ \lambda_P \\ \lambda_R \\ \lambda_N \\ \lambda_{UK} \\ \lambda_U \end{bmatrix} w_t + \begin{bmatrix} \gamma_{A,Lat} & 0 & 0 \\ \gamma_{B,Lat} & 0 & 0 \\ \gamma_{M,Lat} & 0 & 0 \\ 0 & \gamma_{I,As} & 0 \\ 0 & \gamma_{K,As} & 0 \\ 0 & \gamma_{T,As} & 0 \\ 0 & 0 & \gamma_{BU,Eur} \\ 0 & 0 & \gamma_{P,Eur} \\ 0 & 0 & \gamma_{R,Eur} \\ 0 & 0 & 0 \\ 0 & 0 & 0 \\ 0 & 0 & 0 \end{bmatrix}
$$

$$
\times \begin{bmatrix} R_{Lat,t} \\ R_{As,t} \\ R_{Eur,t} \end{bmatrix} + \begin{bmatrix} \phi_A & 0 & 0 & \cdots & 0 \\ 0 & \phi_B & 0 & \cdots & 0 \\ \vdots & \vdots & \ddots & \cdots & \vdots \\ 0 & 0 & 0 & \cdots & \phi_U \end{bmatrix} \begin{bmatrix} u_{A,t} \\ u_{B,t} \\ \vdots \\ u_{U,t} \end{bmatrix}, \tag{3.3}
$$

where the countries are: Argentina (A), Brazil (B), Mexico (M), Indonesia (I), Korea (K), Thailand (T), Bulgaria (BU), Poland (P), Russia (R), Netherlands (N), United Kingdom (UK), and the United States (U).

To incorporate the large movements in the premia over the sample period identified in 3.2, the common factor is specified as integrated of order one

$$
w_t = w_{t-1} + \eta_t, \tag{3.4}
$$

where η_t is a stationary disturbance term. The regional factors in (3.3) are also specified as integrated processes of order one

$$
R_{k,t} = R_{k,t-1} + v_{k,t}, \quad where\ k = Lat,\ As,\ Eur, \tag{3.5}
$$

where $v_{k,t}$ are stationary disturbance terms. In addition, equation (3.3) shows that each premium has a unique idiosyncratic error, or country-specific factor, $u_{i,t}$. To complete the specification of the non-contagion model, the disturbance processes are assumed to be distributed as

$$\eta_t, v_{Lat,t}, v_{As,t}, v_{Eur,t}, u_{1,t}, u_{2,t}, \ldots, u_{12,t} \sim N(0, H_t), \qquad (3.6)$$

where in general H_t is a 16-variate system of independent GARCH processes normalized to have unit unconditional variances. Whilst the factors are assumed to be independent, the model nonetheless is able to capture the comovements in bond spreads in the mean, as well as in the variance. An important advantage of adopting a factor structure is that it provides a parsimonious representation of the data, thereby circumventing the need to estimate highly parameterized multivariate GARCH models. Here we restrict the GARCH to the world factor, following the preliminary GARCH results reported in Appendix 3.B, Table B.4, which showed a high degree of commonality amongst the conditional variance structure of the premia.[8]

Using the definition of contagion given in Chapter 2, equation (3.3) is now augmented to allow for contagion by including the idiosyncratic shocks from Russia ($u_{R,t}$) and the United States ($u_{U,t}$) into each equation of the factor model. The full factor model is represented by

$$
\begin{bmatrix} P_{A,t} \\ P_{B,t} \\ P_{M,t} \\ P_{I,t} \\ P_{K,t} \\ P_{T,t} \\ P_{BU,t} \\ P_{P,t} \\ P_{R,t} \\ P_{N,t} \\ P_{UK,t} \\ P_{U,t} \end{bmatrix}
=
\begin{bmatrix} \lambda_A \\ \lambda_B \\ \lambda_M \\ \lambda_I \\ \lambda_K \\ \lambda_T \\ \lambda_{BU} \\ \lambda_P \\ \lambda_R \\ \lambda_N \\ \lambda_{UK} \\ \lambda_U \end{bmatrix} w_t
+
\begin{bmatrix}
\gamma_{A,Lat} & 0 & 0 \\
\gamma_{B,Lat} & 0 & 0 \\
\gamma_{M,Lat} & 0 & 0 \\
0 & \gamma_{I,As} & 0 \\
0 & \gamma_{K,As} & 0 \\
0 & \gamma_{T,As} & 0 \\
0 & 0 & \gamma_{BU,Eur} \\
0 & 0 & \gamma_{P,Eur} \\
0 & 0 & \gamma_{R,Eur} \\
0 & 0 & 0 \\
0 & 0 & 0 \\
0 & 0 & 0
\end{bmatrix}
\begin{bmatrix} R_{Lat,t} \\ R_{As,t} \\ R_{Eur,t} \end{bmatrix}
$$

---

8. The three regional factors were initially assumed to exhibit GARCH processes, but were found to be statistically insignificant.

$$+ \begin{bmatrix} \phi_A & 0 & 0 & \cdots & 0 \\ 0 & \phi_B & 0 & \cdots & 0 \\ \vdots & \vdots & \ddots & \cdots & \vdots \\ 0 & 0 & 0 & \cdots & \phi_U \end{bmatrix} \begin{bmatrix} u_{A,t} \\ u_{B,t} \\ \vdots \\ u_{U,t} \end{bmatrix}$$

$$+ \begin{bmatrix} \kappa_{A,R} & \kappa_{A,U} \\ \kappa_{B,R} & \kappa_{B,U} \\ \kappa_{M,R} & \kappa_{M,U} \\ \kappa_{I,R} & \kappa_{I,U} \\ \kappa_{K,R} & \kappa_{K,U} \\ \kappa_{T,R} & \kappa_{T,U} \\ \kappa_{BU,R} & \kappa_{BU,U} \\ \kappa_{P,R} & \kappa_{P,U} \\ 0 & \kappa_{R,U} \\ \kappa_{N,R} & \kappa_{N,U} \\ \kappa_{UK,R} & \kappa_{UK,U} \\ \kappa_{U,R} & 0 \end{bmatrix} \begin{bmatrix} u_{R,t} \\ I_t u_{U,t} \end{bmatrix}, \tag{3.7}$$

where the strength of contagion from both Russia and LTCM are controlled by the parameters $\kappa_{i,R}$ and $\kappa_{i,U}$, whilst the other parameters are as defined in equation (3.3). For identification reasons there are no own effects, that is $\kappa_{R,R} = \kappa_{U,U} = 0$.

Given the global dominance of U.S. financial markets, it is desirable to isolate the LTCM shock from other U.S.-based news. To achieve this the contagion effects of LTCM, $(u_{U,t})$, in equation (3.7) is multiplied by the indicator variable I_t. This takes the value of 1 for the period of the LTCM recapitalization announcement shock, September 23, 1998, to October 15, 1998, and 0 for the non-LTCM crisis period.[9] This choice of dates is consistent with the Committee on the Global Financial System (1999, pp.8–9). It begins with the recapitalization package announced on September 23, and ends with the inter-FOMC rate cut by the Federal Reserve on October 15, a date supported by Kumar and Persaud (2001). Whilst it is apparent that there were signals that LTCM was in difficulty before September 1998, reports suggest that the true size of the problem became clearer around the time of the meetings coordinated

9. In Dungey, Fry, González-Hermosillo, and Martin (2002b), the indicator variable, I_t, was omitted — the influence of the U.S. economy in global markets means that the impact of the LTCM shock was somewhat overstated. We thank Charles Goodhart for his suggestions on the structure of the dummy variable.

by the Federal Reserve, see for example Shirreff (1998). As the clearest signal to the market of LTCM's difficulties was the recapitalization announcement, this is used as the starting date.

A useful way of examining the results from estimating a model such as (3.7) is to consider the contribution that each factor makes to total volatility in the movement of the premium of each country. As the factors are independent, the total variance of the change in the premia for each economy can be conveniently decomposed as[10]

$$Var(\Delta P_{i,t}) = \lambda_i^2 + \gamma_i^2 + 2\kappa_{i,R}^2 + 2\kappa_{i,U}^2 + 2\phi_i^2. \qquad (3.8)$$

The results of interest are then given as the proportion of the total volatility in the changes in the premium for country i due to the:

(i)   Contribution of the world factor $\qquad = \quad \dfrac{\lambda_i^2}{Var(\Delta P_i)}$

(ii)   Contribution of the regional factor $\qquad = \quad \dfrac{\gamma_i^2}{Var(\Delta P_i)}$

(iii)   Contribution of the country-specific factor $\qquad = \quad \dfrac{\phi_i^2}{Var(\Delta P_i)}$

(iv)   Contribution of contagion from Russia $\qquad = \quad \dfrac{2\kappa_{i,R}^2}{Var(\Delta P_i)}$

(v)   Contribution of contagion from the United States $\qquad = \quad \dfrac{2\kappa_{i,U}^2}{Var(\Delta P_i)}$

3.5 Estimation Method

Gourieroux and Monfort (1994) have shown that direct estimation of the factor model in equation (3.4) by likelihood methods based on existing deterministic numerical procedures is infeasible as a result of the nonlinearization arising from the GARCH conditional variance structure. Estimation procedures based on the Kalman filter or GMM only produce an approximation to the likelihood and thereby yield inconsistent parameter estimates. To circumvent problems of parameter

---

10. The expression in equation (3.8) is based on rewriting equation (3.7) as an error correction model; for details see Dungey, Fry, González-Hermosillo, and Martin (2002b) equations (3.10) to (3.16).

inconsistency we adopt the indirect estimation techniques of Gourieroux, Monfort, and Renault (1993) and Gourieroux and Monfort (1994) to estimate the models specified in equation (3.4). A recent alternative numerical simulation approach focusing on the direct likelihood is Fiorentini, Sentana, and Shephard (2004).

Indirect estimation belongs to a class of techniques whereby the parameters are estimated by matching the characteristics of the sample data, with those of data simulated from the hypothesized model. The key to this technique is that while the model is analytically complex to evaluate directly, it is relatively straightforward to simulate. Other forms of this technique are known as Simulated Method of Moments (SMM) and Efficient Method of Moments (EMM). SMM is associated with the work of Duffie and Singleton (1993) and EMM with Gallant and Tauchen (1996). The differences between the three methods lie in the way in which the matching of moments between actual and simulated data proceeds.

In indirect estimation, the matching of moments is accomplished via specifying an auxiliary model that acts as an approximation to the true likelihood function. The auxiliary model is chosen to capture the key empirical characteristics of the data that are needed to identify the unknown parameters. The first set of conditions is based on a VAR(1) of the levels of the premia, where the moments are given by the product of the residuals and the lagged values of all premia in the VAR, P_{t-1}. That is

$$k_t^0 = \left\{ u_{1t}P'_{t-1}, u_{2t}P'_{t-1}, u_{3t}P'_{t-1}, \ldots, u_{12t}P'_{t-1} \right\} \qquad (3.9)$$

This is of dimension (1×144).

The second set of moment conditions corresponds to the variance of the level of the premia. Formally

$$k_t^1 = P_{i,t}^2, \quad i = 1, 2, \ldots, 12. \qquad (3.10)$$

The third set of moment conditions captures the AR(1) structure of the changes in the premia

$$k_t^2 = \left(\Delta P_{i,t} - \Delta \overline{P}_{i,t} \right) \left(\Delta P_{i,t-1} - \Delta \overline{P}_{i,t-1} \right), \quad i = 1, 2, \ldots, 12. \qquad (3.11)$$

The fourth and fifth set of moment conditions capture conditional volatility in the premia arising from the GARCH characteristics of the data discussed in equation (3.3). It comprises AR(1) and AR(2) loadings for the squared changes in the premia. In a similar manner to Diebold and Nerlove (1989), the number of overidentifying conditions is controlled by including only the "own" squared autocorrelations of the change in the premium. These additional expressions contain a total of 12 elements each

$$k_t^3 = \left(\Delta P_{i,t}^2 - \Delta \overline{P}_{i,t}^2\right)\left(\Delta P_{i,t-1}^2 - \Delta \overline{P}_{i,t-1}^2\right), \quad i = 1, 2, \ldots, 12.$$

(3.12)

$$k_t^4 = \left(\Delta P_{i,t}^2 - \Delta \overline{P}_{i,t}^2\right)\left(\Delta P_{i,t-2}^2 - \Delta \overline{P}_{i,t-2}^2\right), \quad i = 1, 2, \ldots, 12.$$

(3.13)

Collecting all $(144 + 12 + 12 + 12 + 12)$ time series from (3.9) to (3.13) into a (1×192) vector

$$g_t = \left\{k_t^0, k_t^1, k_t^2, k_t^3, k_t^4\right\},$$

(3.14)

and taking the sample average of g_t defines all of the moment conditions that summarize the auxiliary model at time t.

Analogous to the moment conditions based on the sample data, a set of moment conditions based on the simulated data is given by taking the sample averages of

$$v_h = \left\{k_h^0, k_h^1, k_h^2, k_h^3, k_h^4\right\},$$

(3.15)

where k_h^0, k_h^1, k_h^2, k_h^3, and k_h^4 are the analogs of equations (3.9) to (3.13) with the actual data replaced by the simulated data for the hth simulation of the premia, $P_{i,h}$.

Letting θ be the set of unknown parameters of the latent factor model, the indirect estimator, $\widehat{\theta}$, is the solution of

$$\widehat{\theta} = \arg\min_{\theta} \left[\overline{g} - \frac{1}{H}\sum_{h=1}^{H}\overline{v}_h\right]' W^{-1} \left[\overline{g} - \frac{1}{H}\sum_{h=1}^{H}\overline{v}_h\right],$$

(3.16)

where $\bar{g}$ and $\bar{v}$ are respectively the sample means of equations (3.14) and (3.15). The matrix W is the optimal weighting matrix computed as follows, see Gourieroux, Monfort, and Renault (1993)

$$W = \frac{1}{T}g_t'g_t + \frac{1}{T}\sum_{l}^{L}\omega_l(g_t'g_{t-l} + g_{t-l}'g_t),\qquad(3.17)$$

where

$$\omega_t = 1 - \frac{1}{L+1},\qquad(3.18)$$

are the Newey-West weights. In constructing this weighting matrix, the blocks are assumed to be independent.

The indirect estimator in equation (3.16) is solved using the gradient algorithms in OPTMUM, GAUSS version 3.2, where the gradients are computed numerically. The simulations are based on normal random numbers using the GAUSS procedure RNDN.[11]

3.6 Empirical Results

To examine the differences between the transmission of contagion from the Russian crisis and the LTCM recapitalization announcement, the unconditional variance decomposition estimates using equation (3.8) are presented in table 3.2 and summarized in figure 3.3.[12] Total volatility is decomposed into the contribution due to the world factor, regional factors, country-specific factors, and the contagion effects from Russia and the LTCM recapitalization announcement shocks.

The results in table 3.2 indicate that the dominant factor in the volatility decomposition of the change in the bond premia

11. All results are based on $H = 500$ simulation paths in (3.16) with a convergence tolerance of 0.001 and a lag window of $L = 5$ in equation (3.17).
12. Experiments extending this class of models to allow for contagion from the Latin American and Asian regions, in conjunction with contagion from the U.S. and Russia, were undertaken to allow for the most general specification. However, this line of research was not pursued due to an undesirable amount of parameter instability inherent in estimating the larger models. The present model is an extension of the model investigated in Dungey, Fry, González-Hermosillo, and Martin (2002b), which allowed for contagion effects just from Russia.

Table 3.2
Volatility decomposition of changes in the premia (contribution to total volatility, in percent).

Country	World	Country	Regional	Contagion From		
				Russia	US	Total
Latin America						
Argentina	86.83	12.68	0.05	0.35	0.10	0.45
Brazil	83.15	0.18	0.05	16.41	0.25	16.66
Mexico	99.74	0.00	0.01	0.15	0.11	0.26
Asia						
Indonesia	98.85	0.27	0.21	0.30	0.38	0.68
Korea	88.85	4.95	0.88	1.57	3.75	5.32
Thailand	90.52	1.32	0.38	6.18	1.60	7.78
Eastern Europe						
Bulgaria	91.33	0.20	0.52	7.57	0.37	7.95
Poland	93.71	0.05	0.66	5.31	0.27	5.59
Russia	94.73	5.06	0.11	–	0.10	0.10
Industrial						
Netherlands	82.29	0.52	–	16.94	0.25	17.19
UK	99.74	0.01	–	0.10	0.15	0.25
US	84.97	11.83	–	3.20	–	3.20

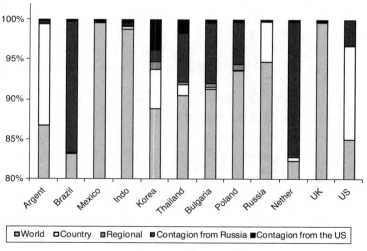

Figure 3.3 Volatility decomposition of changes in the premia.

is the world factor, pointing strongly towards commonality in the movements in premia experienced over the sample period (figures 3.1 and 3.2). This result is consistent with the view that increasing financial market integration has led to high (and expected) co-movements in asset prices. The world factor accounts for between 82% (Netherlands) and 99.7% (United Kingdom and Mexico) of total volatility. A corollary of this is that the regional factors have little influence on volatility, with all accounting for less than one percentage point of total volatility. Country-specific factors are relatively important for the United States (11.8%) and Argentina (12.7%), with the contribution to all the other countries being relatively small at less than 6% of total volatility.

The contagion effects recorded in table 3.2 are consistent with Proposition A in 3.2.2, that contagious links exist during the crisis period. Most of the contagion effects in the results are sourced from Russia. The empirical results also show that contagion affects a wide range of countries across the regions investigated. Of the industrial nations, the Netherlands experiences almost 17% of its total volatility from contagion originating in Russia. The other developed markets experience less than 4%. These results provide support for Proposition B in 3.2.2, that financial exposure to the Russian markets made economies vulnerable to contagion. The United States financial exposure to Russia is also partly evident in the results, with contagion representing 3% of the total volatility in the United States.

The Russian crisis results provide some support for the regional proposition, Proposition C in 3.2.2. Contagion from the Russian crisis was most consistently present in Eastern Europe, where it represents 5% and 7% of volatility for Poland and Bulgaria respectively.

In contrast, contagion from the LTCM recapitalization announcement shock is very small as a proportion of total volatility, although its effects are nonetheless widespread across countries and regions. The largest contagion effect from the LTCM recapitalization announcement shock is under 4% of total volatility, experienced by Korea. It is possible that the relatively small LTCM recapitalization announcement effects are the result of the coordinated action of the U.S. Fed to halt its spread. The results for Indonesia, Brazil, and Argentina are worthy of further examination. Indonesia drew comment as the hardest hit by contagion effects in currency markets during the 1997 Asian crisis; see for example discussions by Radelet and Sachs (1998) and Goldstein, Kaminsky, and Reinhart (2000). However, the contagion effects in Indonesian bond markets during 1998, as measured here, are relatively small. Contagion may still have been transmitted to Indonesia through asset markets other than the bond market, possibly due to illiquidity in the sovereign bond market during the political turmoil prevailing in Indonesia. An alternative interpretation is that Indonesia became extremely sensitive to global financial events in this period, consistent with a large value of λ_i in equation (3.7), compared with the East Asian crisis; see also the Indonesian results in Dungey, Milunovich, and Thorp (2010) for further discussion.

The Brazilian results show a relatively large proportionate effect of contagion, predominantly sourced from Russia, consistent with the view developed by Baig and Goldfajn (2001) that the withdrawal of foreign capital from Brazil during the Russian crisis precipitated the Brazilian crisis of January 1999. The relatively large contagion effect to Brazil may be a reflection of the vulnerability of Brazilian fundamentals, consistent with Proposition D in 3.2.2. Brazil at the time had recently managed to reenter global markets as a sovereign issuer and let domestic interest rates fall to stimulate the economy. In response to the Russian shock, it experienced sharp capital outflows as foreign investors withdrew, which eventually promoted higher domestic interest rates and a tighter fiscal stance. However, the relief was short-lived as these reforms came to be viewed as unsustainable in the light of the depreciation of the Brazilian real (International Monetary Fund 2001).

Argentina experienced relatively small contagion effects in 1998. Krueger (2002) notes that Argentina appeared in relatively good economic condition at that time, which is consistent with the fundamentals proposition. The International Monetary Fund (2001, p. 9) pointed out that Argentina had not had to access financial markets to meet its current financing commitments during the crisis period. It was only later that the combination of policy settings was revealed to be unsustainable. In light of this it is noteworthy that the factors determining total volatility in the sample period for Argentina are more like those determining the United States than the other countries examined. In particular, the contributions to total volatility coming from the country-specific factors in Argentina and the United States are the largest of the countries examined. This may reflect the fact that Argentina was the only emerging economy in our sample with a currency board regime that appeared to be credible during this time.

The results provide little evidence to support the proposition that contagion emanating from Russia is confined to developing nations, or that contagion emanating from the LTCM recapitalization announcement was confined to developed markets, as suggested by the Committee on the Global Financial System (1999, p.7–8). However, it is difficult to derive any stylized facts to support or refute the contention that emerging markets are more affected by contagion than developed markets. The evidence presented here suggests that both types of markets can be affected by contagion to varying degrees. For example, countries where the effect of contagion from Russia is less than one percentage point include the United Kingdom, Mexico, Argentina, and Indonesia.

To address these issues further, we transform the results in table 3.2 into their squared basis point equivalent by multiplying the values in table 3.2 by the variance in the changes in the premia for each country (i.e. the square of the standard deviations that are reported in table B.2 in Appendix 3.B). The estimated variance decompositions in squared basis points are reported in table 3.3.

Comparing the results in tables 3.2 and 3.3 highlights the differences between emerging and developed markets. Consider the Netherlands. In proportionate terms in table 3.2, contagion contributes 17% to volatility in the Netherlands. However, in table 3.3, this corresponds to 5 squared basis points[13], only greater than the other developed markets and Mexico. On the other hand, Brazil, which had the second greatest proportionate contribution from contagion, also has the second greatest squared basis point contribution, at around 590 squared basis points. The largest squared basis point contribution from contagion was experienced by Bulgaria. Bulgaria had a proportionate contribution from contagion of almost 8%, similar to that for Thailand, but contagion contributed 795 squared basis

---

13. This result may also reflect the choice of the corporate bond used for the Netherlands; it would be interesting to expand the empirical analysis to a wider set of corporates.

Table 3.3

Volatility Decomposition of Changes in the Premia (contribution to total volatility, in squared basis points).

Country	World	Country	Regional	Total Contagion
Latin America				
Argentina	984.34	143.71	0.51	5.12
Brazil	2923.10	6.47	0.14	585.60
Mexico	525.31	0.01	0.03	1.35
Asia				
Indonesia	3085.45	8.39	6.41	21.21
Korea	728.81	40.60	7.22	43.62
Thailand	452.58	6.59	1.88	38.92
Eastern Europe				
Bulgaria	9138.90	20.38	51.62	795.11
Poland	494.42	0.25	3.48	29.48
Russia	55685.89	2973.20	62.97	59.94
Industrial				
Netherlands	23.91	0.15	–	4.99
UK	13.88	0.00	–	0.04
US	6.38	0.89	–	0.24

points in Bulgaria, compared with 39 squared basis points in Thailand. The bond markets of emerging countries experienced a greater squared basis point contribution from contagion than the developed countries due to their absolute higher levels of volatility.

3.7 Conclusion

The international spillover effects stemming from the Russian debt default and the LTCM recapitalization announcement in 1998 seemed to be different from those of other financial crises in the 1990s. In 1998, bond markets in both developed and emerging economies experienced a significant widening of spreads between long-term bonds and their corresponding risk-free rate of return. In other episodes of financial crisis during the 1990s, the impact of crises seemed to be limited to emerging markets, or even a regional subset of them.

This chapter examined the crises associated with the Russian bond default in August 1998, and the LTCM recapitalization announcement in September 1998. Using a latent factor model, the change in the premia of 12 bond markets was decomposed into components associated with a common world factor, country-specific factors, regional factors, and contagion effects. Contagion was defined as the contemporaneous effect of idiosyncratic shocks transmitting across country borders. This definition of contagion is consistent with those offered in a substantial portion of the literature on this topic, including Masson (1999a,b,c), Favero and Giavazzi (2002), Forbes and Rigobon (2001; 2002), and introduced in Chapter 2. The contribution of this chapter is both in the application to bond markets and that we provide numerical estimates of the contribution of contagion to volatility in those markets.

The results show clear evidence of contagion effects from Russia, to both emerging and developed countries, while the global contagion effects from the LTCM recapitalization announcement tended to be smaller. In proportionate terms, contagion effects from Russia were particularly substantial for the Netherlands, Brazil, Bulgaria, and Thailand, ranging from 8% to about 17% of total volatility. The results showed that the strength of market fundamentals and the extent of offshore exposures of countries to Russia were important factors in determining the strength of contagion across national borders. Further, there is also strong evidence that contagion operated within regions, with the Russian bond default affecting the bonds markets of Poland and Bulgaria.

The absence of substantial contagion from the LTCM recapitalization announcement, as a global liquidity shock, is somewhat surprising given the anecdotal evidence offered by traders surveyed by the Committee on the Global Financial System (1999, Chapter 3). However, these results may reflect the short duration of the LTCM recapitalization announcement period (spanning about three weeks) as the Fed acted to contain a potential credit crunch by easing monetary policy aggressively. The evidence also suggests that while the United States experienced some contagion from Russia, contagion from the LTCM recapitalization announcement crisis to Russia was very small.

The proportion of volatility in the premia attributed to contagion did not provide clear evidence as to whether the crises had a greater effect on emerging or developed markets. When the results were transformed to squared basis point effects, the evidence generally supported the contention that contagion was greater in emerging markets, due to the overall higher degree of volatility typically experienced in those markets. While most of the literature on contagion generally espouses the notion that contagion is only a concern for emerging countries, the results in this chapter suggest that contagion can also be meaningful for developed economies, at least in the bond market.

The results also give support to the view that Brazil was affected by contagion prior to its currency crisis in January 1999. The relatively large contagion effects from Russia to Brazil, may be a reflection of the vulnerability of this country. That the contagion to Brazil is evident in the data prior to its own crisis provides scope for interesting future work in establishing at what point pre-crisis jitters are evident in financial markets.

3.A Data Definitions and Sources

The definition of the data and sources are given in table 3.4. The data obtained from the U.S. Federal Reserve was for the Bank for International Settlements, Committee on Global Financial System to aid in their enquiry into the turmoil of 1998 (Bank for International Settlements, Committee on the Global Financial System 1999). The data will not necessarily represent trades enacted. The estimation is based on daily data on spreads from February 12 to January 1, 1999. The bond spreads, or "risk premia," are constructed by taking a representative long-term sovereign bond issued in U.S. dollars by an emerging country and subtracting from it a U.S. Treasury bond of comparable maturity. For developed economies, the risk premia are constructed by taking a representative long-term corporate bond in domestic currency and subtracting from it a Government Treasury bond of comparable maturity.

Missing observations were dealt with by removing all contemporaneous observations for that date across countries. The original sample of 231 observations was reduced to 209 observations after accounting for missing observations. The exact details of the missing observations are contained in Dungey, Fry, González-Hermosillo, and Martin (2002b).

Table 3.4

Data definitions and sources of bond risk premia.

Country	Description	Source
Argentina	Republic of Argentina bond spread over US Treasury	US Fed. Res.
Brazil	Republic of Brazil bond spread over US Treasury	US Fed. Res.
Mexico	JP Morgan Eurobond Index Mexico Sovereign spread over US Treasury	US Fed. Res.
Indonesia	Indonesian Yankee Bond Spread over US Treasury	US Fed. Res.
Korea	Government of Korea 8 7/8% 4/2008 over US Treasury	Bloomberg (50064FAB0)
Thailand	Kingdom of Thailand Yankee Bond Spread over US Treasury	US Fed. Res.[a]
Bulgaria	Bulgarian Discount Stripped Brady Bond Yield Spread over US Treasury	US Fed. Res.
Poland	Poland Par Stripped Brady Bond Yield Spread over US Treasury	US Fed. Res.
Russia	Government of Russia 9.25% 11/2001 over US Treasury	Bloomberg (007149662)
Netherlands	Akzo Nobel NV 8% 12/2002 yield spread over NETHER 8.25% 6/2002	US Fed. Res.
UK	UK Industrial BBB Corporate 5-year Bond Spread over Gilt	Bloomberg (UKBF3B05)
US	US Industrial BBB1 Corporate 10-year Bond Spread over US Treasury	Bloomberg (IN10Y3B1)

(a) The longer series used in 3.1, 7.75% 15/04/07, comes from Credit Swiss First Boston.

3.B Descriptive Statistics

Table 3.5
Descriptive statistics of bond risk premia (in levels).

Statistics	Latin America			Asia		
	Arg.	Bra.	Mex.	Indo.	Korea	Thai.
Mean	534.70	744.07	469.70	959.67	486.26	423.17
Max.	1061.00	1438.00	868.33	1865.80	965.88	916.30
Min.	374.00	415.00	297.66	537.10	306.70	270.20
SD	140.62	291.13	155.61	369.50	163.88	167.48
AR(1)	0.97	0.98	0.99	0.99	0.98	0.99
AR(2)	0.94	0.96	0.97	0.97	0.96	0.98
Skew.	1.26	0.61	0.66	0.97	1.26	1.16
Kurt.	4.38	2.12	2.16	2.58	3.84	3.32
JB	71.84	19.71	21.10	34.05	61.44	47.79
(pv)	(0.00)	(0.00)	(0.00)	(0.00)	(0.00)	(0.00)

Statistics	Eastern Europe			Industrial		
	Bul.	Pol.	Rus.	Nether.	UK	US
Mean	951.72	261.21	2871.81	58.59	122.92	106.06
Max.	2279.00	521.00	6825.78	109.10	203.00	153.00
Min.	535.00	162.00	392.35	34.20	76.00	67.00
SD	431.92	75.73	2512.65	20.38	36.26	28.85
AR(1)	0.97	0.95	0.99	0.96	0.99	0.99
AR(2)	0.94	0.90	0.98	0.93	0.98	0.98
Skew.	1.35	0.95	0.28	0.95	0.72	0.44
Kurt.	4.26	3.17	1.20	2.42	2.03	1.38
JB	77.52	31.53	30.96	34.24	26.11	29.51
(pv)	(0.00)	(0.00)	(0.00)	(0.00)	(0.00)	(0.00)

Table 3.6
Standard deviations of the change in the bond risk premia.

Latin America			Asia		
Arg.	Bra.	Mex.	Indo.	Korea	Thai.
33.67	59.29	22.95	55.87	28.64	22.36

Eastern Europe			Industrial		
Bulgaria	Poland	Russia	Netherlands	UK	US
100.03	22.97	242.45	5.39	3.73	2.74

3.C Unit Root Tests

Table 3.7 gives the results of performing unit root tests on the bond risk premia. Both Augmented Dickey Fuller (ADF) and Phillips Perron (PP) unit root tests are reported.

Table 3.7
Augmented Dickey Fuller (ADF) and Phillips Perron (PP) unit root tests of the bond risk premia. The p-values are based on the MacKinnon critical values for rejection of the hypothesis of a unit root.[a]

Statistics	Latin America			Asia		
	Arg.	Bra.	Mex.	Indo.	Korea	Thai.
ADF	−1.70	−1.14	−1.18	−1.22	−1.30	−1.13
PP	−1.82	−1.28	−1.27	−1.22	−1.43	−1.08
Statistics	Eastern Europe			Industrial		
	Bul.	Pol.	Rus.	Nether.	UK	US
ADF	−1.38	−2.29	−0.73	−1.26	−0.61	−0.60
PP	1.69	−2.30	−0.74	−1.54	−0.58	−0.64

(a) MacKinnon critical values for the ADF test are:
   1% critical value −3.46 (* represents rejection at the 1% level of significance)
   5% critical value −2.88 (** represents rejection at the 5% level of significance)

   MacKinnon critical values for the PP test are:
   1% critical value −3.46 (* represents rejection at the 1% level of significance)
   5% critical value −2.88 (** represents rejection at the 5% level of significance)

3.D Estimated GARCH Models

Table 3.8 presents the results from estimating an integrated GARCH(1,1) model for changes in each of the bond risk premia. The changes are examined to highlight the properties of the short-term adjustment process in the data. The estimated GARCH model is

$$\Delta P_{i,t} = \rho_0 + e_{i,t}$$

$$e_{i,t} = \sqrt{h_{i,t}u_{i,t}}$$

$$h_{i,t} = \alpha_0 + \alpha_1 e_{i,t-1}^2 + (1-\alpha)h_{i,t-1}$$

$$u_{i,t} \sim N(0,1),$$

(3.19)

Table 3.8

Univariate Integrated GARCH (1,1) parameter estimates of bond risk premia based on equation (3.19) (QMLE standard errors in brackets).

Country	ρ_0	α_0	α_1	ln L
Latin America				
Argentina	0.32	12.60	0.29	−916.04
	(0.90)	(6.99)	(0.07)	
Brazil	1.02	26.71	0.24	−1023.26
	(1.52)	(18.61)	(0.06)	
Mexico	0.15	11.53	0.34	−854.15
	(0.65)	(6.98)	(0.098)	
Asia				
Indonesia	−1.22	251.21	0.41	−1088.47
	(2.55)	(212.66)	(0.164)	
Korea	−0.54	20.81	0.20	−947.49
	(1.21)	(11.06)	(0.04)	
Thailand	−0.70	32.43	0.25	−906.89
	(0.86)	(30.41)	(0.14)	
Eastern Europe				
Bulgaria	0.15	59.09	0.32	−1088.00
	(2.15)	(37.83)	(0.07)	
Poland	−0.21	22.95	0.33	−896.91
	(0.90)	(30.52)	(0.254)	
Russia	−0.02	1.58	0.21	−636.67
	(0.37)	(1.61)	(0.14)	
Industrial				
Netherlands	−0.02	1.58	0.21	−626.67
	(0.32)	(1.60)	(0.14)	
UK	0.07	1.63	0.41	−553.96
	(0.23)	(0.78)	(0.11)	
US	0.06	1.06	0.60	−467.88
	(0.12)	(1.32)	(0.45)	

where $\Delta P_{i,t}$ is the change in the premium for country i recorded at time t.

4

Contagion in Global Equity Markets

4.1 Introduction

While the primary shocks in the Russian and LTCM crises began in bond markets, as discussed in Chapter 3, their repercussions were felt throughout the financial sector, and much volatility appeared in international equity markets. This chapter looks at the transmission of crises during 1998 in international equity markets and finds results that differ substantially to the results on international bond markets presented in Chapter 3. In equity markets the majority of the transmission of the shocks across international borders is attributable to contagion effects whereas in bond markets contagion effects are relatively small, although in both cases contagion effects are significant.

The empirical results also show that the most influential source of contagion effects differs across the two asset types during this period: The majority of the contagion effects in equity markets are sourced through the United States equity market, while in bond markets contagion is primarily associated with events in Russia (see Chapter 3, and Dungey, Fry, González-Hermosillo, and Martin 2006). The importance of the United States market in distributing equity market shocks supports the hypothesis of Kaminsky and Reinhart (2002) that large markets act as centers in distributing shocks to the periphery markets.

The empirical results of this chapter contribute to the existing literature that focusses on the role of equity markets in acting as a conduit during the Russian bond crisis and the LTCM near collapse, by adopting a more general model that looks at a range of factors linking both industrial and emerging equity markets during the financial crises of 1998. The earlier work of the Committee on the Global Financial System (1999) focuses on industrial countries, whereas Rigobon (2003b) and Hernández and Valdés (2001) concentrate on emerging markets. Kaminsky and Reinhart (2003) look at the interrelationships between industrial and emerging markets, while Baig and Goldfajn (2001) specifically focus on the transmissions to Brazil.

To identify the linkages across international equity markets during financial crises, the factor model introduced in Chapters 2 and 3 is extended to equity markets. A feature of the model is that it allows for not only common and regional factors but also for contagion, according to the definition discussed in Chapter 2.

The remainder of this chapter is organized as follows. A multi-regime factor model of financial crises is specified in Section 4.2. A number of preliminary empirical issues are discussed in Section 4.3, including data filtering, identification of equity market shocks, and estimation strategies. The main empirical results are presented in Section 4.4, while Section 4.5 contains some concluding comments and suggestions for future research.

4.2 A Model of Financial Turmoil in Equity Markets During 1998

In this section a multi-regime factor model of equity markets is specified to identify the transmission mechanisms of financial crises between international equity markets. The model builds on the earlier work of Solnik (1974), and in particular, the factor model of King, Sentana and Wadhwani (1994) and Chapters 2 and 3 of this book, by allowing for additional linkages arising from contagion during the Russian and LTCM crises. An important theoretical extension of the previous work is the identification of contagion during the crisis periods by allowing for multiple regime shifts in the factor structures.

Let $s_{i,t}$ represent the equity returns of country i at time t. A total of 10 equity markets is used in the empirical analysis including six emerging equity markets (Argentina (A), Brazil (B), Hong Kong SAR (H), Thailand (T), Poland (P) and Russia (R)) and four industrial equity markets (Germany (G), Japan (J), United Kingdom (UK) and the United States (U)). Defining s_t as a (10×1) vector of all equity returns, the dynamics of equity markets are assumed to be represented by the following vector autoregression (VAR)

$$s_t = \mu + A_1 s_{t-1} + A_2 s_{t-2} + \cdots + A_p s_{t-p} + v_t, \qquad (4.1)$$

where μ is a (10×1) vector of parameters to allow for non-zero means in equity returns, A_i is a (10×10) matrix of autoregressive parameters corresponding to the ith lag, and v_t is a (10×1) multivariate disturbance process with zero mean, variance-covariance matrix Ω, and $Ev_t v_{t-k} = 0, \forall k \neq 0$. The length of the lag distribution of the VAR is given by p.

The disturbance term v_t in (4.1) represents shocks to equity markets that are assumed to be derived from a set of factors. In specifying the factor structure, the model distinguishes between a benchmark period where the factors represent the market fundamentals that link international equity markets, and a crisis period where the benchmark factor structure is augmented with additional linkages that capture contagion caused by shocks that increase the comovements of international equity markets. These factor structures are formally specified below.

4.2.1 A Benchmark Model

The factor structure of v_t in (4.1) during the benchmark period is specified as

$$v_t = \left[\begin{array}{ccc} A & \vdots & \Phi_1 \end{array} \right] f_t = \Gamma_1 f_t, \qquad (4.2)$$

where f_t represents the full set of factors

$$f_t = \left[w_t, e_t, d_t, R_t, u_{A,t}, u_{B,t}, \cdots, u_{U,t} \right], \qquad (4.3)$$

and

$$
A = \begin{bmatrix}
\lambda_A & \gamma_A & 0 & \psi_A \\
\lambda_B & \gamma_B & 0 & \psi_B \\
\lambda_H & \gamma_H & 0 & 0 \\
\lambda_T & \gamma_T & 0 & 0 \\
\lambda_P & \gamma_P & 0 & 0 \\
\lambda_R & \gamma_R & 0 & 0 \\
\lambda_G & 0 & \delta_G & 0 \\
\lambda_J & 0 & \delta_J & 0 \\
\lambda_{UK} & 0 & \delta_{UK} & 0 \\
\lambda_U & 0 & \delta_U & \psi_U
\end{bmatrix}, \quad
\Phi_1 = diag \begin{bmatrix}
\phi_A \\
\phi_B \\
\phi_H \\
\phi_T \\
\phi_P \\
\phi_R \\
\phi_G \\
\phi_J \\
\phi_{UK} \\
\phi_U
\end{bmatrix}.
$$

(4.4)

The factor w_t in (4.3) represents shocks that simultaneously impact upon all equity markets with the size of the impact determined by the loading parameter λ_i. For this reason this factor is referred to as a world factor. Typical examples of world factors would be the global effects of changes in United States monetary policy on world equity markets (Forbes and Rigobon 2002), or the simultaneous impact on international equity markets of an oil price shock. One important difference between these choices of factors is that w_t in (4.3) is not assumed to be observable, but is treated as a latent factor.

The model in (4.3) contains two factors to distinguish emerging and developed markets, which are represented by e_t and d_t respectively (see also Kaminsky and Reinhart 2002, and the Committee on the Global Financial System 1999). The factor e_t, captures those shocks that specifically affect the six emerging markets where the size of the impact is governed by the parameter γ_i. The factor d_t captures those shocks that just affect the four industrial equity markets, with the size of the impact controlled by the parameter δ_i.

To allow for shocks that solely capture a common regional interest, such as proposed by Glick and Rose (1999), the factor R_t impacts only upon Argentina (A), Brazil (B) and the United States (U), with loading parameters given by ψ_i. There are insufficient countries in any other common regional grouping to warrant the inclusion of further regional factors in the set of equity markets used in the empirical application.

The last set of factors in (4.3) are given by $u_{i,t}$, which represent shocks that are specific to each of the 10 equity markets with loading parameters given by ϕ_i. The full set of factors can be classified into two broad groups, with the first four factors (w_t, e_t, d_t, R_t) representing systematic factors whose risks are not diversifiable, whilst the country specific factors ($u_{i,t}$) represent idiosyncratic factors whose risks are diversifiable (Solnik 1974).[1]

To complete the specification of the benchmark model, the set of systematic and idiosyncratic factors are assumed to be independent with zero means and unit variances

$$f_t \sim (0, 1). \tag{4.5}$$

In this specification the series are assumed to be homoskedastic.[2] This choice of the normalization of the factors provides a convenient decomposition of equity volatility into the contributions of each of the underlying factors during the benchmark period

$$Var\left(v_{i,t}\right) = \lambda_i^2 + \gamma_i^2 + \delta_i^2 + \psi_i^2 + \phi_i^2. \tag{4.6}$$

4.2.2 A Model Incorporating Contagion

The crisis model of equity shocks is characterized by the inclusion of additional transmission mechanisms linking global equity markets during periods of crisis, over and above the mechanisms identified by the benchmark model in (4.2). The approach to modeling these additional linkages is to include the Russian ($u_{R,t}$) and United States ($u_{U,t}$) idiosyncratic shocks defined in (4.3), into the factor structure of the remaining countries during periods in which crises are present. Given the definition of contagion presented in Chapter 2, these linkages are referred to as contagion as they represent additional shocks over and above the shocks that occur during the benchmark period linking equity markets, which contribute to the volatility of asset markets during periods of crisis.

---

1. The choice of factors is based on some preliminary empirical analysis. Some robustness checks and tests of the specified factors stucture are discussed in the empirical section.
2. Some preliminary ARCH tests on equity returns during the benchmark period find no strong evidence of time-varying volatility. However, to guard against potential time varying volatility, the GMM standard errors are adjusted for heteroskedasticity.

Incorporating Contagion from Russia   To incorporate contagion from Russia, the factor model in (4.2) is specified as

$$u_t = \begin{bmatrix} A & \vdots & \Phi_2 \end{bmatrix} f_t = \Gamma_2 f_t, \tag{4.7}$$

where A and f_t are respectively given in (4.4) and (4.3), and Φ_2 is specified as

$$\Phi_2 = \begin{bmatrix} \phi_A & & & & & \kappa_A \\ & \phi_B & & & & \kappa_B \\ & & \phi_H & & & \kappa_H \\ & & & \phi_T & & \kappa_T \\ & & & & \phi_P & \kappa_P \\ & & & & & \kappa_R \\ & & & & & \kappa_G & \phi_G \\ & & & & & \kappa_J & & \phi_J \\ & & & & & \kappa_{UK} & & & \phi_{UK} \\ & & & & & \kappa_U & & & & \phi_U \end{bmatrix}, \tag{4.8}$$

where blank cells represent zeros. The strength of contagion from Russia to international equity markets is controlled by the parameter κ_i. Equation (4.7) also allows for the effect of Russian idiosyncratic shocks to differ across regimes by allowing the parameter ϕ_R in (4.4) to differ from κ_R in (4.8). Dungey, Fry, González-Hermosillo, and Martin (2005b) interpret this as an idiosyncratic structural break.

Following the benchmark decomposition of the variance in (4.6), equity market volatility with contagion from Russia is decomposed as

$$Var\left(v_{i,t}\right) = \lambda_i^2 + \gamma_i^2 + \delta_i^2 + \psi_i^2 + \phi_i^2 + \kappa_i^2. \tag{4.9}$$

This suggests that the contribution of contagion to volatility in the *ith* country when there is potentially contagion from Russia compared with the benchmark model is simply

$$\Delta Var\left(v_{i,t}\right) = \kappa_i^2. \tag{4.10}$$

Hence, a test of contagion emanating from the Russian equity market can be performed by testing the restriction

$$H_0 : \kappa_i = 0, \qquad \forall i \neq R. \tag{4.11}$$

The specification in (4.8) allows for an exogenous change in the volatility of idiosyncratic shocks in Russia between the benchmark and Russian crisis period. This constitutes a structural break in the Russian idiosyncratic factor, which can be tested via the restriction

$$H_0 : \phi_R = \kappa_R. \tag{4.12}$$

Incorporating Contagion from LTCM   An important feature of the LTCM crisis is that it occurs in conjunction with the Russian crisis, but is of shorter duration. The LTCM liquidity crisis is viewed to have ended at the time of the surprise inter-FOMC meeting to cut interest rates on October 15 (see Committee on the Global Financial System 1999). The implication of this characteristic of the twin-crisis periods, is that the contagious channel used to model the transmission of shocks from Russia is still active during the LTCM crisis period. This feature of the problem imposes additional structure on the factors across the regimes.

Following the approach to modeling contagion during the Russian period, contagion emanating from the LTCM crisis is modeled by including United States equity shocks $u_{U,t}$ during the time of the LTCM crisis as well as the Russian shocks $u_{R,t}$ in the factor representation of the other equity markets. The LTCM crisis model is specified as

$$u_t = \left[\; A \; \vdots \; \Phi_3 \; \right] f_t = \Gamma_3 f_t. \tag{4.13}$$

where A and f_t are respectively given in (4.4) and (4.3), and Φ_3 is specified as

$$\Phi_3 = \begin{bmatrix} \phi_A & & & & & \kappa_A & & & \bar{\kappa}_A \\ & \phi_B & & & & \kappa_B & & & \bar{\kappa}_B \\ & & \phi_H & & & \kappa_H & & & \bar{\kappa}_H \\ & & & \phi_T & & \kappa_T & & & \bar{\kappa}_T \\ & & & & \phi_P & \kappa_P & & & \bar{\kappa}_P \\ & & & & & \kappa_R & & & \bar{\kappa}_R \\ & & & & & \kappa_G & \phi_G & & \bar{\kappa}_G \\ & & & & & \kappa_J & & \phi_J & \bar{\kappa}_J \\ & & & & & \kappa_{UK} & & \phi_{UK} & \bar{\kappa}_{UK} \\ & & & & & \kappa_U & & & \bar{\kappa}_U \end{bmatrix}, \tag{4.14}$$

where blank cells represent zeros. The strength of contagion from LTCM to international equity markets is controlled by the parameter $\bar{\kappa}_i$. As in the case of the model including contagion from Russia, the specification of the LTCM crisis model allows for a structural break in the idiosyncratic shock of the United States, with the parameter $\bar{\kappa}_U$ in (4.14) being allowed to differ from the parameter ϕ_U in (4.4). As the LTCM crisis coincides with potential contagion from the Russian crisis, the Russian idiosyncratic shock $u_{R,t}$ is also included in the factor specification of the other equity markets to reflect the twin nature of the crises during the time of the LTCM crisis. A comparison of (4.7) and (4.13) shows that the parameters measuring the strength of contagion from Russia (κ_i) to equity markets are the same across the two regimes.

During the LTCM crisis the decomposition of equity market volatility is given by

$$Var\left(v_{i,t}\right) = \lambda_i^2 + \gamma_i^2 + \delta_i^2 + \psi_i^2 + \phi_i^2 + \kappa_i^2 + \bar{\kappa}_i^2. \tag{4.15}$$

The change in volatility between the benchmark and LTCM crisis periods is

$$\Delta Var\left(v_{i,t}\right) = \kappa_i^2 + \bar{\kappa}_i^2, \tag{4.16}$$

which shows that the total contribution of contagion to volatility during the LTCM crisis period can be decomposed into two elements, emanating from the Russian-based shocks and the United States-based LTCM shocks. A test of contagion emanating from the LTCM shock can be performed by testing the restriction

$$H_0 : \bar{\kappa}_i = 0, \qquad \forall i \neq U. \tag{4.17}$$

A joint test of contagion from both Russia and the United States is given by

$$H_0 : \kappa_i = 0; \bar{\kappa}_j = 0, \qquad \forall i \neq R, \quad \forall j \neq U. \tag{4.18}$$

A test of a structural break in the United States idiosyncratic factor is given by testing the restriction

$$H_0 : \phi_U = \bar{\kappa}_U. \tag{4.19}$$

4.3 Empirical Issues

4.3.1 Data

The sample consists of daily share prices $(P_{i,t})$ on 10 countries, beginning January 2, 1998, and ending December 31, 1998, a total of $T = 260$ observations. Local equity market data are used that are sourced from Bloomberg.[3] Extending the sample period either before or after 1998 would complicate estimating the model as it would involve including additional regimes to capture the East Asian currency crisis and the Brazilian crisis of 1999 respectively.

Daily percentage equity returns of the ith country at time t are computed as

$$s_{i,t} = 100 \left(\ln \left(P_{i,t} \right) - \ln \left(P_{i,t-1} \right) \right). \qquad (4.20)$$

Missing observations are treated by using the lagged price.[4] To capture differences in time zones of equity markets, a two-day moving average is chosen following the approach of Forbes and Rigobon (2002), with the first observation of the moving average set equal to the realized returns on January 5.[5] Thus, the effective sample of returns data begins January 5, 1998, and ends December 31, 1998, a total of $T = 259$ observations. A plot of the filtered equity returns is given in Figure 4.1.

The benchmark period is chosen to begin on January 5 and end July 31, while the crisis period is taken as the second half of 1998, beginning August 3 and ending December 31. The start of the Russian crisis on August 3 is chosen to begin before Russia's unilateral debt restructuring on August 17, and to take into account the early concerns of investors about the underlying

---

3. The particular equity market indices used are: Argentina Merval Index, Brazil Bovespa Stock Exchange, Hang Seng Stock Index, Thai SET Index, Warsaw Stock Exchange Total Return Index, Russian RTS Index $, Deutsche Borse DAX Index, Nikkei 225 Index, FTSE 100, Dow Jones Industrial Index.

4. Filling in missing observations by use of a linear interpolation between observed prices does not change the qualitative results of the estimated factor model.

5. Another approach to addressing the problem of different time zones is to follow Dungey, Fry, González-Hermosillo, and Martin (2003b) and treat time zones as a missing observation problem. This makes estimation more involved as it requires simulating a high-frequency model to generate hourly data which is converted into daily data and then calibrated with the actual data.

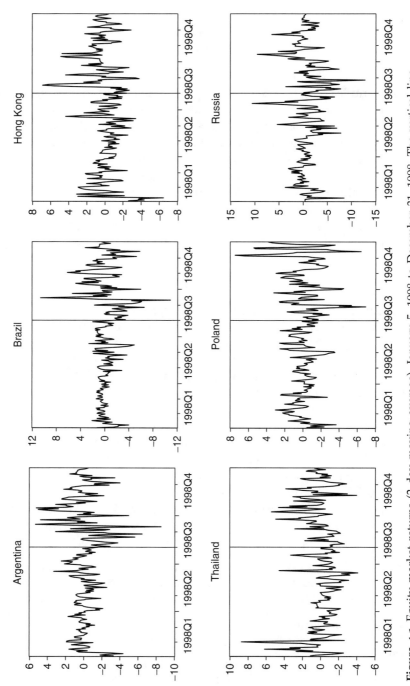

Figure 4.1 Equity market returns (2 day moving average), January 5, 1998 to December 31, 1998. The vertical line represents July 31, 1998, which corresponds to the end of the benchmark period.

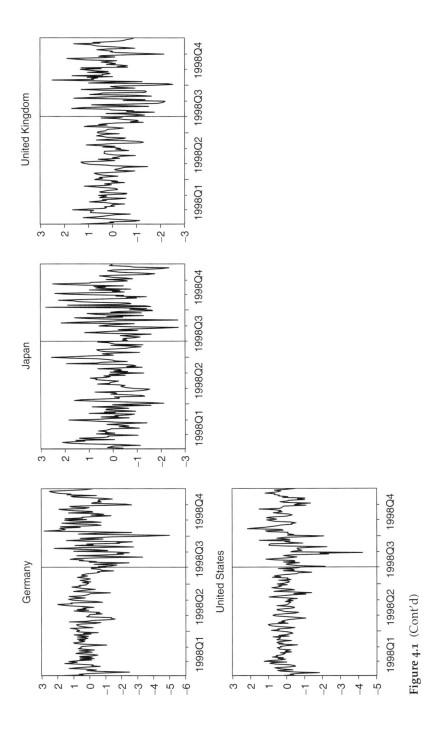

Figure 4.1 (Cont'd)

stability of the Russian GKO debt market, as well as the ongoing problems in the Russian economy.[6]

The LTCM crisis period is chosen as a sub-period of the overall crisis period, running from August 31 to October 15. The start of this crisis is chosen to reflect that the plight of LTCM had gradually became more public by the end of August, culminating in the public announcement of a recapitalization package in late September. The LTCM crisis is taken to end with the surprise cut in United States interest rates between FOMC meetings on October 15, 1998 (see Kumar and Persaud 2002, Upper and Werner 2002, and Committee on the Global Financial System 1999). A full chronology of these events is given by Lowenstein (2001), Jorion (2000) and Kharas, Pintos, and Ulatov (2000).

The choice of the crisis dates is clearly partly subjective. This choice is also complicated by the occurrence of other events over the period, such as the period of August 14 to 28, where the Hong Kong Monetary Authority intervened in the Hong Kong equity market to support the Hong Kong currency board (Goodhart and Dai 2003). As the dating of the regimes is important in identifying the parameters of each regime, some robustness checks are discussed in the empirical section where the model is reestimated for alternative crisis dates.

Some descriptive statistics of the data are presented in table 4.1 for the three sample periods, with variances and covariances given in table 4.2. Inspection of the covariances show the increase in comovements between equity returns between the benchmark and crisis periods. The diagonal elements in table 4.2 reveal that volatility in equity returns increased for most countries in the Russian crisis period, and increased even further during the LTCM crisis.

4.3.2 GMM Estimator

The model is estimated using generalized method of moments (GMM); see also Rigobon and Sack (2004) for an application, and Sentana and Fiorentini (2001) for identification conditions. This has the advantage of not having to specify the distribution

---

6. Even though many of the investments in Russia were hedged by forward rouble contracts with the Russian banking system, those very exposures contributed to the fragility of the banking system itself (Steinherr 2006).

Table 4.1

Descriptive statistics of daily percentage filtered equity returns in 1998 for selected sample periods.[a] The sample mean (Mean), the standard deviation (S.D.), the maximum (Max.) and the minimum (Min.).

Stat.	Country									
	Arg.	Brz.	HK	Thl.	Pol.	Rus.	Ger.	Jap.	UK	US
Benchmark Period: Jan. 5 to Jul. 31										
Mean	−0.01	0.05	−0.26	−0.20	0.02	−0.56	0.25	0.01	0.13	0.09
S.D.	1.12	1.28	1.55	1.78	1.22	2.55	0.71	0.83	0.60	0.51
Max.	3.30	2.64	4.32	8.76	3.04	10.55	1.20	2.56	1.66	1.25
Min.	−4.36	−4.91	−6.46	−4.11	−3.69	−8.48	−2.49	−2.12	−1.47	−1.81
Russian Crisis Period: Aug. 3 to Dec. 31										
Mean	−0.41	−0.35	0.47	0.03	−0.21	−0.95	0.07	−0.10	0.05	0.06
S.D.	1.86	2.51	1.85	1.72	2.60	3.10	1.25	1.09	0.90	0.77
Max.	3.10	6.21	6.89	4.65	7.50	6.47	2.50	2.50	1.90	1.79
Min.	−6.44	−6.55	−2.87	−3.98	−6.92	−12.83	−3.32	−2.73	−2.16	−2.33
LTCM Crisis Period: Aug. 31 to Oct. 15										
Mean	0.51	−0.20	0.51	0.77	−0.45	−0.76	−0.47	−0.13	−0.28	−0.21
S.D.	2.99	4.13	1.96	1.83	2.05	3.48	1.78	1.22	1.26	1.17
Max.	5.34	10.65	4.87	5.42	3.22	9.50	2.84	2.79	2.52	2.17
Min.	−8.52	−10.84	−3.78	−2.09	−5.35	−7.48	−5.00	−2.72	−2.52	−4.23

(a) Equity returns are filtered for time-zone effects using a 2-day moving average.

of the factors in (4.5). Let the sample periods for the three regimes be respectively T_1 (benchmark), T_2 (Russian crisis), and T_3 (LTCM crisis). Associated with each regime is the empirical variance-covariance matrix

$$\Omega_1 = \frac{1}{T_1} \sum_{t \in T_1} v_t v_t', \quad \Omega_2 = \frac{1}{T_2} \sum_{t \in T_2} v_t v_t', \quad \Omega_3 = \frac{1}{T_3} \sum_{t \in T_3} v_t v_t',$$

$$(4.21)$$

where v_t is the (10×1) vector of shocks from the VAR in (4.1). The factor model is compactly written as

$$v_t = \Gamma_k f_t, \qquad k = 1, 2, 3, \tag{4.22}$$

where Γ_1, Γ_2 and Γ_3 are defined in equations (4.2), (4.7), and (4.13) respectively, and f_t is the set of all factors defined

Table 4.2

Variance-covariance matrices of daily percentage filtered equity returns in 1998 for selected sample periods.

	Arg.	Brz.	HK	Thl.	Pol.	Rus.	Ger.	Jap.	UK	US
Benchmark Period: Jan. 5 to Jul. 31										
Arg.	1.25									
Brz.	0.87	1.64								
HK	0.84	0.82	2.38							
Thl.	0.60	0.86	1.64	3.14						
Pol.	0.61	0.49	1.05	0.97	1.49					
Rus.	1.02	1.51	1.31	1.49	1.37	6.47				
Ger.	0.14	0.27	0.51	0.40	0.21	0.51	0.50			
Jap.	0.14	0.21	0.48	0.47	0.26	0.10	0.12	0.68		
UK	0.21	0.38	0.37	0.48	0.28	0.68	0.25	0.10	0.36	
US	0.29	0.39	0.39	0.35	0.21	0.44	0.19	0.06	0.20	0.26
Russian Crisis Period: Aug. 3 to Dec. 31										
Arg.	3.41									
Brz.	3.73	6.20								
HK	1.05	0.86	3.38							
Thl.	1.73	1.94	1.22	2.90						
Pol.	1.58	1.98	1.11	1.01	6.65					
Rus.	3.95	4.78	0.33	2.05	1.31	9.48				
Ger.	1.57	1.55	0.97	1.09	0.58	1.97	1.55			
Jap.	1.12	1.51	0.52	0.76	1.03	1.61	0.32	1.17		
UK	1.08	0.98	0.91	0.74	0.84	1.29	0.81	0.47	0.81	
US	1.06	1.30	0.60	0.67	0.657	1.16	0.62	0.39	0.45	0.58
LTCM Crisis Period: Aug. 31 to Oct. 15										
Arg.	8.70									
Brz.	10.41	16.55								
HK	1.72	0.49	3.71							
Thl.	0.69	0.45	1.98	3.23						
Pol.	1.16	0.02	2.23	1.34	4.09					
Rus.	3.59	2.53	2.54	0.95	2.20	11.72				
Ger.	2.98	2.45	1.83	0.34	2.57	3.73	3.08			
Jap.	0.99	0.60	0.83	0.43	1.35	0.64	1.02	1.44		
UK	1.97	1.89	1.59	0.72	1.74	2.44	1.91	0.75	1.53	
US	2.67	3.40	0.91	0.67	0.76	1.52	1.04	0.27	0.80	1.34

in equation (4.3). Using the property that the factors are independent with zero means and unit variances, as in equation (4.5), the theoretical variance-covariance matrices for the three regimes are conveniently given by

$$E\left[v_t v_t'\right] = \Gamma_k \Gamma_k', \qquad k = 1, 2, 3. \qquad (4.23)$$

The total number of unknown parameters in $\Gamma_1, \Gamma_2,$ and Γ_3 is 53. The GMM estimator is obtained by choosing the parameters of the factor model in $\Gamma_1, \Gamma_2,$ and Γ_3, and matching the empirical moments in (4.21) with the theoretical moments in (4.23). Associated with each empirical variance-covariance matrix are $10 \times 11/2 = 55$ unique moments. In total there are $3 \times 55 = 165$ moments across all three regimes. As the LTCM crisis period is relatively short, it is necessary to control the number of moments used in the GMM procedure. The strategy is to choose for the LTCM crisis period the 10 variances, the 9 covariances between the United States and the remaining countries, and the 8 covariances between Russia and the remaining countries, excluding the United States. This means that there are $2 \times 55 + 27 = 137$ empirical moments used to identify the 53 unknown parameters, a total of 84 excess moment conditions.

Defining the set of excess moment matrices for the three regimes as

$$M_1 = vech\,(\Omega_1) - vech\,(\Gamma_1 \Gamma_1')$$
$$M_2 = diag\,(\Omega_2) - diag\,(\Gamma_2 \Gamma_2') \qquad (4.24)$$
$$M_3 = diag\,(\Omega_3) - diag\,(\Gamma_3 \Gamma_3'),$$

the GMM estimator is obtained by choosing the parameters of the factor model to minimize the following objective function

$$Q = M_1' W_1^{-1} M_1 + M_2' W_2^{-1} M_2 + M_3' W_3^{-1} M_3, \qquad (4.25)$$

where $W_1, W_2,$ and W_3 represent the optimal weighting matrices corresponding to the respective regimes (Hamilton 1994), which correct the standard errors for heteroskedasticity in each regime. Equation (4.25) is minimized with v_t in (4.21) replaced by the residuals of the estimated VAR in (4.1) where the lag structure is set at $p = 1$ lags. The computations are performed using the BFGS algorithm in GAUSS Version 7, with a convergence criterion of 0.00001.

4.4 Empirical Results

4.4.1 Parameter Estimates

The GMM point estimates of the factor model in (4.2), (4.7), and (4.13) are given in table 4.3 with standard errors reported in parentheses. An overall test of the model is given by testing the 84 overidentifying restrictions. Under the null hypothesis that the restrictions are satisfied, the value of the objective function in (4.25) is asymptotically distributed as χ^2 with 84 degrees of freedom. The reported value of the test statistic is 97.79.

Table 4.3
GMM parameter estimates of the multi regime factor model in equations (4.2), (4.7) and (4.13), with standard errors based on the optimal weighting matrix in parentheses.

Ctry	Common Factors				Idio.	Contagion from	
	World λ_i	Emerging γ_i	Industrial δ_i	Regional ψ_i	ϕ_i	Russia κ_i	LTCM $\bar{\kappa}_i$
Arg.	0.37 (0.15)	0.27 (0.14)	—	0.64 (0.09)	0.37 (0.12)	0.29 (0.31)	1.46 (0.31)
Brz.	0.44 (0.16)	0.22 (0.16)	—	0.61 (0.12)	0.68 (0.07)	−0.08 (0.48)	2.23 (0.53)
HK	0.70 (0.11)	0.54 (0.13)	—	—	0.66 (0.08)	0.09 (0.22)	−0.64 (0.34)
Thl.	0.59 (0.17)	0.60 (0.14)	—	—	0.96 (0.11)	−0.31 (0.17)	−0.55 (0.58)
Pol.	0.34 (0.09)	0.40 (0.10)	—	—	0.71 (0.06)	0.08 (0.18)	0.99 (0.36)
Rus.	0.53 (0.17)	0.60 (0.18)	—	—	1.32 (0.14)	2.27 (0.32)	0.16 (0.36)
Ger.	0.42 (0.07)	—	0.14 (0.12)	—	0.40 (0.03)	0.69 (0.13)	−0.70 (0.20)
Jap.	0.35 (0.09)	—	−0.32 (0.36)	—	0.43 (0.32)	0.13 (0.19)	1.12 (0.19)
UK	0.36 (0.05)	—	0.16 (0.08)	—	0.26 (0.04)	0.46 (0.10)	−0.46 (0.16)
US	0.26 (0.06)	—	0.18 (0.12)	0.24 (0.04)	0.22 (0.05)	0.08 (0.12)	0.11 (0.06)

This yields a p-value of 0.14, showing that the restrictions are not rejected at conventional significance levels. A test of the factor specification of the benchmark model is given by testing the $55 - 33 = 22$ overidentifying restrictions in the non-crisis period. The test statistic is given by the first term in (4.25), which has a value of 29.18. The p-value is 0.14, showing that the benchmark factor structure is not rejected at the 5% level.

The parameter estimates associated with the common factors highlight the factor structure underlying international equity returns during the benchmark period. The parameter estimates of the common factor (λ_i) show that all equity markets react in the same direction to world shocks, with the effects on emerging equity markets tending to be larger than they are on industrial equity markets. A similar result occurs for the emerging market factor where the parameter estimates (γ_i) show that all emerging equity markets respond in the same direction. The parameter estimates of the industrial factor (δ_i), show that Germany, the United Kingdom, and the United States all respond in the same way by a similar amount. In contrast, Japan moves in the opposite direction ($\delta_J = -0.32$), although this parameter estimate is statistically insignificant with a standard error of 0.36. The parameter estimates of the regional factor (ψ_i) show that the Latin American countries experience more than double the impact of shocks to this factor compared with the United States.

A comparison of the contagion parameter estimates stemming from Russia (κ_i) shows that the effects of contagion on international equity markets during the Russian crisis is selective, although it does affect both emerging and industrial equity markets. The largest (absolute) impact is felt by Germany (0.69) and the United Kingdom (0.46), which are both statistically significant at conventional significance levels. This result picks up the fact that most international lenders to Russia were European-based. Van Rijckeghem and Weder (2003) document that German banks had a heavy exposure of loans to Russia. Performing a joint test of no contagion from Russia to all four industrial equity markets in table 4.4 shows that these restrictions are rejected at the 5% level.

Of the emerging markets during the Russian crisis, the strongest contagion channels from Russia are to Argentina (0.29) and Thailand (-0.31), although table 4.3 shows that neither parameter estimates are statistically significant at the

Table 4.4

Joint tests of contagion and structural breaks. Wald statistics based on the unconstrained parameter estimates reported in Table 4.3.

Null Hypothesis		Stat.	DOF	pv
No contagion from Russia to:				
All other	$\kappa_i = 0, \forall i, i \neq R$	78.11	9	0.00
Industrial	$\kappa_i = 0, i = G, J, UK, U$	31.05	4	0.00
Emerging	$\kappa_i = 0, i = A, B, H, T, P$	16.57	5	0.01
No contagion from LTCM to:				
All other	$\overline{\kappa}_i = 0, \forall i, i \neq U$	151.83	9	0.00
Industrial	$\overline{\kappa}_i = 0, i = G, J, UK$	56.32	3	0.00
Emerging	$\overline{\kappa}_i = 0,$ $i = A, B, H, T, P, R$	45.45	6	0.00
Joint test of				
No contagion	$\kappa_i = \overline{\kappa}_j = 0, i \neq R, j \neq U$	250.96	18	0.00
No structural break in idiosyncratic factor of				
Russia	$\phi_R = \kappa_R$	7.04	1	0.01
US	$\phi_U = \overline{\kappa}_U$	1.81	1	0.18

5% level. However, a joint test of no contagion from Russia to the five emerging equity markets given in table 4.4, is rejected at the 5% level.

In contrast to the Russian contagion results, the effects of contagion from the LTCM crisis $(\overline{\kappa}_i)$ on emerging and industrial countries are more widespread. The greatest impact of contagion during the LTCM crisis is on the two Latin American countries. An overall test of contagion from the United States to all emerging equity markets presented in table 4.4 is found to be statistically significant. The industrial countries, Germany, Japan and the United Kingdom, experience contagion levels less than the two Latin American countries, but these linkages are nonetheless individually (table 4.3) and jointly (table 4.4) statistically significant.

4.4.2 Volatility Decompositions

An alternative way of identifying the relative importance of contagion is by computing the variance decompositions in (4.6) for the benchmark period, and (4.9) and (4.15) in the Russian and LTCM crisis periods respectively. The results of the volatility decomposition in the benchmark period are given in

Table 4.5
Variance decomposition of equity returns in proportions (%):
Benchmark period. Row totals sum to 100%. Based on (4.6).

Ctry	Common Factors				Idio.
	World	Emerging	Industrial	Regional	
Arg.	18.32	9.45	–	54.04	18.19
Brz.	18.45	3.91	–	34.79	42.85
HK	40.03	24.24	–	–	35.74
Thl.	21.42	22.30	–	–	56.28
Pol.	14.95	20.60	–	–	64.45
Rus.	11.61	14.93	–	–	73.45
Ger.	49.07	–	5.20	–	45.73
Jap.	29.13	–	25.57	–	45.31
UK	59.07	–	11.57	–	29.36
US	32.28	–	14.90	28.66	24.16

table 4.5, where the decompositions are expressed as a percentage of the total. This table shows the importance of idiosyncratic shocks in explaining equity market volatility in many of the countries investigated, with Russia (73.45%) followed by Poland (64.45%) exhibiting the highest proportions.

The volatility decompositions during the Russian crisis reported in table 4.6 support the previous results showing that equity markets in Germany (57.18%) and the United Kingdom (48.67%) are the most affected of all equity markets by contagion from Russia. The maximum affect of contagion from Russia on the emerging markets during this period is felt by Argentina (10.38%). In contrast, United States equity markets (3.05%) appear to be hardly affected by contagion from Russia.

The volatility decompositions during the LTCM crisis reported in table 4.7 further highlight the relative importance and widespread effects of contagion from the United States during this period. Of the emerging markets, Argentina (71.74%) and Brazil (82.16%) are particularly affected by contagion from the United States, as is Poland (55.76%). Hong Kong (24.90%) and Thailand (14.86%) are proportionately less affected by contagion from the United States, suggesting that an important component of their volatilities is the result of idiosyncratic factors. This is particularly true for Thailand where the contribution of the idiosyncratic shock is 45.22% during the

Table 4.6
Variance decomposition of equity returns in proportions (%):
Russian crisis period. Row totals sum to 100%. Based on (4.9).

Ctry	Common Factors				Idio.	Contagion From Russia
	World	Emerging	Industrial	Regional		
Arg.	16.42	8.47	–	48.44	16.30	10.38
Brz.	18.34	3.89	–	34.57	42.58	0.63
HK	39.76	24.07	–	–	35.49	0.68
Thl.	20.22	21.04	–	–	53.11	5.63
Pol.	14.83	20.43	–	–	63.92	0.83
Rus.	4.80	6.17	–	–	89.04	0.00
Ger.	21.01	–	2.23	–	19.58	57.18
Jap.	28.03	–	24.60	–	43.60	3.76
UK	30.32	–	5.94	–	15.07	48.67
US	31.30	–	14.45	27.79	23.43	3.05

Table 4.7
Variance decomposition of equity returns in proportions (%): LTCM
crisis period. Row totals sum to 100%. Based on (4.15).

Ctry	Common Factors				Idio.	Contagion Form	
	World	Emerging	Industrial	Regional		Russia	US
Arg.	4.64	2.39	–	13.69	4.61	2.93	71.74
Brz.	3.27	0.69	–	6.17	7.60	0.11	82.16
HK	29.86	18.08	–	–	26.66	0.51	24.90
Thl.	17.21	17.92	–	–	45.22	4.80	14.86
Pol.	6.56	9.04	–	–	28.28	0.37	55.76
Rus.	4.78	6.14	–	–	88.64	0.00	0.44
Ger.	13.16	–	1.39	–	12.26	35.80	37.39
Jap.	7.12	–	6.25	–	11.08	0.96	74.59
UK	20.42	–	4.00	–	10.15	32.78	32.66
US	38.08	–	17.58	33.81	6.82	3.71	0.00

LTCM crisis. Russian equities (0.44%) show no effect of contagion from the United States, which are still dominated by their
own idiosyncratic shocks (88.64%). Of the industrials, Japanese
(74.59%) equity markets are the most affected by contagion
from the United States, followed by Germany (37.39%) and the
United Kingdom (32.66%).

4.4.3 Structural Break Tests

Table 4.4 also gives the results of two structural break tests. The first is a test of a structural break in the Russian idiosyncratic parameter. The increase in volatility caused by the Russian crisis is highlighted in table 4.3, where the idiosyncratic parameter estimate nearly doubles in magnitude from ($\phi_R = 1.32$) in the benchmark period to ($\kappa_R = 2.27$) in the Russian crisis period. The p-value of this structural break test is 0.01 showing evidence of a significant structural break. The second structural break test reported in table 4.3 is for the United States idiosyncratic parameter. The test yields a p-value of 0.18 showing that the null of no structural break is not rejected at conventional significance levels.

4.4.4 Robustness Checks

The robustness of the empirical results are investigated by subjecting the multi-regime factor model to a number of robustness checks. To save space, the results are summarized in the following with the output available from the authors upon request.

The first robustness check consists of extending the factor structure to allow for an additional common factor in the benchmark model. The results of the variance decompositions show no qualitative change to the results reported above. The biggest contribution to the variance decomposition in the second common factor is for Russia, where the weight is 6.93%.

The second robustness check consists of reestimating the model for different crisis dates. In each case, the variance decompositions reported above did not change qualitatively. In addition, for the alternative sample periods investigated, the value of the objective function from the GMM procedure is maximized using the sample period chosen above.

4.4.5 Comparison with Bond Market Transmissions

In Chapter 3 the effects of contagion on international bond markets were studied using a similar framework to the approach adopted here. However, the LTCM sample period in the bond market chapter is slightly shorter than in the current chapter, where the start of the LTCM crisis period is defined to coincide with the public recapitalization announcement on September 23. To enable a comparison of the results for the two markets, the model in Chapter 3 is reestimated using the same definition of the LTCM crisis period used in this chapter.[7] The results are given in Table 4.8 which gives the contribution of contagion as a proportion of total volatility during the Russian and LTCM crisis periods for the bond market, together with the equity market results, which are taken from table 4.7. Blank cells indicate countries not included in a particular study.

Inspection of table 4.8 shows that contagion from both Russia and the United States dominates the observed volatility in equity market returns of most countries, while the effects in bond markets are smaller, but still not insubstantial. In the case of Argentina, Brazil, Poland, Germany, Japan, and the United Kingdom, the contribution of contagion to total volatility in equities is over 50%. The largest contributions of contagion to bond market volatility are in Argentina, Poland, and Russia, where the total contribution is just under 50%.

The main source of contagion in most equity markets is from the United States. In the case of Germany and the United Kingdom, the contributions of contagion from Russia and the United States are similar at between 32% and 37%. A similar result occurs in bond markets where the main contributor to bond market volatility is contagion from the United States. Two exceptions are Brazil, where the contribution from Russia is 23.64% compared to 1.31% from the United States, and to a lesser extent, the Netherlands, where the contribution from Russia is 11.04% compared to 4.6% from the United States.

A comparison of the equity market and bond market results shows that Brazil is a recipient of contagion from the United States in equity markets, and from Russia in bonds. This suggests that in the case of Brazil, at least, crises may be propagated differently through different asset markets, across the same geographical borders. This also implies that the influences of trade and other regional considerations, such as suggested in Glick and Rose (1999) and Van Rijckeghem and Weder (2001), where transmission is based on trade or financial linkages, cannot constitute the entire story. The evidence presented suggests that the nature of particular assets or asset

7. Consistent with the previous chapter, the bond market model is reestimated using Gauss v.3.2.

Table 4.8
Variance decomposition of daily equity returns and daily bond market premia in proportions (%) for various countries during the LTCM crisis period.[a]

Country	Contagion from:	Equity Markets			Bond Markets		
		Russia	US	Total	Russia	US	Total
Argentina		2.93	71.74	74.67	0.03	45.37	45.40
Brazil		0.11	82.16	82.27	23.64	1.31	24.95
Mexico		—	—	—	0.01	2.74	2.75
Hong Kong		0.51	24.90	25.41	—	—	—
Indonesia		—	—	—	0.08	0.01	0.09
Korea		—	—	—	0.36	2.10	2.46
Thailand		4.80	14.86	19.66	1.41	27.78	29.19
Bulgaria		—	—	—	8.32	1.22	9.54
Poland		0.37	55.76	56.13	0.05	46.18	46.23
Russia		—	0.44	0.44	—	42.00	42.00
Netherlands		—	—	—	11.04	4.60	15.64
Germany		35.80	37.39	73.19	—	—	—
Japan		0.96	74.59	75.55	—	—	—
UK		32.78	32.66	65.44	0.22	6.67	6.89
US		3.71	—	3.71	1.65	—	1.65

(a) The bond market results are based on reestimating the model of Chapter 3, by extending the LTCM period from September 23, 1998 to October 15, 1998, to August 31, 1998 to October 15, 1998. Some of the bond market results reported in this table differ to those originally reported by Dungey, Fry, González-Hermosillo and Martin (2006). Given the robustness properties of the equity markets presented above, this suggests that the bond markets are more sensitive to changes in crisis dates. The equity market results are based on Table 4.7.

markets may hold important information on the transmission of shocks.

4.5 Conclusions

This chapter has provided a framework for modeling the transmission of contagion in international equity markets during the complex period of the Russian bond default and the LTCM crisis in 1998. The model was based on extending the existing latent factor model allowing for additional transmission mechanisms between global equity markets during periods of financial crises arising from contagion. Contagion was identified as the impact of shocks from either Russia or the United States on global equity markets, having conditioned on both world and regional factors, as well as country-specific shocks in equity markets. A property of the model was that the volatility of equity returns could be decomposed in terms of the underlying factors, thereby providing a measure of the relative strength of contagion. A number of hypothesis tests of contagion and structural breaks were also carried out. The model was applied to 10 equity markets consisting of four developed markets, and six emerging markets from three regions (Latin America, Asia, and Eastern Europe), using daily equity returns over 1998. A GMM estimator, which matched the theoretical moments of the factor model with the empirical moments of the data across regimes, was presented.

The key result of the chapter was that contagion was significant and widespread to a variety of international equity markets during the LTCM crisis, with the effects of contagion being strongest on the industrial markets and the geographically close Latin American markets. The contagion transmission mechanisms emanating from the Russian equity market tended to be more selective during the Russian crisis, but nonetheless still impacted upon both emerging and industrial equity markets. Moreover, rather than the Russian crisis being seen as an emerging market phenomenon, as suggested by the Committee on the Global Financial System (1999, pp.7-8), contagion from Russia was found to be more statistically significant in industrial countries than in emerging markets.

Chapter 3 found that contagion in bond markets also affected a wide variety of economies. The combination of the results from that chapter and the current one suggest that it would be informative to construct a more general model of asset markets, combining both bonds and equities to test the importance of contagious transmission mechanisms between markets across international borders. A step in this direction, for different case studies, has been recently undertaken in Ehrmann, Fratzscher, and Rigobon (2005), while Granger, Huang, and Yang (2000), and Hartmann, Straetmans, and de Vries (2004) focused on bivariate relationships between asset markets during financial crises.

An important feature of the proposed model is the specification of a multiple regime model to allow for multiple crises. This suggests that the framework could be applied to model several crises simultaneously by extending the sample period adopted in the current application. By extending the sample period backwards to include 1997 would enable the Asian financial crisis to be modeled, while extending the sample period forwards would enable the Brazilian crisis of 1999 to be modeled for example. This latter extension is particularly interesting given the empirical results presented here, as Brazil was the next country to experience a financial crisis in January 1999. Moreover, Brazilian financial markets seem to have experienced several hits from the Russian and LTCM crises during 1998: The Brazilian bond market was impacted by the Russian crisis (see Chapter 3, as well Dungey, Fry, González-Hermosillo, and Martin 2006, and Baig and Goldfajn 2001) and the equity market by the LTCM near-collapse as shown here. The extension to multiple markets and multiple crises is the focus of the next chapter.

Arguably the most policy-relevant finding of this chapter is the significant contagion effects across countries evident in the Russian and LTCM crises. Contagion effects were shown to be larger for emerging markets in absolute value, but proportionate results are less clear. Discussions with policy makers indicate that they would be concerned by a 17% contribution of contagion to volatility whether that translates to 5 basis points squared (Netherlands) or over 500 (Brazil). The results also clearly point to the regional nature of crises. This suggests a coordinated crisis prevention policy may well be appropriate; Brunnemeier, Crockett, Goodhart, Persaud, and Shin (2009) suggest coordinated global regulatory policy is essential for crisis prevention. However, from a crisis management perspective, it is not likely that identical policy responses will be appropriate globally. Chapter 2 suggested a number of themes to be explored in building the blocks of a contagion model. The current chapter has examined the behavior of one market (fixed interest), region specific effects, emerging market effects, and nested crises, as well as volatility clustering. In Chapter 5 these features will be brought together in a single model across a number of crises for fixed interest and equity markets.

5

Are Crises Alike? Comparing Financial Crises

Co-written with Chrismin Tang

5.1 Introduction

There is a common presumption that financial crises are not alike as the triggers of crises differ, and the economic and institutional environments in which crises take place vary amongst countries. Recent triggers for crises include sovereign debt default (the Russian crisis in August 1998), risk management strategies (the near collapse of Long-Term Capital Management, LTCM, in September 1998), sudden stops in capital flows (Brazil in early 1999), collapses of speculative bubbles (the dot-com crisis in 2000), inconsistencies between fundamentals and policy settings (as in Argentina in 2001) and a liquidity squeeze (associated with the pressure in the U.S. subprime mortgage market from mid-2007).[1] These examples include countries with highly developed financial markets as well as a number of emerging markets.

This lack of commonality amongst crisis-affected countries is reflected in the development of theoretical models of financial turmoil, where there now exist three broad classes of models. The first generation models emphasize the role

---

1. Further analysis of these crises are given in Lowenstein (2001); Jorion (2000); Baig and Goldfajn (2001); and del Torre, Levy, Yeyati, and Schmulker (2003).

of macroeconomic variables in causing currency crises when countries adopted fixed exchange rates (Flood and Marion 1999); the second generation models focus on the role of speculative attacks; while the third generation of models focus on institutional imbalances and information asymmetries (Allen and Gale 2000, Kaminsky and Reinhart 2003, Kodres and Pritsker 2002, Pavlova and Rigobon 2007, and Yuan 2005).

The identification of shocks triggering a crisis is just one dimension to understanding financial crises. A second, and arguably more important dimension, is to identify the transmission mechanisms that propagate shocks from the source country across national borders and across financial markets. These links are emphasized in third-generation crisis models, where channels over and above the market fundamental mechanisms that link countries and asset markets during noncrisis periods appear during a crisis. As discussed in Chapter 2, these additional linkages are broadly known as contagion.

It is not entirely straightforward to combine existing theoretical models into a general empirical framework in which to model and test the relative strengths of alternative transmission mechanisms operating during financial crises.[2] The strategy followed in this chapter is to adopt a broader approach and focus on the factor structures of the transmission mechanisms linking international asset markets. Formally the model is based on the theoretical framework of Kodres and Pritsker (2002). This leads to a latent factor structure that is transformed into a model that admits three broad contagious transmission mechanisms according to the classification proposed by Dungey and Martin (2007) and extends the latent factor model of Chapters 2 to 4. The first corresponds to shocks originating in a particular asset market within a particular country (Idiosyncratic) that transmit to all financial markets. The second represents mechanisms originating in a specific asset market class (Market), for example equities or bonds, that jointly impact alternative classes of asset markets. The third mechanism represents shocks beginning in a particular country that impact upon the asset markets

---

2. Some previous attempts are by van Rijckeghem and Weder (2001), who focus on banking channels; Glick and Rose (1999), who look at regional linkages; and Boyer, Kumagai, and Yuan (2006), who emphasise liquidity effects. Perhaps the most extensive recent work is by Kaminsky (2006), who considers a broad range of variables, classified according to alternative theoretical crisis models.

of other countries (Country). If the structure of these three transmission mechanisms is found to be common across different financial crises, this would suggest that all crises are indeed alike regardless of the nature of the initial shock and the economic and institutional environments of the affected country. Alternatively, if the propagation mechanisms vary across crises, perhaps as a result of the development of new strains of contagion, this would suggest that crises are indeed unique at least across their source and their transmission mechanism.

The factor model is estimated for a series of five crises across six countries over the period 1998 to 2007: the Russian/LTCM crisis, the Brazilian crisis, the dot-com crisis, the Argentinian crisis, and the recent U.S. subprime mortgage and credit crisis.[3] A key empirical result is that a general model can be specified to explain the contagious linkages operating over a broad array of financial crises. Moreover, as all possible transmission mechanisms are found to be statistically significant in each crisis investigated, this suggests that the answer to the title of the chapter is "Yes." The crises that generated the most contagion are the Russian/LTCM and U.S. subprime crises, which both began in credit markets and spread to equity markets. However, this conclusion needs qualification as the relative contribution of each channel to the volatility of returns in asset markets does vary across crises.

The rest of the chapter proceeds as follows. The theoretical model is specified in Section 5.2 where asset returns are specified in term of a set of latent factors. The form of these factors are discussed in Section 5.3. The factors are expressed (rotated) in terms of the classification proposed by Dungey and Martin (2007). Section 5.4 provides a discussion of the data, key empirical results are reported in Section 5.5, while some additional robustness checks and sensitivity analyses are conducted in Section 5.6. Concluding comments are provided in Section 5.7. The appendices contain details of the derivation of the theoretical model, data sources, and additional empirical results.

---

3. Other financial crises have also occured during this period including Iceland and Turkey (mid 2006) and China (late February 2007). To control the dimension of the empirical application the approach is to condition the empirical results on these crisis.

5.2 A Model of Contagion

In this section a theoretical model of contagion is developed whereby excess returns on financial assets for N countries are expressed in terms of a set of latent factors. These factors capture a range of channels that link asset markets including common factors that simultaneously impact upon all asset markets, idiosyncratic factors that are specific to a single market, and contagion that transmits through additional channels arising during times of financial stress. The approach is related to the work of Kodres and Pritsker (2002) with one important difference: the solution is derived in terms of asset returns instead of asset prices. Formally this is achieved by changing the preference function of agents and the underlying distributional assumptions of the model.

The model consists of heterogenous international agents who choose portfolios from N risky assets with return vector R, and a risk-free asset Rf, across a set of countries. The three groups of agents consist of informed investors (denoted as I), uninformed investors (denoted as U), and noise traders. The informed and uninformed investors are assumed to derive portfolios based on optimizing behavior, whereas the noise traders do not. In the specification of the model, each country is assumed to be a two-period endowment economy with a fixed net supply X_T, that provides one risky asset. This assumption is relaxed in the empirical application where the number of risky assets of each country is extended to two assets. Investors in each economy trade assets in the current period at a price vector P, and consume the liquidation value v, of assets in the next period. Market equilibrium is where the supply of the risky asset X_T, equals the sum of the demands of the three groups of agents

$$X_T = \mu_I \alpha_I^* W + \mu_U \alpha_U^* W + \ln \epsilon, \qquad (5.1)$$

where μ_I and μ_U are respectively the number of informed and uninformed investors, α_k^* is a $(N \times 1)$ vector of the optimal proportions of risky assets held by investor $k = I, U$, and W is current period wealth. The term $\mu_I \alpha_I^* W$ is the optimal demand for risky assets of informed agents, $\mu_U \alpha_U^* W$ is the optimal demand for risky assets of uninformed agents, and $\ln \epsilon$ is the total demand of risky assets of noise traders.

In the current period, the informed and uninformed investors are assumed to choose between the proportion of the portfolio held in risky assets and the proportion of the portfolio held in a risk-free asset $(1 - \alpha'_k \iota)$, that maximizes expected utility from wealth in the next period (W_+)

$$\max_{\alpha_k} E[V\left(W_+\right)|\Omega_k] = \max_{\alpha_k}\left\{\ln E\left[W_+^{(1-\gamma)}\middle|\Omega_k\right]\right\}, \qquad k = I, U, \tag{5.2}$$

subject to the wealth constraint

$$W_+ = \left(1 + R_p\right)W, \tag{5.3}$$

where γ is the relative risk aversion parameter, W is current period wealth, and

$$R_p = \alpha'_k R + (1 - \alpha'_k \iota)\, Rf, \tag{5.4}$$

is the return on the portfolio where ι is a $(N \times 1)$ vector of ones. The information set of investor $k = I, U$, is represented by Ω_k.

The return on the ith risky asset is defined as the percentage difference between the unknown liquidation value of the asset in the next period (v_i) and its price in the current period (P_i)

$$R_i = \frac{v_i - P_i}{P_i}, \qquad i = 1, 2, \cdots, N. \tag{5.5}$$

The liquidation values of the asset are determined by two factors, θ and u, according to

$$\ln v = \ln \theta + \ln u. \tag{5.6}$$

The factor θ represents an information factor with the following distribution

$$\ln \theta \sim N\left(\bar{\theta}, \Sigma_\theta\right),$$

while u is driven by a set of K macroeconomic ($\ln f$) and N idiosyncratic ($\ln \eta$) factors

$$\ln u_{t+1} = \beta \ln f_{t+1} + \ln \eta_{t+1}, \qquad (5.7)$$

with loadings β, and

$$\ln f_{t+1} = \ln f_t + \ln \delta_{t+1}$$
$$\ln \eta_{t+1} \sim N\left(0, \Sigma_\eta\right) \qquad (5.8)$$
$$\ln \delta_{t+1} \sim N\left(0, I_N\right),$$

show that the macroeconomic factors are integrated processes of order one.

The optimal solution to the portfolio problem of the informed and the uninformed investors is of the form (see Appendix 5.A.1)

$$\alpha_k^* = \frac{1}{\gamma}\left[E\left[r|\Omega_k\right] - rf + \frac{1}{2}\text{Covar}\left[r|\Omega_k\right]\right]\text{Covar}\left[r|\Omega_k\right]^{-1},$$
$$k = I, U, \qquad (5.9)$$

where $r = \ln(1 + R)$ and $rf = \ln(1 + Rf)$ represent logarithmic returns. In contrast to the informed and uninformed investors, noise traders are assumed to buy and sell assets based solely on their own idiosyncratic need for liquidity, which does not depend upon the fundamental value of assets (v).

The information set of the informed investor is defined as

$$\Omega_I = \left\{\ln \theta, \ln P\right\}, \qquad (5.10)$$

where P represents a N vector of prices. The conditional moments in (5.9) are given by (see Appendix 5.A.2)

$$E\left[r|\Omega_I\right] = \ln \theta + \beta \ln f - \ln P$$
$$Var\left[r|\Omega_I\right] = \beta\beta' + \Sigma_\eta. \qquad (5.11)$$

The information set of the uninformed investor is defined as

$$\Omega_U = \{\ln P\},\tag{5.12}$$

so the conditional moments in (5.9) are given by (see Appendix 5.A.3)

$$E[r|\Omega_U] = \ln P + \bar{\theta} + \Sigma_\theta$$

$$\times \left[\Sigma_\theta + \left(\frac{\gamma}{\mu_I W}\right)^2 (\beta\beta' + \Sigma_\eta) \Sigma_\epsilon (\beta\beta' + \Sigma_\eta)'\right]^{-1}$$

$$\times \left[\ln \theta + \frac{\gamma (\beta\beta' + \Sigma_\eta)}{\mu_I W} \ln \epsilon - \bar{\theta}\right],\tag{5.13}$$

$$Var[r|\Omega_U] = [\Sigma_\theta + \Sigma_u] - \Sigma_\theta \left[\Sigma_\theta + \left(\frac{\gamma}{\mu_I W}\right)^2\right.$$

$$\left.(\beta\beta' + \Sigma_\eta) \Sigma_\epsilon (\beta\beta' + \Sigma_\eta)'\right]^{-1} \Sigma_\theta'.$$

To complete the specification of the demand for risky assets in (5.1), the net demand of noise traders, $\ln \epsilon$, is assumed to have the distribution

$$\ln \epsilon \sim N(0, \Sigma_\epsilon).$$

To derive an expression of the model in terms of asset returns, let

$$y = \ln P_+ - \ln P - rf,$$

represent the vector of N realized excess returns, where P and P_+ are the price vectors in the current period and the next period respectively. In Appendix 5.A.4, it is shown that in equilibrium the solution of the model is characterized by y being expressed in terms of the latent factors $\{\ln \theta, \ln \epsilon, \ln f, \ln \zeta\}$

$$y = C_0 + C_1 \ln \theta + C_2 \ln \epsilon + C_3 \ln f + C_4 \ln \zeta,\tag{5.14}$$

where $\ln \zeta = \ln P_+ - E[\ln v|_U]$ is an expectations error that is assumed to be iid. The C_i matrices are functions of the parameters of the model and the conditional expectations expressions in (5.11) and (5.13) (see Appendix 5.A.4 for details). This specification represents a multifactor model of asset markets similar to the class of empirical contagion models proposed by Dungey and Martin (2007). An important implication of this equation is that the effect of contagion during financial crises is to change the structure of the C_i matrices. For example, in a noncrisis period where there is no contagion, this is represented by $\beta\beta'$ and Σ_η in (5.7) and (5.8) being diagonal matrices, with the model reducing to the class of factor models used in international finance to price assets in "normal times" as proposed by Bekaert and Hodrick (1992), Solnik (1974), Dumas and Solnik (1995), and Longin and Solnik (1995), as well as the factor models developed for international bond and equity markets in Chapter 3 and Chapter 4 respectively.

5.3 Empirical Factor Specification

The empirical factors are identified using the approach of Dungey and Martin (2007), which involves expressing the N excess returns (y_t) by rotating the factors in (5.14) into global (w_t), market (m_t), country (c_t), and idiosyncratic (u_t) components. In the empirical analysis $N = 12$, which consists of six countries Argentina (A), Brazil (B), Canada (C), Mexico (M), Russia (R), and the United States (U), each with two asset markets, equities (s_t) and bonds (b_t). Of the six countries used in the empirical analysis, Argentina, Brazil, Mexico, and Russia represent the emerging financial markets, and the United States and Canada represent the industrial financial markets. In the second quarter of 2007, Mexico, Brazil, and Argentina accounted for 46 percent of total emerging market bond trading. Russia accounted for an additional 4 percent. Thus, the four emerging countries examined here account for about 50 percent of the total emerging market debt (see EMTA Survey 2007).

In specifying the empirical factor model, care is taken to distinguish between the factors operating during noncrisis and crisis periods. Five crisis specifications are considered corresponding to the Russia/LTCM crisis in 1998, the Brazilian crisis in early 1999, the dot-com crisis in 2000, the Argentinian crisis 2001-2005, and the recent U.S. subprime crisis beginning mid 2007. The choice of crisis dates is discussed in Section 5.4.2 below.

5.3.1 Noncrisis Specification

The factor specification during the noncrisis period is

$$
\begin{bmatrix}
s_{A,t} \\
s_{B,t} \\
s_{C,t} \\
s_{M,t} \\
s_{R,t} \\
s_{U,t} \\
b_{A,t} \\
b_{B,t} \\
b_{C,t} \\
b_{M,t} \\
b_{R,t} \\
b_{U,t}
\end{bmatrix}
=
\underbrace{
\begin{bmatrix}
\lambda_A^s & \beta_A^s & \pi_A^s \\
\lambda_B^s & \beta_B^s & \pi_B^s \\
\lambda_C^s & \beta_C^s & \\
\lambda_M^s & \beta_M^s & \\
\lambda_R^s & \beta_R^s & \pi_R^s \\
\lambda_U^s & \beta_U^s & \\
\lambda_A^b & \beta_A^b & \pi_A^b \\
\lambda_B^b & \beta_B^b & \pi_B^b \\
\lambda_C^b & \beta_C^b & \\
\lambda_M^b & \beta_M^b & \\
\lambda_R^b & \beta_R^b & \pi_R^b \\
\lambda_U^b & \beta_U^b &
\end{bmatrix}
\begin{bmatrix}
w_t^1 \\
w_t^2 \\
w_t^3
\end{bmatrix}
}_{\text{Common}}
+
\underbrace{
\begin{bmatrix}
\gamma_A^s \\
\gamma_B^s \\
\gamma_C^s \\
\gamma_M^s \\
\gamma_R^s \\
\gamma_U^s \\
\gamma_A^b \\
\gamma_B^b \\
\gamma_C^b \\
\gamma_M^b \\
\gamma_R^b \\
\gamma_U^b
\end{bmatrix}
\begin{bmatrix}
m_t^s \\
m_t^b
\end{bmatrix}
}_{\text{Market}}
$$

$$
+
\underbrace{
\begin{bmatrix}
\delta_A^s \\
& \delta_B^s \\
& & \delta_C^s \\
& & & \delta_M^s \\
& & & & \delta_R^s \\
& & & & & \delta_U^s \\
& & & & & & \delta_A^b \\
& & & & & & & \delta_B^b \\
& & & & & & & & \delta_C^b \\
& & & & & & & & & \delta_M^b \\
& & & & & & & & & & \delta_R^b \\
& & & & & & & & & & & \delta_U^b
\end{bmatrix}
\begin{bmatrix}
c_{A,t} \\
c_{B,t} \\
c_{C,t} \\
c_{M,t} \\
c_{R,t} \\
c_{U,t}
\end{bmatrix}
}_{\text{Country}}
+
\underbrace{
\mathrm{diag}
\begin{pmatrix}
\phi_A^s \\
\phi_B^s \\
\phi_C^s \\
\phi_M^s \\
\phi_R^s \\
\phi_U^s \\
\phi_A^b \\
\phi_B^b \\
\phi_C^b \\
\phi_M^b \\
\phi_R^b \\
\phi_U^b
\end{pmatrix}
\begin{bmatrix}
\upsilon_{A,t}^s \\
\upsilon_{B,t}^s \\
\upsilon_{C,t}^s \\
\upsilon_{M,t}^s \\
\upsilon_{R,t}^s \\
\upsilon_{U,t}^s \\
\upsilon_{A,t}^b \\
\upsilon_{B,t}^b \\
\upsilon_{C,t}^b \\
\upsilon_{M,t}^b \\
\upsilon_{R,t}^b \\
\upsilon_{U,t}^b
\end{bmatrix}
}_{\text{Idiosyncratic}}
.
$$

$$(5.15)$$

All variables on the right-hand side of (5.15) are classified into the four sets of factors. The first set of factors are referred to as the common factors. The first two factors within this set (w_t^1, w_t^2) impact upon all asset markets, across all countries with loadings given by $\left(\lambda_i^j, \beta_i^j\right)$ for asset market $j = s, b$, in country i. The third factor in the common set of factors $\left(w_t^3\right)$ represents the set of emerging markets where crises originated during the sample period: Argentina, Brazil, and Russia, with loadings $\left(\pi_i^j\right)$. The second set of factors is the market factor, which captures respectively shocks to equity markets (m_t^s) and bond markets (m_t^b) with loadings (γ_i^s) and (γ_i^b). The set of country factors are given by $c_{A,t}, c_{B,t}, c_{C,t}, c_{M,t}, c_{R,t}, c_{U,t}$, which represent shocks specific to both the equity and bond market of each of the six countries where the loadings for the ith country are δ_i^s (equities) and δ_i^b (bonds). Finally, the set of idiosyncratic are given by the $v_{i,t}^j$ factors with loading $\left(\phi_i^j\right)$, which represent shocks that are specific to a particular asset market in a particular country.

The noncrisis factor specification in (5.15) is conveniently expressed as

$$y_t = A_w w_t + A_m m_t + A_c c_t + A_u u_t, \qquad (5.16)$$

where y_t is the (12×1) vector of excess returns, w_t is the (3×1) vector of common factors, m_t is the (2×1) vector of market factors, c_t is the (6×1) vector of country factors, and u_t is the (12×1) vector of idiosyncratic factors. The A_j, $j = w, m, c, u$, are parameter matrices of conformable order to the empirical factors w_t, m_t, c_t and u_t, and correspond to those in (5.15).

5.3.2 Crisis Specification

The crisis model is an extension of the noncrisis model by allowing for additional channels representing contagion, which link international asset markets during financial crises. Three broad channels are specified following Dungey and Martin (2007):

1. Market shock: the shock originates in a specific class of asset markets globally, which impacts simultaneously on all other asset markets.
2. Country shock: the shock originates in a particular country that transmits to the asset markets of other countries.

3. Idiosyncratic shock: the shock originates in a specific asset market of a country that impacts upon global asset markets.

The Russian/LTCM Crisis The Russian crisis is specified to begin in the Russian bond market. The LTCM crisis is interpreted as a credit shock and is assumed to originate in the United States bond market. As seen in Chapters 3 and 4, it is not possible to separate out the two crises and model the full set of transmission mechanisms for each as a result of the shortness of the LTCM crisis period. The strategy adopted is to model both crises jointly by including idiosyncratic shocks arising from the Russian bond market and the United States bond market, together with the asset market and country contagion channels. The sample period is taken as the Russian crisis period, namely August to the end of 1998. This may have the effect of underestimating the importance of the LTCM crisis as its effects may be diluted by using a longer sample period than is necessary.

The Russian/LTCM crisis model is specified as

$$y_t = B_w w_t + B_m m_t + B_c c_t + B_u u_t, \qquad (5.17)$$

where the parameter matrices are defined as

$$
B_w = \begin{bmatrix}
\lambda_A^s & \beta_A^s & \pi_A^s \\
\lambda_B^s & \beta_B^s & \pi_B^s \\
\lambda_C^s & \beta_C^s & \\
\lambda_M^s & \beta_M^s & \\
\lambda_R^s & \beta_R^s & \pi_R^s \\
\lambda_U^s & \beta_U^s & \\
\cdots & \cdots & \cdots \\
\lambda_A^b & \beta_A^b & \pi_A^b \\
\lambda_B^b & \beta_B^b & \pi_B^b \\
\lambda_C^b & \beta_C^b & \\
\lambda_M^b & \beta_M^b & \\
\lambda_R^b & \beta_R^b & \pi_R^b \\
\lambda_U^b & \beta_U^b &
\end{bmatrix}, \quad
B_m = \begin{bmatrix}
\gamma_A^s + \theta_A^s & \kappa_{A,b}^s \\
\gamma_B^s + \theta_B^s & \kappa_{B,b}^s \\
\gamma_C^s + \theta_C^s & \kappa_{C,b}^s \\
\gamma_M^s + \theta_M^s & \kappa_{M,b}^s \\
\gamma_R^s + \theta_R^s & \kappa_{R,b}^s \\
\gamma_U^s + \theta_U^s & \kappa_{U,b}^s \\
\cdots & \cdots \\
\kappa_{A,s}^b & \gamma_A^b + \theta_A^b \\
\kappa_{B,s}^b & \gamma_B^b + \theta_B^b \\
\kappa_{C,s}^b & \gamma_C^b + \theta_C^b \\
\kappa_{M,s}^b & \gamma_M^b + \theta_M^b \\
\kappa_{R,s}^b & \gamma_R^b + \theta_R^b \\
\kappa_{U,s}^b & \gamma_U^b + \theta_U^b
\end{bmatrix},
$$

$$B_c = \begin{bmatrix} \delta_A^s & & & & & \kappa_{A,R}^s & \\ & \delta_B^s & & & & \kappa_{B,R}^s & \\ & & \delta_C^s & & & \kappa_{C,R}^s & \\ & & & \delta_M^s & & \kappa_{M,R}^s & \\ & & & & \delta_R^s + \theta_{R,R}^s & \\ & & & & & \kappa_{U,R}^s & \delta_U^s \\ \cdots & \cdots & \cdots & \cdots & & \cdots & \cdots \\ \delta_A^b & & & & & \kappa_{A,R}^b & \\ & \delta_B^b & & & & \kappa_{B,R}^b & \\ & & \delta_C^b & & & \kappa_{C,R}^b & \\ & & & \delta_M^b & & \kappa_{M,R}^b & \\ & & & & \delta_R^b + \theta_{R,R}^b & \\ & & & & & \kappa_{U,R}^b & \delta_U^b \end{bmatrix},$$

and

$$B_u = \begin{bmatrix} \phi_A^s & & & & & & & & & & & & \kappa_{A,Rb}^s & \kappa_{A,Ub}^s \\ & \phi_B^s & & & & & & & & & & & \kappa_{B,Rb}^s & \kappa_{B,Ub}^s \\ & & \phi_C^s & & & & & & & & & & \kappa_{C,Rb}^s & \kappa_{C,Ub}^s \\ & & & \phi_M^s & & & & & & & & & \kappa_{M,Rb}^s & \kappa_{M,Ub}^s \\ & & & & \phi_R^s & & & & & & & & \kappa_{R,Rb}^s & \kappa_{R,Ub}^s \\ & & & & & \kappa_U^s & & & & & & & \kappa_{U,Rb}^s & \kappa_{U,Ub}^b \\ & & & & & & \phi_A^b & & & & & & \kappa_{A,Rb}^b & \kappa_{A,Ub}^b \\ & & & & & & & \phi_B^b & & & & & \kappa_{B,Rb}^b & \kappa_{B,Ub}^b \\ & & & & & & & & \phi_C^b & & & & \kappa_{C,Rb}^b & \kappa_{C,Ub}^b \\ & & & & & & & & & \phi_M^b & & & \kappa_{M,Rb}^b & \kappa_{M,Ub}^b \\ & & & & & & & & & & \phi_R^b + \theta_{R,Rb}^b & & \kappa_{R,Ub}^b \\ & & & & & & & & & & & \kappa_{U,Rb}^b & \phi_U^b + \theta_{U,Ub}^b \end{bmatrix}.$$

The parameter matrices are specified by augmenting the noncrisis parameter matrices in (5.15) and (5.16) to allow for contagion as well as structural breaks in the factor structures during the crisis period. The market contagion channels are represented by the parameter $\kappa_{i,s}^b$ in the matrix B_m, which measures the strength of the equity market factor in the crisis period on the bond market in country i, while the parameter $\kappa_{i,b}^s$ measures the strength of the bond market factor on the equity market in country i. The country contagion channel from Russia to asset market j in country i is controlled by the parameter $\kappa_{i,R}^j$. The strength of the idiosyncratic contagion channel from the Russian (U.S.) bond market to asset market j in country i is determined by the parameter $\kappa^j_{i,Rb}$ $\left(\kappa^j_{i,Ub}\right)$. All structural breaks in the factors during the crisis period are controlled by the parameter θ. For example, the effects of a structural break in the equity and bond market factors during the crisis period on country i are respectively given by θ^s_i and θ^b_i. The common factors (w_t) are assumed not to exhibit structural breaks during the crisis period.

The Brazilian Crisis   The specification of the Brazilian crisis model is similar to the Russian/LTCM crisis model in (5.17), with the exception that there is just one idiosyncratic shock now arising from the Brazilian bond market. The two market channels of contagion are as before, which are represented by the 4th and 5th columns of the B_m matrix in (5.17). The country channel of contagion switches from the 5th column (Russian country factor) to the 2nd column (Brazilian country factor) of B_c. The idiosyncratic contagion channel arising from the Brazilian bond market shock is specified by switching column 11 in B_u in (5.17) to column 8 (Brazilian bond), and deleting column 12 with the exception of the parameter ϕ^b_U.

The Dot-Com Crisis   The dot-com crisis model has a similar structure to the Brazilian crisis model. The country channel of contagion is now found in the 6th column of B_c (U.S. country factor), and the idiosyncratic contagion channel is specified in column 6 of the B_u matrix (U.S. equity) in (5.17).

The Argentinian Crisis   The Argentinian crisis model follows the same form as the previous two models. The country channel of contagion is now found in the 1st column of B_c (Argentinian country factor), and the idiosyncratic contagion channel is specified in column 7 of the B_u matrix (Argentinian bond) in (5.17).

The U.S. Subprime Mortgage and Credit Crisis   The specification of the U.S. subprime mortgage and credit crisis is similar to the dot-com crisis specification with one exception. In the dot-com crisis there is a single idiosyncratic channel of contagion operating through the U.S. equity market as it is clear that this crisis originated in the U.S. equity market. The U.S. subprime mortgage and credit crisis is characterized by turbulence that spread from subprime mortgage markets to credit markets more generally, and then to short-term interbank markets as liquidity dried up in certain segments of the markets, particularly in structured credits. As the U.S. crisis manifested itself mainly in credit markets, this suggests that contagion should run from bond markets to equity markets in the model specified here. To test this proposition, both bond and equity idiosyncratic channels of contagion are allowed for in the subprime crisis specification.

5.4 Data

The data consist of daily excess returns on equities and bonds, all expressed in U.S. dollars, beginning March 31, 1998, and ending December 31, 2007, at the time of writing this chapter. The daily data are constructed from bond yields and equity indices. All data sources and formal definitions of the variables are given in Appendix 5.B. The data as well as computer codes used to generate the empirical results of this chapter, are available from

http://www.dungey.bigpondhosting.com

The United States and Canadian bonds are modeled using 10-year corporate BBB yields, with the Canadian yields converted into U.S. dollars. Bond returns are constructed for the two developed markets as

$$b_t = -n\left(r_{n,t} - r_{n-1,t-1}\right),$$ (5.18)

where $r_{n,t}$ is the yield on a bond with term to maturity, $n = 10$ years. That is, returns are computed simply by taking the first difference of the yields, multiplying this change in yields by the maturity and then changing the sign (Campbell, Lo, and MacKinlay 1997).[4]

---

4. The formula for converting bond yields into returns is just an approximation, but as the data are daily the error from using the approximation should be small (Craine and Martin 2008).

As in Chapter 3 emerging market bonds are represented by U.S. dollar denominated sovereign debt to avoid the lack of liquidity in emerging market domestic currency denominated bonds. As bonds are issued only sporadically in the emerging countries, it is not possible to derive a daily 10-year bond series as with the developed countries. The approach adopted is to choose a 10-year bond issued near the start of the sample period for an emerging country and track this bond over the sample period. For these bonds, the returns are computed using (5.18) with the term to maturity, n, now declining monotonically over the sample. However, as the sample covers approximately nine years, this bond will become less liquid as it approaches maturity near the end of the sample. In the case of the Argentinian bond used, this bond actually matures before the end of the sample period. To circumvent potential liquidity problems the approach is to choose another set of 10-year bonds beginning 1st of July, 2004, and track these bonds through the remaining part of the sample. Although this involves using bonds of differing maturities, by working with returns instead of yields, or even yield changes, makes the returns data on bonds commensurate.

The equity market indices are those for the major indices in each country, given in Appendix 5.B. All indices are expressed in domestic currencies and converted into USD equivalents using daily exchange rates. Missing observations arising from the terrorist attacks of September 11, 2001, are replaced by the previously observed price. Equity returns are computed by taking the first difference of the natural logarithm of the equity prices.

All bond and equity returns are expressed in terms of excess returns by subtracting the returns on a risk-free rate, as represented by the U.S. Treasury 10-year benchmark bond yield. The excess returns are expressed in percentage terms by multiplying each series by 100. Time series plots of the excess returns on equities and bonds are presented in figure 5.1. The shaded regions presented in the figure correspond to the period of the five crises investigated, whose dates are discussed below.

5.4.1 Filters

Two filters are applied to the raw returns before estimating the model. First, all excess returns are adjusted for any dynamics by

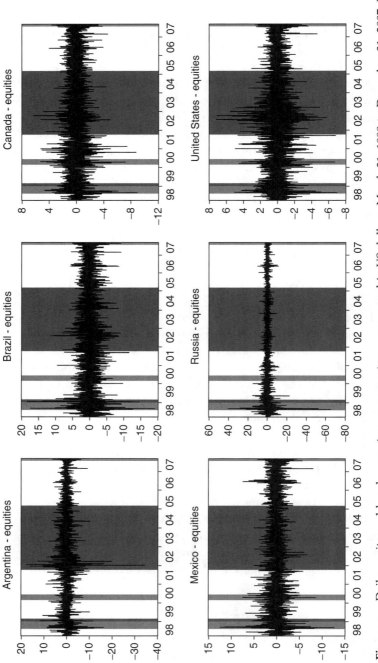

Figure 5.1 Daily equity and bond percentage excess returns, expressed in US dollars, March 31, 1998 to December 31, 2007. Data are unfiltered. The shaded regions correspond to the crisis periods in the following order: Russia/LTCM, Brazil, dot-com, Argentina, US subprime.

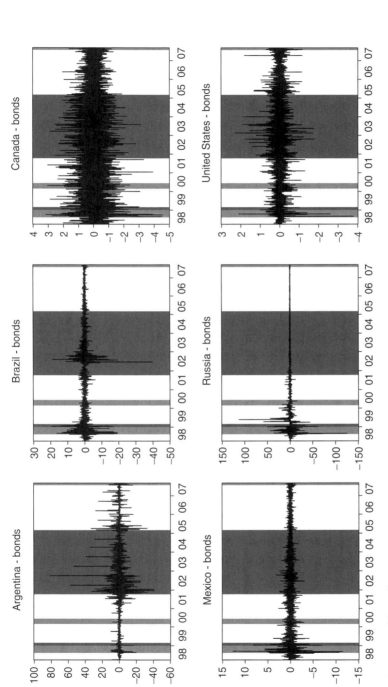

Figure 5.1 (Cont'd)

estimating a 12-variate VAR(1) consisting of all six equity and bond excess returns, together with a constant. Higher order lags do not qualitatively change the empirical properties of the model.

Second, the VAR contains a set of dummy variables to capture institutional changes that have a once-off big impact on excess returns. A dummy variable is included in the Russian bond equation of the VAR to account for the large fall in excess bond returns from 57.73% to 44.97%, arising from the change in the Russian finance minister on May 25, 1999. Inspection of the excess returns of Argentinian bonds shows that there are five large spikes that occur during the Argentinian crisis: the dates are April 4 and October 4, 2002, April 4 and October 6, 2003, and April 6, 2004. These dates correspond to the coupon dates after all Argentinian sovereign debt went into default, with the price for these bonds declining because of uncertainty surrounding the scheduled coupon payment. To correct for these outliers, a dummy variable is included in the Argentinian bond equation of the VAR, which has a value of one on the five dates and zero otherwise. Finally, there are a number of crises that have occurred that are potentially too small to be able to model individually. To condition the results on these crises additional dummy variables are also included into the VAR specification. The dummy variables consist of the Turkish crisis May 1 to June 30, 2006, and the large movements in asset returns on February 27 and March 13, 2007 during the concerns over Chinese equity markets.

The residuals from estimating the VAR are taken to be the filtered excess returns subsequently used in the empirical analysis. Further filtering of the data could be entertained, such as allowing for time-varying volatility during each sub-period. Some strategies would be to incorporate GARCH specifications either using the approach of Bekaert, Harvey and Ng (2005), or the factor GARCH specification of Dungey and Martin (2004) and Dungey, Fry, González-Hermosillo and Martin (2006); also see the discussion in Chapter 2 on autoregressive and heteroskedastic dynamics in models of contagion. However, conditional moment tests of conditional volatility applied to the VAR standardized residuals given in Section 5.6.2 of this chapter, show little evidence of time-varying volatility within asset markets during the crisis periods.

Empirically this result is partly a reflection of the small duration of the crisis periods. The final data set of filtered excess returns comprises 2544 observations across bond and equity markets for the six countries.

5.4.2 Crisis Dates

The choice of the dates of the crisis periods are summarized in table 5.1. This choice is based on important institutional events surrounding each crisis, together with empirical pretesting and sensitivity analysis to fine-tune the timing of the crisis dates. Details of the empirical methods together with some additional sensitivity analysis of the chosen dates, are presented in Section 5.6. The Russian crisis is chosen to begin with the announcement of the Russian government's deferral of its bond repayments on August 17, 1998, while the end of the crisis is taken as the end of 1998, following the crisis dates given in Chapter 3, as well as Dungey, Fry, González-Hermosillo, and Martin (2006) for commensurability. The LTCM crisis begins when the Federal Reserve orchestrated the bailout of LTCM on September 23, and ends with the inter-FOMC Federal Reserve rate cut on October 15; see also Committee on the Global Financial System (1999) and Chapters 3 and 4.

The start of the Brazilian crisis is chosen as January 7, 1999, before the effective devaluation of the real on January 15, 1999, which followed the loss of nearly USD$14 billion of reserves in two days. The end of the crisis occurs in the next month on February 25, after several new governors of the Central Bank had been appointed and prior to the agreement of a revised IMF program in early March 1999.

Table 5.1
Summary of the crisis dates.

Crisis	Origin of Shock	Start of Crisis	End of Crisis
Russia	Russian bonds	Aug. 17, 1998	Dec. 31, 1998
LTCM	US bonds	Sept. 23, 1998	Oct. 15, 1998
Brazil	Brazilian bonds	Jan. 7, 1999	Feb. 25, 1999
Dot-com	US equities	Feb. 28, 2000	June 7, 2000
Argentina	Argentinian bonds	Oct. 11, 2001	March 3, 2005
US subprime	US bonds, equities	July 26, 2007	Dec. 3, 2007

The dating of the dot-com crisis is based on inspection of equity returns, which shows that the main impact of the crisis occurs in the second quarter of 2000, especially in the case of the equity markets of the United States, Canada, and Mexico. Combined with econometric sensitivity analysis, the dot-com crisis is chosen to begin on February 28, 2000, and end on June 7, of the same year.

The start of the crisis in Argentina is chosen to begin October 11, 2001. This date occurs one month prior to the introduction of the partial deposit freeze (corralito) and capital controls (Cifarelli and Paladino 2004), but occurs after the increase in volatility that began following the "mega-swap" announced on June 3, 2001. The end of the crisis is taken as March 3, 2005, commensurate with the agreement for debt rescheduling and Argentina's return to the voluntary market.[5]

Turbulence in the U.S. subprime mortgage markets began in mid 2007, which burgeoned into the global financial crisis throughout 2008 and 2009. A broad range of markets worldwide experienced heightened risk aversion and a sharp fall in liquidity. By early August, credit spreads had widened substantially, equity markets had fallen significantly, and term premia in interbank markets rose. The U.S. Federal Reserve reduced the federal funds rate sharply by 50 basis points on August 18, reducing volatility in equity and credit markets, however liquidity concerns persisted. The U.S. subprime crisis model in this chapter contains data from July 26, 2007, until the end of the sample period, December 31, 2007.

The noncrisis period is constructed by combining together all of the data between the crisis dates in table 5.1. Selected descriptive statistics of the filtered excess returns on equities and bonds during the noncrisis and crisis periods are presented in tables 5.2 and 5.3, respectively. All filtered returns have zero sample means as a result of including a constant in the VAR to filter returns for lags and the identified institutional changes discussed above.

---

5. The period of the Argentinian crisis also coincides with an increase in volatility in the Brazilian asset markets during the Brazilian presidential election campaign of the first part of 2002. As the duration of this increase in volatility is very short and primarily limited to Brazil, it is not modeled here as a separate regime.

Table 5.2
Descriptive statistics of filtered excess equity returns for selected periods.

Period/Crisis	Statistic	Arg.	Brz.	Can.	Mex.	Rus.	US
Russia			August 17, 1998 to December, 31, 1998				
	Max.	7.84	10.79	4.93	11.50	40.09	4.03
	Min.	−9.41	−9.60	−6.91	−11.96	−58.85	−3.58
	SD	3.13	3.97	1.68	3.34	11.84	1.45
LTCM			September 23, 1998 to October 15, 1998				
	Max.	6.73	5.22	4.93	6.33	9.96	3.72
	Min.	−6.49	−6.14	−5.25	−8.92	−12.27	−3.58
	SD	3.43	3.46	2.48	3.88	6.76	1.69
Brazil			January 7, 1999 to February 25, 1999				
	Max.	6.85	12.61	2.54	6.01	9.06	2.56
	Min.	−8.37	−11.56	−2.23	−6.14	−10.21	−4.24
	SD	2.73	5.05	1.15	2.40	4.22	1.27
Dot-com			February 28, 2000 to June 7, 2000				
	Max.	2.84	4.73	4.42	6.94	6.95	4.36
	Min.	−5.24	−5.71	−4.85	−8.51	−7.19	−4.32
	SD	1.62	1.92	1.71	2.66	3.34	1.47
Argentina			October 11, 2001 to March 3, 2005				
	Max.	15.93	13.38	5.07	4.90	8.43	6.04
	Min.	−32.55	−8.12	−3.99	−6.34	−10.75	−5.37
	SD	3.01	2.33	1.13	1.34	2.04	1.31
US Subprime			July 26, 2007 to December 31,2007				
	Max.	7.29	6.48	4.25	5.81	4.41	3.67
	Min.	−5.50	−7.55	−5.58	−5.18	−4.14	−3.84
	SD	2.01	3.04	1.83	2.17	1.68	1.66
Non-crisis							
	Max.	11.28	9.84	5.15	7.46	16.43	3.97
	Min.	−9.39	−11.80	−8.57	−5.72	−21.79	−6.25
	SD	1.91	2.13	1.22	1.66	2.95	1.02

5.5 Empirical Results

The crisis and noncrisis models specified in the previous section are estimated using a generalized method of moments (GMM) estimator. This involves computing the unknown parameters by equating the theoretical moments of the model to the empirical moments of the data for both the noncrisis and the crisis periods. As a result of the large number of parameters in

Table 5.3

Descriptive statistics of filtered excess bond returns for selected periods.

Period/Crisis	Statistic	Arg.	Brz.	Can.	Mex.	Rus.	US
Russia			*August 17, 1998 to December, 31, 1998*				
	Max.	9.24	15.38	3.14	9.40	42.38	1.81
	Min.	−16.80	−15.03	−4.64	−8.66	−115.15	−3.44
	SD	3.36	5.52	1.10	2.40	19.21	0.58
LTCM			*September 23, 1998 to October 15, 1998*				
	Max.	9.24	8.89	3.14	4.88	17.25	1.81
	Min.	−2.95	−13.98	−3.33	−3.64	−12.52	−1.30
	SD	2.94	5.23	1.65	2.14	8.89	0.65
Brazil			*January 7, 1999 to February 25, 1999*				
	Max.	9.88	16.82	1.57	7.87	30.43	0.57
	Min.	−11.25	−12.80	−2.71	−4.95	−58.98	−0.84
	SD	3.07	5.67	0.85	2.24	13.89	0.30
Dot-com			*February 28, 2000 to June 7, 2000*				
	Max.	7.15	2.97	1.74	1.68	19.39	0.59
	Min.	−3.70	−3.60	−2.06	−2.24	−15.04	−0.74
	SD	1.37	1.22	0.72	0.78	3.87	0.26
Argentina			*October 11, 2001 to March 3, 2005*				
	Max.	29.18	17.26	2.81	2.67	11.60	2.23
	Min.	−40.62	−38.08	−1.79	−2.70	−4.75	−1.43
	SD	6.39	2.60	0.64	0.60	1.26	0.35
US Subprime			*July 26, 2007 to December 31, 2007*				
	Max.	20.03	3.78	2.15	1.86	3.23	0.80
	Min.	−14.57	−2.60	−2.59	−1.98	−1.84	−1.37
	SD	3.63	1.09	0.88	0.68	0.94	0.36
Non-crisis							
	Max.	33.36	10.58	2.89	5.06	55.57	1.85
	Min.	−33.70	−5.69	−2.96	−4.26	−44.35	−1.35
	SD	3.42	1.20	0.58	0.65	4.36	0.26

the model, the full system containing the noncrisis model and the five crisis models are not estimated jointly. The approach is to estimate the noncrisis model jointly with each of the crisis models one at a time.[6]

---

6. In estimating the model the parameters

$$\pi_B^b, \delta_U^s, \delta_U^b, \phi_U^s,$$

The objective function of the GMM estimator is specified as

$$Q = M'W^{-1}M, \tag{5.19}$$

where M is a vector containing the differences between the empirical and theoretical moments and W is the optimal weighting matrix. All calculations are undertaken using the library MAXLIK in GAUSS Version 7.0. The GMM estimates are computed by iterating over the parameters and optimal weighting matrix W, using the BFGS algorithm with the gradients computed numerically.

An overall test of the model is based on testing the number of overidentification restrictions using Hansen's J-statistic

$$J = TQ, \tag{5.20}$$

where Q is defined in (5.19) and T is the sample size. The results of the overidentification test for the full model are presented in table 5.4 for each crisis, in the column corresponding to three common factors. The specification of the model satisfies this test at the 1% level for all crises and at the 5% level for all but the dot-com and Argentinian crises.

Further tests of the number of common factors underlying the factor structure of each crisis model are presented in table 5.4. Apart from testing the most general common factor structure, which corresponds to a three common factor model, tests of two, one, and no common factors are also presented. These tests amount to imposing restrictions on the parameters in the matrices A_w and B_w in (5.16) and (5.17) and testing if the restrictions are consistent with the data using the J-statistic in (5.20). Reducing the number of common factors from 3 to 2 is satisfied for the Brazilian and U.S. subprime crisis models at the 5% level where the p-values of both tests are 0.62. This restriction is also satisfied for the Russian/LTCM and Argentinian crises at the 1% level, but not for the dot-com crisis model. Further restricting the number of common factors from two to one leads to a clear rejection of the null hypothesis for all

were found to be small, in which case they were restricted to be zero. The restriction $\delta_U^s = \delta_U^b = 0$, means that there is no U.S. country factor. Setting $\phi_U^s = 0$ in (5.15) has the effect of making the U.S. equity market the common equity market factor.

Table 5.4
Overidentification tests for common factors based on the J-statistic. Unrestricted model given by the column headed "Three common factors". The restrictions for "Two common factors" are based on $\pi_i^j = 0$. The restrictions for "One common factor" are based on $\pi_i^j = 0$, $\beta_i^j = 0$. The restrictions for "No common factors" are based on $\pi_i^j = 0$, $\beta_i^j = 0$, $\lambda_i^j = 0$. The last set of restrictions amounts to restricting the matrices A_w and B_w in (5.16) and (5.17) respectively, as null matrices.

Crisis	Statistic	Number of Common Factors			
		Three	*Two*	*One*	*None*
Russia/	J-statistic	25.63	42.82	71.99	339.74
LTCM	dof	22	27	39	51
	p-value	0.27	0.03	0.00	0.00
Brazil	J-statistic	22.50	35.64	67.94	334.12
	dof	34	39	51	63
	p-value	0.93	0.62	0.06	0.00
Dot-com	J-statistic	49.39	66.46	98.37	363.58
	dof	34	39	51	63
	p-value	0.04	0.01	0.00	0.00
Argentina	J-statistic	50.83	54.88	143.81	369.57
	dof	34	39	51	63
	p-value	0.03	0.05	0.00	0.00
US Subprime	J-statistic	20.86	35.76	67.56	333.51
	dof	34	39	51	63
	p-value	0.96	0.62	0.06	0.00

crisis models at the 5% level with the exceptions of the Brazilian and U.S. subprime crisis models where the p-values are both 0.06. Further testing of the Brazilian and U.S. subprime crisis models for no common factors is clearly rejected where both the p-values are 0.00. Given that the approach adopted in this paper is to specify a model that is common for all crises, for the rest of the paper the number of common factors is chosen to be three for all crisis models.

5.5.1 Evidence of Contagion

In presenting the results, the relative strength of contagion is highlighted in terms of its contribution to the total volatility of asset returns during the crisis periods. Given the independence and normalization assumptions of the factors, the (12×12) theoretical variance-covariance matrix of returns during the crisis period is immediately obtained from (5.17), as

$$E\left[y_t y_t'\right] = B_w B_w' + B_m B_m' + B_c B_c' + B_u B_u', \qquad (5.21)$$

where it is assumed that y_t is standardized to have zero mean. The variance decompositions are simply the individual components of the diagonal terms of (5.21), expressed as a percentage of the total, with the parameter values replaced by their GMM parameter estimates. For example, from (5.17) the contribution of the bond market factor to the variance of equities in Argentina during the Russian/LTCM crisis, is

$$Var = \frac{100 \times \left(\kappa_{A,b}^s\right)^2}{Total},$$

where

$$Total = (\lambda_A^s)^2 + (\beta_A^s)^2 + (\pi_A^s)^2 + (\gamma_A^s + \theta_A^s)^2 + \left(\kappa_{A,b}^s\right)^2$$
$$+ (\delta_A^s)^2 + \left(\kappa_{A,R}^s\right)^2 + (\phi_A^s)^2 + \left(\kappa_{A,Rb}^s\right)^2 + \left(\kappa_{A,Ub}^s\right)^2.$$

Complete variance decompositions, which contain both non-crisis and crisis factor contributions for the five crisis periods, are given in Appendix 5.C.

Table 5.5 gives the percentage contribution of contagion to total volatility in equity and bond markets for the five crisis periods. Complete variance decompositions, which contain both noncrisis and crisis factor contributions for the five crisis periods, are given in Appendix 5.C. For comparative purposes, the table also gives the sample variance. This table highlights three important points concerning the overall size of contagion from 1998 to 2007. First, the Russian/LTCM crisis is widespread as it affects all countries, developed and emerging, and both classes of asset markets, equities and bonds. The equity markets hit hardest during this crisis are Brazil (98.63%), the United States (63.74%), Argentina (43.98%), Canada (41.46%), and Mexico (35.65%), with Russia (25.88%) being the least affected. The bond markets most affected during this crisis are Brazil (89.33%), Mexico (85.67%), Canada (45.92%), the United States

Table 5.5

Contribution of contagion to equity and bond market volatility during financial crises: percentage of total volatility. For comparison the variance of actual returns for equity and bonds for each country are also reported.

Crisis	Factor	Arg.	Brz.	Can.	Mex.	Rus.	US
		Equity Markets					
Russia/	Contagion (%)	43.98	98.63	41.46	35.65	25.88	63.74
LTCM	Variance	9.79	15.78	2.83	11.18	140.12	2.09
Brazil	Contagion (%)	62.26	7.04	14.92	20.47	27.20	55.9
	Variance	7.45	25.52	1.33	5.78	17.84	1.62
Dot-com	Contagion (%)	92.47	39.63	2.97	88.50	0.46	2.12
	Variance	2.62	3.69	2.92	7.09	11.18	2.15
Argentina	Contagion (%)	4.59	61.93	7.04	1.91	0.02	6.90
	Variance	9.07	5.42	1.28	1.80	4.16	1.73
Subprime	Contagion (%)	28.20	42.64	44.97	44.49	3.86	13.62
	Variance	4.05	9.22	3.33	4.72	2.83	2.77
		Bond Markets					
Russia/	Contagion (%)	31.01	89.33	45.92	85.67	4.55	31.38
LTCM	Variance	11.29	30.52	1.21	5.74	369.17	0.33
Brazil	Contagion (%)	14.73	4.73	12.28	82.48	65.09	7.58
	Variance	9.40	32.17	0.72	5.03	192.80	0.09
Dot-com	Contagion (%)	0.12	94.06	1.17	1.97	0.27	1.08
	Variance	1.88	1.49	0.52	0.60	14.95	0.07
Argentina	Contagion (%)	3.97	2.20	16.52	11.63	0.11	34.59
	Variance	40.77	6.77	0.41	0.36	1.58	0.12
Subprime	Contagion (%)	94.31	14.16	24.71	21.14	30.17	92.19
	Variance	13.18	1.19	0.78	0.47	0.89	0.13

(31.38%), and Argentina (31.01%). The low contribution of contagion to Russian bonds (4.55%) in table 5.5, simply reflects that the Russian crisis originated in this market. In the case of Brazil, these results support Baig and Goldfajn (2001) and the discussion in Chapter 4.

Second, comparison of the relative importance of contagion during the financial crises chronologically between Russia/ LTCM in 1998 and the U.S. subprime crisis in 2007 shows that the strength of contagion tends to become weaker in the intervening crises, with the effects becoming more fragmented across asset markets and national borders. The Brazilian crisis mainly impacts emerging markets, with the effects on the developed markets, except U.S. equities, being relatively small. In particular, the effects on Russian equity (27.20%) and bond (65.09%) markets, potentially reflect effect of an overhang of the Russian crisis. There are also important effects on the equity market in Argentina (62.26%) and the bond market in Mexico (82.48%). During the dot-com and Argentinian crises, the main effects are on equities, with very little impact on bond markets, although the dot-com crisis affects the Brazilian bond market markedly (94.06%). The South American equity markets are affected most during the dot-com crisis, where the contributions of contagion to total volatility are Argentina (92.47%), Mexico (88.50%), and Brazil (39.63%). The Canadian and Russian equity markets are not particularly affected by the dot-com crisis. These results not only confirm that the dot-com crisis is a crisis in equities, but also suggest that Russian asset markets had finally settled down after the Russian crisis. There is a further reduction in the overall relative impact of contagion on South American equity markets during the Argentinian crisis compared to the dot-com and previous crises, with the exception of Brazil. The largest impact occurs in Brazilian equities (61.93%) and U.S. bond markets (34.59%).

Third, and in stark contrast to the diminishing strength of contagion channels during the previous financial crises and the apparent far lower impact of contagion on bond markets during the dot-com and Argentinian financial crises, the effects of contagion during the U.S. subprime crisis are widespread with no country immune. In bond markets the contagion effects in Argentina (94.31%) and the United States (92.19%) account for almost all of the volatility in these markets, while in equity markets three of the six countries, Brazil, Canada, and Mexico, have contagion effects greater than 40.00% of volatility. A similar result occurs during the Russian/LTCM crisis, where the contribution of contagion to equity market volatility is greater than 40% for four equity markets and four bond markets. Given that the Russian asset markets are largely immune to the dot-com and Argentinian crises, it is interesting to observe that Russia is also affected by the subprime crisis in bond markets, where approximately 30% in Russian bonds is the result of contagion.[7]

---

7. Both the Argentine and Russian central banks injected liquidity into their respective financial systems during this period (see Fitch Ratings 2007a,b).

5.5.2 *Comparison of Contagion Channels Across Crises*

The previous discussion highlights the changes in the relative importance of contagion in contributing to asset market volatility across crises. In this section the estimated factor model is used to break-down the relative contribution of contagion into its separate components. Tables 5.6 and 5.7 provide the variance decompositions of the contagion transmission mechanisms for equities and bonds respectively, due to market, country, and idiosyncratic channels, across the five crisis periods.

Table 5.6
Breakdown of the contribution of contagion channels in equity markets during financial crises: percentage of total volatility. A "n.a." represents not applicable.

Crisis	Factor	Arg.	Brz.	Can.	Mex.	Rus.	US
Russia/	Market (bond)	1.16	37.65	11.48	9.16	18.82	0.32
LTCM	Country (Rus.)	38.05	2.57	6.92	13.48	n.a.	40.97
	Idio. (Rus. bond)	4.35	51.95	1.49	2.36	6.32	0.90
	Idio. (US bond)	0.42	6.46	21.57	10.65	0.74	21.57
	Total contagion	43.98	98.63	41.46	35.65	25.88	63.74
	Variance	9.79	15.78	2.83	11.18	140.12	2.09
Brazil	Market (bond)	0.73	0.07	5.61	6.16	22.48	21.21
	Country (Brz.)	51.51	n.a.	1.43	10.50	0.13	2.46
	Idio. (Brz. bond)	10.02	6.97	7.88	3.81	4.59	32.23
	Total contagion	62.26	7.04	14.92	20.47	27.2	55.9
	Variance	7.45	25.52	1.33	5.78	17.84	1.62
Dot-com	Market (bond)	0.10	13.64	0.97	76.35	0.19	2.12
	Country (US)	85.40	5.63	0.27	1.96	0.02	n.a.
	Idio. (US equity)	6.93	20.36	1.72	10.20	0.25	n.a.
	Total contagion	92.47	39.63	2.97	88.50	0.46	2.12
	Variance	2.62	3.69	2.92	7.09	11.18	2.15
Argentina	Market (bond)	4.58	18.70	0.98	0.28	0.00	0.65
	Country (Arg.)	n.a.	0.00	4.30	1.55	0.01	6.14
	Idio. (Arg. bond)	0.01	43.23	1.76	0.08	0.01	0.11
	Total contagion	4.59	61.93	7.04	1.91	0.02	6.9
	Variance	9.07	5.42	1.28	1.80	4.16	1.73
Subprime	Market (bond)	10.14	15.77	17.34	17.33	0.67	7.94
	Idio. (US equity)	5.31	7.74	8.11	7.28	1.18	n.a.
	Idio. (US bond)	12.75	19.13	19.52	19.88	2.01	5.68
	Total contagion	28.20	42.64	44.97	44.49	3.86	13.62
	Variance	4.05	9.22	3.33	4.72	2.83	2.77

Table 5.7

Breakdown of the contribution of contagion channels in bond markets during financial crises: percentage of total volatility. A "n.a." represents not applicable.

Crisis	Factor	Arg.	Brz.	Can.	Mex.	Rus.	US
Russia/	Market (equity)	12.11	26.68	4.92	27.57	4.50	5.85
LTCM	Country (Rus.)	0.44	26.90	1.00	16.24	n.a.	22.88
	Idio. (Rus. bond)	13.62	15.67	8.36	17.01	n.a.	2.65
	Idio. (US bond)	4.85	20.09	31.64	24.85	0.05	n.a.
	Total contagion	31.01	89.33	45.92	85.67	4.55	31.38
	Variance	11.29	30.52	1.21	5.74	369.17	0.33
Brazil	Market (equity)	0.06	4.73	0.41	2.39	25.37	0.31
	Country (Brz.)	14.57	n.a.	7.12	77.52	5.10	4.27
	Idio. (Brz bond)	0.10	n.a.	4.75	2.57	34.62	3.00
	Total contagion	14.73	4.73	12.28	82.48	65.09	7.58
	Variance	9.40	32.17	0.72	5.03	192.80	0.09
Dot-com	Market (equity)	0.09	42.91	0.58	1.55	0.00	0.47
	Country (US)	0.03	0.33	0.02	0.32	0.00	n.a.
	Idio. (US equity)	0.00	50.82	0.57	0.09	0.27	0.61
	Total contagion	0.12	94.06	1.17	1.97	0.27	1.08
	Variance	1.88	1.49	0.52	0.60	14.95	0.07
Argentina	Market (equity)	3.97	0.53	5.12	5.14	0.01	13.43
	Country (Arg.)	n.a.	0.04	2.74	2.82	0.10	17.59
	Idio. (Arg. bond)	n.a.	1.63	8.66	3.67	0.00	3.57
	Total contagion	3.97	2.2	16.52	11.63	0.11	34.59
	Variance	40.77	6.77	0.41	0.36	1.58	0.12
Subprime	Market (equity)	4.64	9.94	5.96	14.40	0.03	87.98
	Idio. (US equity)	84.90	1.75	3.56	2.72	0.03	4.21
	Idio. (US bond)	4.77	2.47	15.19	4.02	30.11	n.a.
	Total contagion	94.31	14.16	24.71	21.14	30.17	92.19
	Variance	13.18	1.19	0.78	0.47	0.89	0.13

The Russian/LTCM crisis results in table 5.6 show that idiosyncratic bond shocks and Russian country shocks are important in transmitting contagion to equity markets. The dominant mechanism is the country channel where equities in the United States (40.97%) and Argentina (38.05%) are hardest hit, whilst Brazilian equities (51.95%) are affected by the direct link from Russian bonds, and U.S. and Canadian equities (both 21.57%) are affected by the direct link from U.S. bonds. In the case of bond markets, table 5.7 shows that all channels are operating. The most affected country during the LTCM phase of the Russian/LTCM crisis is Brazil, where equities (51.95%)

and bonds (15.67%) are affected directly by Russian bonds. The Mexican bond market is also particularly affected by the Russia/LTCM crisis, with almost one quarter (24.85%) coming through the idiosyncratic U.S. bond channel. Mexican equity markets are much less affected by this source of contagion.

The effects on the Russian asset markets during the Brazilian crisis can be attributed to an idiosyncratic channel from the Brazilian bond market in the case of Brazilian bonds (34.62%) and channels through the bond and equity market channels. In other asset markets affected by this crisis it is the country channel that transmits contagion to the Argentinian equity market (51.51%) and the Mexican bond market (77.52%).

All three contagion channels are at play in transmitting the dot-com crisis to equity markets. The largest effect is on the equity markets in Argentina (85.40%) through the country channel, and Mexico (76.35%) through the bond market channel. Effects via the idiosyncratic channel from U.S. equities on Brazilian (20.36%) and Mexican (10.20%) equities, are relatively larger than they are for Argentina and Canada. Russian equities are immune to the dot-com crisis, as are all but the Brazilian bond markets, where strong effects come from the equity market (42.91%) and idiosyncratic channel from U.S. equities (50.82%).

The contagion channels operating during the Argentinian crisis are even more selective than they are in the previous crises, with just the equity market in Brazil being affected (18.77%) through the bond market channel, and (43.23%) through the Argentinian bond channel. However, as the results in table 5.7 show that, with the exception of the United States, most bond markets are immune to the Argentinian crisis, suggesting that the market linkage transmitting contagion to the Brazilian equity market is being transmitted via the developed U.S. markets. This result is in line with the role of developed markets in spreading crises between developing markets highlighted in Kaminsky and Reinhart (2003).

Table 5.6 shows that during the subprime crisis in the United States all channels are operating to transmit the crisis to equity markets. No one channel dominates, although the idiosyncratic link from U.S. equity markets is of lesser importance than the remaining links. The results for the bond markets in table 5.7 show that the effects of the subprime crisis are also widespread, with the main effects felt by Argentina (84.90%) through the idiosyncratic U.S. equity market channel, and Russia (30.11%) through the U.S. bond market idiosyncratic channel. The U.S. bond market (87.98%) is affected through the equity market channel, which represents a second-round effect of the credit market shock that occurred first in the U.S. bond market.

5.5.3 Testing the Channels of Contagion

The variance decompositions discussed above provide a descriptive measure of the relative impact of contagion on the volatility of asset returns during financial crises. To formalize the strength of these mechanisms, Wald tests of the statistical significance of the market, country, and idiosyncratic contagion channels for each crisis period are presented in table 5.8. As an

Table 5.8
Wald tests of contagion channels: p-values in brackets.

Test	DOF	Crisis				
		Russia/ LTCM	Brazil	Dot-com	Argentina	Subprime
Market (equity)	6	43.20 (0.00)	1457611.98 (0.00)	3391.14 (0.00)	2884.24 (0.00)	122980.11 (0.00)
Market (bond)	6	40.06 (0.00)	174942.09 (0.00)	252266.25 (0.00)	294191.71 (0.00)	305.38 (0.00)
Country	10	179.53 (0.00)	316208.57 (0.00)	254690.28 (0.00)	5055.81 (0.00)	
Idiosyncratic (Rus. bond)	11	167.97 (0.00)				
Idiosyncratic (US bond)	11	96.72 (0.00)				2254131.29 (0.00)
Idiosyncratic (Brz. bond)	11		2026223.76 (0.00)			
Idiosyncratic (US equity)	11			65483.90 (0.00)		137316.06 (0.00)
Idiosyncratic (Arg. bond)	11				672290.30 (0.00)	
Joint	44[a] 33[b]	762.08 (0.00)	3977390.81 (0.00)	724307.18 (0.00)	1002437.13 (0.00)	2540997.37

(a) $k = 44$ degrees of freedom for the Russian/LTCM crisis.
(b) $k = 33$ degrees of freedom for the Brazilian, Dot-com, Argentinian and US subprime crises.

example of the way the Wald test is performed, in the case of the Russian/LTCM crisis, the Wald test of contagion from the equity market factor to the six bond markets consists of testing that the joint restriction $\delta_{i,s}^b = 0$ $\forall i$ in the matrix B_m in (5.17). Testing in the reverse direction from the bond market factor to the six equity markets is given by testing the joint restriction $\delta_{i,b}^s = 0$ $\forall i$ in the matrix B_m in (5.17). The test of the country channel from Russia to the 10 non-Russian asset markets is given by testing the parameter $\delta_{i,R}^j$ in the matrix B_c in (5.17). The test of the idiosyncratic contagion channel from Russian bonds to the other 11 asset markets is given by testing $\delta_{i,Rb}^s = \delta_{i,Rb}^b = 0$, whereas the test of the idiosyncratic contagion channel from U.S. bonds to the other 11 asset markets during the LTCM crisis, is given by testing $\delta_{i,Ub}^s = \delta_{i,Ub}^b = 0$. The form of the tests is similar for the other three crises.

The results of the Wald tests given in table 5.8 reveal that all contagion channels are statistically significant at the 5% level. These tests provide strong support for the importance of all contagion channels operating during all crises. These results also highlight the fact that whilst some of the channels may not be economically significant given the results of the variance decompositions presented above, nonetheless these channels may still be statistically significant.

5.6 Robustness Checks and Additional Tests

An important feature of the empirical model is that identification of the parameters depends in a fundamental way on the dating of the crisis periods and the set of countries used to identify the common factors. In this section a number of additional robustness checks and diagnostic tests are performed on the factor model specification, with special attention given to looking at the sensitivity of the results to changes in the crisis dates and the choice of countries.

5.6.1 Crisis Dating Sensitivity Analysis

The empirical results presented are based on joint estimation of the model over a noncrisis and crisis period. To examine the sensitivity of these results to the choice of crisis dates,

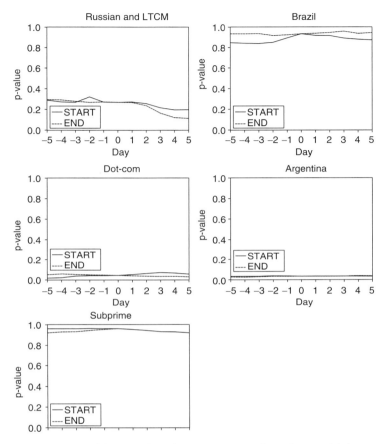

Figure 5.2 Model over-identification test p-values for sensitivity to crisis date selection: −5, 4, ...0, ... + 4, +5 days. Continuous (dashed) line represents the start (end) of the crisis period. The p-values at zero correspond to the values reported in Table 5.4 where the number of common factors is three.

figure 5.2 gives the p-values from performing the moment overidentification test based on the J-statistic in (5.20), for changes in the start and the end dates of the five crises. A maximum window of five days is chosen where either the start of the crisis period (continuous line) or the end of the crisis period (dashed line) are adjusted. A zero day signifies the crisis dates given in table 5.1. The U.S. subprime crisis end date is not extended by five days as this crisis is assumed to continue until the end of the sample. The p-values reported in figure 5.2

in general are qualitatively insensitive to changes in the dating of the five crises.[8]

Given that the Argentinian crisis period (October 11, 2001, to June 3, 2005) is much longer than the other crisis periods identified here, some additional sensitivity analysis is conducted on Argentina by considering shorter crisis periods.[9] Three crisis sub-periods are investigated consisting of the first year of the crisis (October 11, 2001, to October 10, 2002), the first two years of the crisis (October 11, 2001, to October 10, 2003) and the first three years of the crisis (October 11, 2001, to October 10, 2004). The results are in table 5.9, which gives the variance decompositions for the three crisis sub-periods and the total crisis period, where the total period results are taken from tables 5.6 and 5.7.

Comparing the contagion results across the four alternative crisis periods reveals that the qualitative analysis of the contagion effects is in general robust to the different sample periods. The exceptions are mainly for Brazil and the United States asset markets. In the case of the shorter crisis sample, Brazilian equities receive around 4% contagion from the Argentinian bond market channel, compared with 43% from both these channels in the total sample. In the case of the two-year sample, Brazilian bonds receive almost 36% via the Argentinian country channel, compared with less than 1% in the total sample. For the United States, the shorter sample periods result in contagion effects from the idiosyncratic Argentinian bond channel on United States equities being as high as 55%, in the third subsample, compared with the less than 1% for the total sample period. These results suggest that although there are potentially some changes in the way that contagion is transmitted during the Argentinian crisis, especially from late 2004 to mid 2005, nonetheless contagion is important during the total crisis period which provides support for the choice of the crisis dates.

8. For each of the p-values reported in figure 5.2, variance decompositions of the relative importance of the factors are also computed, but not reported here to save space. In general, the variance decompositions are insensitive to the choice of the crisis dates for the window of dates investigated.

9. We would like to thank Roberto Rigobon for suggesting this.

Table 5.9
Sample sensitivity of Argentine crisis dates: equity and bond markets.

Market	Factor	Arg.	Brz.	Can.	Mex.	Rus.	US
Equities			*October 11, 2001 to October 10, 2002*				
	Market (bond)	19.84	25.74	1.47	2.30	0.00	1.44
	Country (Arg.)	n.a.	2.96	2.34	0.13	3.69	5.68
	Idio. (Arg. bond)	0.17	3.59	25.71	5.87	10.09	48.04
			October 11, 2001 to October 10, 2003				
	Market (bond)	3.27	25.75	2.22	3.14	0.28	2.35
	Country (Arg.)	n.a.	2.96	5.75	1.76	1.25	9.37
	Idio. (Arg. bond)	0.49	3.60	23.53	0.56	2.37	37.77
			October 11, 2001 to October 10, 2004				
	Market (bond)	15.40	25.78	0.76	1.23	0.01	0.74
	Country (Arg.)	n.a.	2.97	3.17	0.07	2.16	12.52
	Idio. (Arg. Bond)	0.51	3.60	22.32	6.02	6.02	55.24
			October 11, 2001 to June 3, 2005				
	Market (bond)	4.58	18.70	0.98	0.28	0.00	0.65
	Country (Arg.)	n.a.	0.00	4.30	1.55	0.01	6.14
	Idio. (Arg.bond)	0.01	43.23	1.76	0.08	0.01	0.11
Bonds			*October 11, 2001 to October 10, 2002*				
	Market (equity)	3.25	0.06	0.01	0.00	0.01	27.76
	Country (Arg.)	n.a.	1.96	2.40	0.62	0.28	30.98
	Idio. (Arg. bond)	n.a.	19.31	2.79	3.57	0.75	8.49
			October 11, 2001 to October 10, 2003				
	Market (equity)	2.12	5.42	1.35	1.91	0.07	6.46
	Country (Arg.)	n.a.	35.95	4.17	8.83	0.02	1.95
	Idio. (Arg. bond)	n.a.	4.45	0.54	8.51	0.74	12.49
			October 11, 2001 to October 10, 2004				
	Market (equity)	3.45	0.03	0.03	0.03	0.00	27.91
	Country (Arg.)	n.a.	0.16	0.00	0.02	0.02	28.83
	Idio. (Arg. bond)	n.a.	0.08	1.48	6.22	0.32	10.66
			October 11, 2001 to June 3, 2005				
	Market (equity)	3.97	0.53	5.12	5.14	0.01	13.43
	Country (Arg.)	n.a.	0.04	2.74	2.82	0.10	17.59
	Idio. (Arg. bond)	n.a.	1.63	8.66	3.67	0.00	3.57

5.6.2 Conditional Moment Tests

Conditional moment tests of first order autocorrelation $AR\,(1)$ and first order conditional volatility $ARCH\,(1)$ in the standardized residuals of the VAR, are given in table 5.10. The results of these tests are reported in terms of p-values, for different

Table 5.10

Conditional moment tests of the standardized VAR residuals (z_t) for selected periods: p-values. AR(1) based on testing $E\left[z_t z_{t-1} - 0\right]$, ARCH(1) based on testing $E\left[(z_t^2 - 1)(z_{t-1}^2 - 1) - 0\right]$.

Crisis	Statistic	Asset	Arg.	Brz.	Can.	Mex.	Rus.	US
Russia	AR(1)	Equities	0.312	0.813	0.183	0.900	0.426	0.175
	AR(1)	Bonds	0.099	0.886	0.616	0.591	0.409	0.865
	ARCH(1)	Equities	0.473	0.190	0.386	0.442	0.273	0.179
	ARCH(1)	Bonds	0.325	0.600	0.463	0.109	0.761	0.215
Brazil	AR(1)	Equities	0.848	0.435	0.376	0.305	0.207	0.439
	AR(1)	Bonds	0.132	0.265	0.998	0.036	0.184	0.365
	ARCH(1)	Equities	0.474	0.331	0.831	0.536	0.314	0.299
	ARCH(1)	Bonds	0.229	0.929	0.220	0.652	0.979	0.505
Dot-com	AR(1)	Equities	0.071	0.594	0.992	0.943	0.646	0.928
	AR(1)	Bonds	0.234	0.263	0.353	0.875	0.524	0.478
	ARCH(1)	Equities	0.675	0.038	0.604	0.415	0.016	0.675
	ARCH(1)	Bonds	0.200	0.391	0.220	0.468	0.050	0.595
Argentina	AR(1)	Equities	0.353	0.047	0.756	0.283	0.036	0.411
	AR(1)	Bonds	0.097	0.681	0.185	0.002	0.280	0.383
	ARCH(1)	Equities	0.274	0.080	0.076	0.002	0.052	0.031
	ARCH(1)	Bonds	0.004	0.042	0.269	0.039	0.069	0.001
Subprime	AR(1)	Equities	0.098	0.006	0.054	0.059	0.002	0.023
	AR(1)	Bonds	0.578	0.215	0.166	0.425	0.021	0.400
	ARCH(1)	Equities	0.155	0.727	0.809	0.861	0.280	0.873
	ARCH(1)	Bonds	0.096	0.885	0.997	0.291	0.139	0.112

crisis models. In practically all cases considered, the p-values are greater than 0.01, showing that the null hypothesis of no autocorrelation or no conditional volatility is not rejected at the 1% level, and in most cases is also not rejected at the 5% level.

5.6.3 Structural Break Tests

The specification of the model allows for the idiosyncratic parameters to exhibit a structural break between the noncrisis and crisis periods. Tests of the significance of the structural break are presented in table 5.11 using a Wald test. In the case of the Russian/LTCM crisis, from equation (5.17) the structural break tests are performed on the loadings of the equity market (τ_i^s) and the bond market (τ_i^b) factors where $i = A, B, C, M, R, U$, the loadings of the Russian country factor

Table 5.11
Wald tests of structural breaks: p-values in brackets.

Test	DOF	Russia /LTCM	Brazil	Dot-com	Argentina	Subprime
Market (equity)	6	93.38 (0.00)	246344.01 (0.00)	2968.47 (0.00)	116950.89 (0.00)	64.53 (0.00)
Market (bond)	6	38.17 (0.00)	996631.19 (0.00)	23.54 (0.00)	7199.04 (0.00)	2488.97 (0.00)
Country	2	13.87 (0.00)	34066.68 (0.00)		8120.44 (0.00)	
Idio. (Rus. bond)	1	13.29 (0.00)				
Idio. (US bond)	1	27.86 (0.00)				96.12 (0.00)
Idio. (Brz. bond)	1		131.09 (0.00)			
Idio. (US equity)	1					11.87 (0.00)
Idio. (Arg. bond)	1				1271.66 (0.00)	
Joint	$k^{(a)}$	435.21 (0.00)	1278002.87 (0.00)	3456.12 (0.00)	223229.60 (0.00)	2849.67 (0.00)

(a) $k = 16$ degrees of freedom for the Russian/LTCM crisis; $k = 15$ degrees of freedom for the Brazilian and Argentinian crises; $k = 12$ degrees of freedom for the dot-com crisis; $k = 14$ degrees of freedom for the US subprime crisis.

$\left(\tau_{R,R}^{s}, \tau_{R,R}^{b}\right)$, and the loadings of the Russian and United States idiosyncratic bond factors $\left(\tau_{R,Rb}^{b}, \tau_{U,Ub}^{b}\right)$. Similar restrictions hold for the other three crisis models. All tests are calculated using a Wald test that the parameter θ, is zero. Under the null hypothesis of no structural break, this amounts to the parameters associated with each factor being the same in the noncrisis and crisis periods.

The results in table 5.11 show strong evidence of structural breaks in practically all factors investigated, across all five financial crises, with all p-values being less than 0.05. The strength of these results are consistent with the empirical findings of Forbes and Rigobon (2002), who emphasize the importance of allowing for increases in volatility in the source country when testing for contagion (see also Chapter 2 and

Dungey, Fry, González-Hermosillo, and Martin 2005a, for further discussion of the role of structural breaks in tests of contagion).

5.7 Conclusions

This paper investigated whether financial crises were alike by considering whether a single modeling framework could fit multiple distinct crises. On this basis, financial crises were alike. The framework introduced three potential channels for contagion effects during a financial crisis, and the empiricial evidence showed that statistically each of these operated during every crisis examined — again on this basis, financial crises are alike. Economically, however, the importance of the channels of contagion differs across crises.

The modeling framework was derived by respecifying the theoretical model of Kodres and Pritsker (2002) for solution in terms of the excess returns on assets, rather than prices. The empirical implementation was a latent factor representation of the equilibrium solution of that model. Three potential channels for contagion effects were simultaneously identified and quantified. The channels were: idiosyncratic channels, which provided a direct link from the nominated source asset market to international asset markets; market channels, which operated through either the bond or equity markets; and country channels, which operated through the asset markets of a country jointly.

The empirical investigation considered a common dataset over the period March 1998 to December 2007 consisting of the equity and bond markets of six countries: Argentina, Brazil, Canada, Mexico, Russia, and the United States, although the results were also extended to allow for a broader range of develop countries. The sample period covered five major crisis instances, from the Russian and LTCM crises in 1998, the Brazilian crisis in 1999, the dot-com crisis in 2000, the Argentinian crisis in 2002–2005 to the recent crisis associated with the U.S. subprime market beginning mid 2007.

The Russian/LTCM crises had a widespread impact that is consistent with the results on bond markets in Chapter 3 and equity markets in Chapter 4. All three contagion channels were active in this period. The Brazilian crisis had greater impact on emerging markets than developed markets, with a pronounced effect on Russian asset markets, via all but the country channel. Russian equity markets, however, were immune to the dot-com crisis, which mainly affected equity markets. Although all three contagion channels operated during the dot-com crisis, the effects on bond markets were limited to the Brazilian bond market. Bond markets were also little affected by the Argentinian crisis, despite all three contagion channels being present and statistically significant. This was not the case in the U.S. subprime crisis, where not only were all contagion channels statistically significant, but the effects of contagion were widespread across asset markets and countries.

Contagion effects were greatest in the Russian/LTCM crisis, and dissipated in the subsequent Brazilian, dot-com, and Argentinian crises, but returned with vehemence in the U.S. subprime crisis. Using the extent of contagious effects as a metric, the worst crises of the past decade were the Russian/LTCM crisis in 1998 and the recent U.S. subprime crisis, which interestingly were first evident in bond markets.

The empirical results presented have a number of important lessons for the building of theoretical models of contagion. First, the empirical results suggest that it is feasible to specify a unifying theoretical model that is applicable for modeling a range of crises regardless of the nature of the initiating shock. Second, a number of potential mechanisms will need to be specified to explain asset market returns and the transmission of contagion across international asset markets. In the empirical model these mechanisms were classified broadly as common, market, country, and idiosyncratic transmission mechanisms according to the decomposition proposed by Dungey and Martin (2007), whilst in the theoretical model these mechanisms represented information asymmetries, noise trading, macroeconomic shocks, and expectation errors, following the theoretical framework of Kodres and Pritsker (2002). The empirical results showed that contagion operated via a range of channels, although the relative importance of each channel was found to vary across crises.

This chapter has drawn together the elements of the latent factor model developed in the previous three chapters. The model developed for bond markets in Chapter 3, which examined the effects of regional impacts, controls for properties of the data such as volatility clustering and serial correlation and nesting crises. Following this, Chapter 4 looked to equity markets with nested crises, a more specific model of emerging versus developed markets as well as regional effects, but dropped the controls for GARCH as these had not had a major impact on the results. However, the model was extended to account for potential structural breaks. The conclusions from the explorations in Chapters 3 and 4 led to the formation of the overarching model of Chapter 5, which is able to account for the important aspects of financial market data across distinct crises using a single model framework. Drawing on the outcomes from the earlier chapters, the model incorporates nested crises, regional effects, emerging market effects, specific country effects, specific asset (market) effects as well as potential structural breaks. Each of these elements plays an important role in effectively modeling contagion effects during multiple crises. This chapter presented a model that uniquely incorporates cross asset market and cross country linkages over multiple crises.

The policy implications of the chapter are relatively clear. Each crisis examined was alike in that there are significant contagion effects evident every time. This leads to a role for policies aimed at contagion management and prevention. However, the same policy is unlikely to be appropriate in every crisis, as the extent and channel of shock transmission in each crisis can be quite different. In the Russian/LTCM crises and the current crisis, contagion has a large impact on total volatility. In intervening crises, such as Brazil and the dot-com collapse, this has not been the case. There is a strong argument in these results for retaining a degree of discretion in policy response to individual crises. Crisis management is clearly different to crisis prevention. Brunnemeier et al. (2009) argue that a global approach is an important aspect of crisis prevention. However, once in crisis the appropriate policy direction will be influenced by whether a country is at the center of the crisis and in danger of transmitting contagion effects or a country that is attempting to avoid contagion. The transmitting country is likely to be far less interested in preventing contagion than those who have not yet been infected, for further discussion see Dungey, Milunovich, and Thorp (2010).

Having established that contagion is a significant and some-times substantial component of transmission during crises, the next chapter turns to the issue of time varying effects of contagion and the potential roles of other sources of risk during the precrisis and crisis period, including liquidity, credit and volatility risks. The empirical analysis returns to the bond markets in the Russian/LTCM crisis period to examine a test case where contagion effects have already been shown to be significant. To identify these additional sources of risk, this line of analysis requires a further extension of the latent factor specifications of Chapters 3 to 5, through the inclusion of a set of observable variables to explain bond spreads.

5.A Model Derivations

5.A.1 Optimal Portfolio Weights

For a normally distributed random variable x, $E[\exp x] = \exp(E[x] + \frac{1}{2} Var[x])$. Defining $y \equiv \exp x$, then $\ln E[y] = E[\ln y] + \frac{1}{2} Var[\ln y]$. Assuming that next period wealth W_+ is lognormally distributed, the objective function in (5.2) is reexpressed as

$$\max_{\alpha_k} \left\{ (1 - \gamma) E\left[\ln W_+ | \Omega_k\right] + \frac{1}{2} (1 - \gamma)^2 Var\left[\ln W_+ | \Omega_k\right] \right\},$$

or

$$\max_{\alpha_k} \left\{ (1 - \gamma) \left[E\left[\ln \left(1 + R_p\right) | \Omega_k\right] + \ln W \right] + \frac{1}{2} (1 - \gamma)^2 \right.$$
$$\left. Var\left[\ln \left(1 + R_p\right) | \Omega_k\right] \right\}, \tag{5.22}$$

by substituting out W_+ in the objective function using the budget constraint in (5.3), and where $E[\ln W | \Omega_k] = \ln W$ and $Var[\ln W | \Omega_k] = 0$, as W is known in the current period.

Using the definition of the portfolio return in (5.4) and some algebraic manipulation, the $\ln\left[1 + R_p\right]$ term in the objective function in (5.22) is expressed as

$$\ln\left[1 + R_p\right] = \ln\left[1 + \alpha_k' R + (1 - \alpha_k' \iota) Rf\right]$$
$$= \ln\left[1 + \alpha_k' \left(\exp \ln \left((1 + Rf)^{-1} (1 + R)\right) - 1\right)\right]$$
$$+ \ln\left[1 + Rf\right].$$

or, in terms of log excess returns

$$r_p - rf = \ln\left[1 + \alpha_k'\left[\exp\left(r - rf\right) - 1\right]\right],$$

where $r_p \equiv \ln\left(1 + R_p\right)$; $r \equiv \ln\left(1 + R\right)$; $rf \equiv \ln\left(1 + Rf\right)$ represent the respective logarithm of returns. The excess portfolio return is approximated by taking a Taylor series expansion around zero excess return $(r - rf = 0)$

$$r_p - rf \simeq \alpha_k'\left(r - rf\right) + \frac{1}{2}\alpha_k'\left(r - rf\right)\left(r - rf\right)'\left(1 - \alpha_k' \iota\right),$$

where the third and higher order terms are assumed to be small.

Taking expectations of the excess portfolio return conditional on the information set of the kth investor, and rearranging gives

$$E\left[\left(r_p - rf\right)|\Omega_k\right] \simeq \alpha_k' E\left[\left(r - rf\right)|\Omega_k\right]$$

$$+ \frac{1}{2}\alpha_k' E\left[\left(r - rf\right)\left(r - rf\right)'|\Omega_k\right]\left(1 - \alpha_k'\iota\right)$$

$$E\left[r_p|\Omega_k\right] - rf \simeq \alpha_k'\left(E[r|\Omega_k] - rf\right) + \frac{1}{2}\alpha_k' Var\left[\left(r - rf\right)|\Omega_k\right]\left(1 - \alpha_k'\iota\right)$$

$$E\left[r_p|\Omega_k\right] \simeq \alpha_k'\left(E[r|\Omega_k] - rf\right) + \frac{1}{2}\alpha_k' Var[r|\Omega_k]\left(1 - \alpha_k'\iota\right) + rf,$$

$$(5.23)$$

and

$$Var\left[\left(r_p - rf\right)|\Omega_k\right] \simeq Var\left[\left(\alpha_k'\left(r - rf\right)\right)|\Omega_k\right]$$

$$Var\left[r_p|\Omega_k\right] \simeq \alpha_k' Var\left[r|\Omega_k\right]\alpha_k. \qquad (5.24)$$

Upon substituting (5.23) and (5.24) into (5.22), together with the definition of log portfolio returns $r_p \equiv \ln\left(1 + R_p\right)$, the objective function is rewritten as

$$\max_{\alpha_k}\left\{(1 - \gamma)\left[\alpha_k'\left(E[r|\Omega_k] - rf\right) + \frac{1}{2}\alpha_k' Var[r|\Omega_k]\left(1 - \alpha_k'\iota\right)\right.\right.$$

$$\left.\left. + rf + \ln W\right] + \frac{1}{2}(1 - \gamma)^2 \alpha_k' Var[r|\Omega_k]\alpha_k\right\}. \qquad (5.25)$$

Differentiating (5.25) with respect to α_k yields the optimal solution to the portfolio problem of the informed and the uninformed investors given in (5.9)

$$\alpha_k^* = \frac{1}{\gamma}\left[E\left[r|\Omega_k\right] - rf + \frac{1}{2}Covar\left[r|\Omega_k\right]\right]Covar\left[r|\Omega_k\right]^{-1}.$$

(5.26)

5.A.2 Informed Conditional Expectations

Using $r \equiv \ln(1 + R)$ combined with the definition of R in (5.5) and the liquidation value definition in (5.6), gives

$$r = \ln\theta + \ln u - \ln P,$$

(5.27)

where P is the current price. Now taking conditional expectations based on the information set Ω_I in (5.10) yields the following conditional expectations of the informed investor

$$E\left[r|\Omega_I\right] = \ln\theta + E\left[\ln u|\Omega_I\right] - \ln P = \ln\theta + \beta\ln f_t - \ln P,$$

(5.28)

and

$$Var\left[r|\Omega_I\right] = Var\left[\ln u|\Omega_I\right] = \beta\beta' + \Sigma_\eta,$$

(5.29)

where

$$E[\ln u|\Omega_I] = \beta E\left[\ln f_{t+1}|\Omega_I\right] + E\left[\ln\eta_{t+1}|\Omega_I\right] = \beta\ln f_t,$$
$$Var[\ln u|\Omega_I] = \beta Var\left[\ln f_{t+1}|\Omega_I\right]\beta' + Var\left[\ln\eta_{t+1}|\Omega_I\right] = \beta\beta' + I_N.$$

Substituting (5.28) and (5.29) into the optimal solution of the informed investor's portfolio problem in (5.9) with $k = I$, gives

$$\alpha_I^* = \frac{\ln\theta + \beta\ln f - \ln P - rf + \frac{1}{2}\left(\beta\beta' + \Sigma_\eta\right)}{\gamma\left(\beta\beta' + \Sigma_\eta\right)}.$$

5.A.3 Uninformed Conditional Expectations

The conditional expectations of (5.27) based on the information set Ω_U in (5.12), are

$$E\left[r|\Omega_U\right] = E\left[\ln v|\Omega_U\right] - \ln P,$$

and

$$Var\left[r|\Omega_U\right] = Var\left[\ln v|\Omega_U\right].$$

The solution to the uninformed investor's optimization problem given in (5.9) with $k = U$ is reexpressed using the expressions for the conditional expectations given above

$$\alpha_U^* = \frac{(E\left[\ln v|\Omega_U\right] - \ln P) - rf + \frac{1}{2}Var\left[\ln v|\Omega_U\right]}{\gamma\,Var\left[\ln v|\Omega_U\right]}.$$

Unlike the conditional expectations of the informed investor, calculation of the uninformed investor's conditional expectations are more involved as it is now necessary to form expectations of θ, as well as ϵ. To achieve this, consider the market equilibrium condition where the supply of the risky asset (X_T) equals demand by the market participants

$$X_T = \mu_I \alpha_I^* W + \mu_U \alpha_U^* W + \ln \epsilon,$$

where μ_I and μ_U are respectively the number of informed and uninformed investors. Using the expressions of α_I^* and α_U^* derived above

$$X_T = \mu_I \frac{\ln \theta + \beta \ln f - \ln P - rf + \frac{1}{2}\left(\beta\beta' + \Sigma_\eta\right)}{\gamma\left(\beta\beta' + \Sigma_\eta\right)} W$$
$$+ \mu_U \frac{E\left[\ln v|\Omega_U\right] - \ln P - rf + \frac{1}{2}Var\left[\ln v|\Omega_U\right]}{\gamma\,Var\left[\ln v|\Omega_U\right]} W + \ln \epsilon.$$

$$(5.30)$$

Rearranging this equation in terms of those variables not contained in the information set of the uninformed investor as a function of $\ln P$, gives

$$S(\ln P) = \ln \theta + \frac{\gamma\left(\beta\beta' + \Sigma_\eta\right)}{\mu_I W} \ln \epsilon$$

$$= \frac{\gamma\left(\beta\beta' + \Sigma_\eta\right)}{\mu_I W} \times$$

$$\left[X_T - \mu_U \frac{E\left[\ln v | \Omega_U\right] - \ln P - rf + \frac{1}{2}Var\left[\ln v | \Omega_U\right]}{\gamma\,Var\left[\ln v | \Omega_U\right]} W \right.$$

$$\left. + \mu_I \frac{-\beta \ln f + \ln P + rf - \frac{1}{2}\left(\beta\beta' + \Sigma_\eta\right)}{\gamma\left(\beta\beta' + \Sigma_\eta\right)} W \right].$$

To ensure that uninformed investor's expectations conditional on equilibrium prices are consistent with that conditional on the information revealed by $S(P)$, the following "belief consistency" conditions are imposed

$$E[\ln v | \Omega_U] = E[\ln v | S(\ln P)]$$

$$= E[\ln v] + Cov[\ln v, S(\ln P)](Var[S(\ln P)])^{-1}$$

$$\times (S(\ln P) - E[S(\ln P)]) \tag{5.31}$$

$$= \bar{\theta} + \Sigma_\theta \left[\Sigma_\theta + \left(\frac{\gamma}{\mu_I W}\right)^2 (\beta\beta' + \Sigma_\eta) \Sigma_\epsilon (\beta\beta' + \Sigma_\eta)' \right]^{-1}$$

$$\times \left[\ln\theta + \frac{\gamma(\beta\beta' + \Sigma_\eta)}{\mu_I W} \ln \epsilon - \bar{\theta} \right],$$

and

$$Var[\ln v | \Omega_U] = Var[\ln v | S(\ln P)]$$

$$= Var[\ln v] - Cov[\ln v, S(\ln P)](Var[S(\ln P)])^{-1}$$

$$\times (Cov[\ln v, S(\ln P)])' \tag{5.32}$$

$$= [\Sigma_\theta + \Sigma_u]$$

$$- \Sigma_\theta \left[\Sigma_\theta + \left(\frac{\gamma}{\mu_I W}\right)^2 (\beta\beta' + \Sigma_\eta) \Sigma_\epsilon (\beta\beta' + \Sigma_\eta)' \right]^{-1} \Sigma_\theta',$$

which represent the required conditional expectations of the uninformed investor.

5.A.4 Excess Returns Equation

The derivations of the model given above are based on the return on the asset R, which is unknown as it is a function of the asset's liquidation value v, which by definition is unknown. To derive an expression of the observed or realized return on the asset, the following steps are adopted. Substitute the conditional expectations in (5.31) into the market-clearing condition in (5.30), and rearrange to generate an expression of the current price in terms of the factors

$$\ln P = \varphi + \xi \ln \theta + \chi \ln \epsilon + \delta \ln f, \tag{5.33}$$

where

$$\varphi = M_0 + M_1 \left[I - \Sigma_\theta \left[\Sigma_\theta + \left(\frac{\gamma}{\mu_I W} \right)^2 (\beta\beta' + \Sigma_\eta) \Sigma_\epsilon (\beta\beta' + \Sigma_\eta)' \right]^{-1} \right] \bar{\theta},$$

$$\xi = \left[M_1 \Sigma_\theta \left[\Sigma_\theta + \left(\frac{\gamma}{\mu_I W} \right)^2 (\beta\beta' + \Sigma_\eta) \Sigma_\epsilon (\beta\beta' + \Sigma_\eta)' \right]^{-1} + M_2 \right],$$

$$\chi = \left[M_1 \Sigma_\theta \left[\Sigma_\theta + \left(\frac{\gamma}{\mu_I W} \right)^2 (\beta\beta' + \Sigma_\eta) \Sigma_\epsilon (\beta\beta' + \Sigma_\eta)' \right]^{-1} \right.$$
$$\left. \frac{\gamma (\beta\beta' + \Sigma_\eta)}{\mu_I W} + M_3 \right],$$

$$\delta = M_4.$$

and

$$M_0 = -\Psi^{-1} \left[X_T + \frac{\mu_U}{\gamma} W \left(rf \, Var \, [\ln v | \ln P]^{-1} - \frac{1}{2} \right) \right.$$
$$\left. + \frac{\mu_I}{\gamma} W \left(rf \, (\beta\beta' + \Sigma_\eta)^{-1} - \frac{1}{2} \right) \right],$$

$$M_1 = \Psi^{-1} \frac{\mu_U}{\gamma} W Var \, [\ln v | \ln P]^{-1},$$

$$M_2 = \Psi^{-1} \frac{\mu_I}{\gamma} W (\beta\beta' + \Sigma_\eta)^{-1},$$

$$M_3 = \Psi^{-1},$$

$$M_4 = \Psi^{-1} \frac{\mu_I}{\gamma} W \left(\beta\beta' + \Sigma_\eta\right)^{-1} \beta,$$

$$\Psi = \frac{\mu_I}{\gamma} W \left(\beta\beta' + \Sigma_\eta\right)^{-1} + \frac{\mu_U}{\gamma} W Var\left[\ln v \mid \ln P\right]^{-1}.$$

Now let P_+ be the realized price in the next period, formally the realization from the distribution of v, be given by

$$\ln P_+ = E\left[\ln v \mid \Omega_U\right] + \ln \zeta,$$

where $\ln \zeta$ is the expectations error, which under the assumption of rational expectations is assumed to be *iid*. Then the realized return is

$$\ln P_+ - \ln P = E[\ln v \mid \Omega_U] + \ln \zeta - \ln P$$

$$= \bar{\theta} + \Sigma_\theta \left[\Sigma_\theta + \left(\frac{\gamma}{\mu_I W}\right)^2 (\beta\beta' + \Sigma_\eta)\Sigma_\epsilon (\beta\beta' + \Sigma_\eta)'\right]^{-1}$$

$$\times \left[\ln \theta + \frac{\gamma(\beta\beta' + \Sigma_\eta)}{\mu_I W} \ln \epsilon - \bar{\theta}\right]$$

$$+ \ln \zeta - \varphi - \xi \ln \theta - \chi \ln \epsilon - \delta \ln f,$$

where the last step is based on using the expression for $E\left[\ln v \mid \Omega_U\right]$ in (5.31) and the expression for $\ln P$ in (5.33). Or, in terms of excess returns, $\ln P_+ - \ln P - rf$, the factor equation becomes

$$y = C_0 + C_1 \ln \theta + C_2 \ln \epsilon + C_3 \ln f + C_4 \ln \zeta,$$

where

$$C_0 = \left\{ I - \Sigma_\theta \left[\Sigma_\theta + \left(\frac{\gamma}{\mu_I W}\right)^2 (\beta\beta' + \Sigma_\eta)\Sigma_\epsilon (\beta\beta' + \Sigma_\eta)'\right]^{-1} \right\}$$

$$\bar{\theta} - \varphi - rf$$

$$C_1 = \Sigma_\theta \left[\Sigma_\theta + \left(\frac{\gamma}{\mu_I W}\right)^2 (\beta\beta' + \Sigma_\eta)\Sigma_\epsilon (\beta\beta' + \Sigma_\eta)'\right]^{-1} - \xi$$

$$C_2 = \Sigma_\theta \left[\Sigma_\theta + \left(\frac{\gamma}{\mu_I W} \right)^2 (\beta\beta' + \Sigma_\eta) \Sigma_\epsilon (\beta\beta' + \Sigma_\eta)' \right]^{-1}$$

$$\frac{\gamma (\beta\beta' + \Sigma_\eta)}{\mu_I W} - \gamma$$

$$C_3 = -\delta$$

$$C_4 = I_N.$$

This is the most general factor representation of excess returns during financial crises as it includes both normal and contagious transmission mechanisms. In a non-crisis period where there is no contagion, this is represented by $\beta\beta'$ and Σ_η being diagonal matrices.

5.B Data Sources and Definitions

Table 5.12
Data sources and definitions. In the case of Argentina, Brazil, Mexico and Russia, the bonds returns are computed from two bonds series.

Country	Bonds (issued in U.S. dollars)	Equities (local currency)	Exch. rates (per USD)
Argentina	11% coupon: Issued October 9, 1996 Matures October 9, 2006 Bloomberg 007022140	MERVAL Index ARGMERV(PI)	ARGPES$
	11.375% coupon: Issued March 15, 2000 Matures March 15, 2010 Bloomberg 010909899		
Brazil	9 3/8% coupon: Issued March 31, 1998 Matures April 7, 2008 Bloomberg 105756AG5	BOVESPA Index BRBOVES(PI)	BRACRU$
	10.25% coupon: Issued June 17, 2003 Matures June 17, 2013 Bloomberg 017062875		
Canada	Corporate BBB Bloomberg C28810Y	S&P/TSX Index TTOCOMP(PI)	CNDOLL$

continued

Table 5.12
Cont'ds

Mexico	8 5/8% coupon Issued March 5, 1998 Matures March 12, 2008 Bloomberg 8534713	BOLSA Index MXIPC35(PI)	 MEXPES$
	6.375% coupon Issued January 16, 2003 Matures January 16, 2013 Bloomberg 016113468		
Russia	3% coupon: Issued May 14, 1993 Matures May 14, 2008 Bloomberg TT3182314	RSF EE MT Index RSMTIND(PI)	 CISRUB$
	3% coupon: Issued May 14, 1996 Matures May 14, 2011 Bloomberg 008170363		
U.S.	Corporate BBB bond rate Bloomberg C00910Y	Dow Jones Index DJINDUS(PI)	
Risk free	Yields on the U.S. Treasury 10 year bond Federal Reserve Board of Governors: Table 15 tcm10y		
Sources:	Bloomberg	Datastream	Datastream

5.C Additional Variance Decompositions

Table 5.13

Variance decompositions, Russian/LTCM crisis: percentage of total.

Factors	Arg.	Brz.	Can.	Mex.	Rus.	US
Noncontagion			*Equity Markets*			
Common 1	1.12	0.20	0.03	1.02	0.18	13.79
Common 2	10.91	0.36	13.76	5.57	0.15	15.27
Emerging	1.24	0.27	n.a.	n.a.	0.19	n.a.
Market (equity)	16.03	0.23	5.12	10.60	52.75	7.21
Market (bond)	n.a.	n.a.	n.a.	n.a.	n.a.	n.a.
Country	2.37	0.05	15.23	0.43	19.92	n.a.
Idio.	24.34	0.26	24.40	46.75	0.93	n.a.
Contagion						
Market (equity)	n.a.	n.a.	n.a.	n.a.	n.a.	n.a.
Market (bond)	1.16	37.65	11.48	9.16	18.82	0.32
Country (Russia)	38.05	2.57	6.92	13.48	n.a.	40.97
Idio. (Rus. bond)	4.35	51.95	1.49	2.36	6.32	0.90
Idio. (US bond)	0.42	6.46	21.57	10.65	0.74	21.57
Total	100.00	100.00	100.00	100.00	100.00	100.00
Noncontagion			*Bond Markets*			
Common 1	0.00	0.02	0.27	0.02	0.48	0.22
Common 2	3.79	5.14	5.81	7.12	3.10	5.55
Emerging	0.34	n.a.	n.a.	n.a.	0.78	n.a.
Market (equity)	n.a.	n.a.	n.a.	n.a.	n.a.	n.a.
Market (bond)	6.66	2.86	24.24	4.12	23.82	29.06
Country	1.29	1.26	12.84	2.22	47.14	n.a.
Idio.	56.91	1.38	10.92	0.86	20.13	33.79
Contagion						
Market (equity)	12.11	26.68	4.92	27.57	4.50	5.85
Market (bond)	n.a.	n.a.	n.a.	n.a.	n.a.	n.a.
Country (Russia)	0.44	26.90	1.00	16.24	n.a.	22.88
Idio. (Rus. bond)	13.62	15.67	8.36	17.01	n.a.	2.65
Idio. (US bond)	4.85	20.09	31.64	24.85	0.05	n.a.
Total	100.00	100.00	100.00	100.00	100.00	100.00

Table 5.14

Variance decompositions, Brazilian crisis: percentage of total.

Factors	Arg.	Brz.	Can.	Mex.	Rus.	US
Noncontagion			*Equity Markets*			
Common 1	4.00	0.82	13.54	2.46	0.01	40.02
Common 2	7.26	8.20	7.95	8.01	0.52	0.54
Emerging	1.19	4.27	n.a.	n.a.	0.22	n.a.
Market (equity)	1.23	1.49	0.13	2.40	70.40	3.54
Market (bond)	n.a.	n.a.	n.a.	n.a.	n.a.	n.a.
Country	4.74	74.46	19.77	14.09	0.89	n.a.
Idio.	19.32	3.73	43.70	52.58	0.77	n.a.
Contagion						
Market (equity)	n.a.	n.a.	n.a.	n.a.	n.a.	n.a.
Market (bond)	0.73	0.07	5.61	6.16	22.48	21.21
Country (Brazil)	51.51	n.a.	1.43	10.50	0.13	2.46
Idio. (Brz. bond)	10.02	6.97	7.88	3.81	4.59	32.23
Total	100.00	100.00	100.00	100.00	100.00	100.00
Noncontagion			*Bond Markets*			
Common 1	3.78	2.17	8.46	7.55	0.02	0.95
Common 2	1.35	0.97	7.37	3.19	0.04	0.08
Emerging	0.46	n.a.	n.a.	n.a.	0.01	n.a.
Market (equity)	n.a.	n.a.	n.a.	n.a.	n.a.	n.a.
Market (bond)	0.48	13.74	4.12	2.26	34.23	3.24
Country	1.01	77.54	42.44	0.14	0.00	0.00
Idio.	78.18	0.85	25.34	4.38	0.62	88.15
Contagion						
Market (equity)	0.06	4.73	0.41	2.39	25.37	0.31
Market (bond)	n.a.	n.a.	n.a.	n.a.	n.a.	n.a.
Country (Brazil)	14.57	n.a.	7.12	77.52	5.10	4.27
Idio. (Brz.bond)	0.10	n.a.	4.75	2.57	34.62	3.00
Total	100.00	100.00	100.00	100.00	100.00	100.00

Table 5.15

Variance decompositions, Dot-com crisis: percentage of total.

Factors	Arg.	Brz.	Can.	Mex.	Rus.	US
Noncontagion			*Equity Markets*			
Common 1	0.01	17.60	0.31	0.01	30.89	25.67
Common 2	1.11	39.86	36.55	0.28	18.21	69.87
Emerging	0.03	17.73	n.a.	n.a.	48.69	n.a.
Market (equity)	4.81	6.59	1.57	10.32	0.39	0.71
Market (bond)	n.a.	n.a.	n.a.	n.a.	n.a.	n.a.
Country	0.00	1.42	14.78	0.02	0.10	0.04
Idio.	1.42	0.25	46.02	1.21	1.47	3.66
Contagion						
Market (equity)	n.a.	n.a.	n.a.	n.a.	n.a.	n.a.
Market (bond)	0.07	4.30	0.02	75.71	0.03	0.05
Country (US)	86.06	1.06	0.03	2.05	0.17	n.a.
Idio. (US equity)	6.50	11.19	0.72	10.40	0.04	n.a.
Total	100.00	100.00	100.00	100.00	100.00	100.00
Noncontagion			*Bond Markets*			
Common 1	0.01	0.02	0.43	0.31	0.53	0.00
Common 2	3.41	4.42	8.37	40.09	2.92	0.04
Emerging	0.08	n.a.	n.a.	n.a.	0.60	n.a.
Market (equity)	n.a.	n.a.	n.a.	n.a.	n.a.	n.a.
Market (bond)	0.63	0.88	0.19	9.13	0.22	0.05
Country	93.64	5.15	60.89	13.84	0.05	0.02
Idio.	0.58	0.01	29.31	7.42	95.47	98.91
Contagion						
Market (equity)	1.04	35.66	0.30	17.03	0.13	0.35
Market (bond)	n.a.	n.a.	n.a.	n.a.	n.a.	n.a.
Country (US)	0.27	0.77	0.45	4.23	0.01	n.a.
Idio. (US equity)	0.35	53.08	0.07	7.96	0.07	0.64
Total	100.00	100.00	100.00	100.00	100.00	100.00

Table 5.16

Variance decompositions, Argentinian crisis: percentage of total.

Factors	Arg.	Brz.	Can.	Mex.	Rus.	US
Noncontagion			*Equity Markets*			
Common 1	0.55	0.00	1.02	0.05	0.13	19.05
Common 2	23.59	0.24	36.36	13.68	10.36	73.16
Emerging	1.83	0.12	n.a.	n.a.	12.01	n.a.
Market (equity)	1.49	37.58	0.48	0.01	0.01	0.90
Market (bond)	n.a.	n.a.	n.a.	n.a.	n.a.	n.a.
Country	29.27	0.04	11.64	0.69	11.35	n.a.
Idio.	38.68	0.10	43.47	83.67	66.11	n.a.
Contagion						
Market (equity)	n.a.	n.a.	n.a.	n.a.	n.a.	n.a.
Market (bond)	4.58	18.70	0.98	0.28	0.00	0.65
Country (Arg.)	n.a.	0.00	4.30	1.55	0.01	6.14
Idio. (Arg. bond)	0.01	43.23	1.76	0.08	0.01	0.11
Total	100.00	100.00	100.00	100.00	100.00	100.00
Noncontagion			*Bond Markets*			
Common 1	5.64	18.63	7.08	13.94	1.52	0.00
Common 2	15.87	47.43	11.14	45.42	3.14	0.00
Emerging	1.95	n.a.	n.a.	n.a.	0.00	n.a.
Market (equity)	n.a.	n.a.	n.a.	n.a.	n.a.	n.a.
Market (bond)	10.57	0.01	1.52	0.05	0.01	64.79
Country	62.00	10.16	63.16	10.88	1.52	n.a.
Idio.	0.00	21.58	0.60	18.08	93.69	0.62
Contagion						
Market (equity)	3.97	0.53	5.12	5.14	0.01	13.43
Market (bond)	n.a.	n.a.	n.a.	n.a.	n.a.	n.a.
Country (Arg.)	n.a.	0.04	2.74	2.82	0.10	17.59
Idio. (Arg. bond)	n.a.	1.63	8.66	3.67	0.00	3.57
Total	100.00	100.00	100.00	100.00	100.00	100.00

Table 5.17

Variance decompositions, subprime crisis: percentage of total.

Factors	Arg.	Brz.	Can.	Mex.	Rus.	US
Noncontagion				*Equity Markets*		
Common 1	3.10	9.25	0.20	1.57	12.62	4.08
Common 2	15.58	10.54	7.88	4.05	6.65	8.05
Emerging	1.95	9.34	n.a.	n.a.	7.59	n.a.
Market (equity)	11.43	19.64	23.13	14.70	8.59	65.69
Market (bond)	n.a.	n.a.	n.a.	n.a.	n.a.	n.a.
Country	4.53	0.89	9.52	0.23	0.06	n.a.
Idio.	35.20	7.72	14.31	34.96	60.63	8.57
Contagion						
Market (equity)	n.a.	n.a.	n.a.	n.a.	n.a.	n.a.
Market (bond)	10.14	15.77	17.34	17.33	0.67	7.94
Idio. (US equity)	5.31	7.74	8.11	7.28	1.18	n.a.
Idio. (US bond)	12.75	19.13	19.52	19.88	2.01	5.68
Total	100.00	100.00	100.00	100.00	100.00	100.00
Noncontagion				*Bond Markets*		
Common 1	0.00	0.19	0.60	0.12	0.35	0.34
Common 2	0.06	56.19	11.28	53.81	1.79	4.96
Emerging	0.01	n.a.	n.a.	n.a.	0.49	n.a.
Market (equity)	n.a.	n.a.	n.a.	n.a.	n.a.	n.a.
Market (bond)	4.62	0.89	11.04	2.39	42.32	0.16
Country	0.02	25.06	25.28	22.31	12.32	n.a.
Idio.	0.97	3.50	27.11	0.22	12.57	2.34
Contagion						
Market (equity)	4.64	9.94	5.96	14.40	0.03	87.98
Market (bond)	n.a.	n.a.	n.a.	n.a.	n.a.	n.a.
Idio. (US equity)	84.90	1.75	3.56	2.72	0.03	4.21
Idio. (US bond)	4.77	2.47	15.19	4.02	30.11	n.a.
Total	100.00	100.00	100.00	100.00	100.00	100.00

6

Characterizing Global Risk in Emerging Markets

6.1 Introduction

This chapter turns to the general problem of examining the relative importance of contagion during periods of financial turbulence. In particular, it returns to the bond markets during the Russian and LTCM crises examined with the latent factor model in chapters 3 and 5. The chapter considers to what extent contagion risk is discernible amongst credit, liquidity, and volatility risk measures.

During February 1998 to May 1999, emerging markets experienced an enormous widening of bond spreads. Figure 6.1 highlights this phenomenon, showing the risk premia of nine emerging markets across three regions (Asia, Europe, and Latin America) over this period. All markets show a sharp increase in spreads during the Russian crisis (August to September, 1998). Further increases in spreads occur during the Long Term Capital Management (LTCM) crisis (September to October, 1998) and the Brazilian crisis (January to February, 1999). During the interval between the LTCM and Brazilian crises spreads were broadly declining with the exception of Russia.

The risk premium for Russia is sustained for most of the period at the level reached during the Russian crisis.[1]

Whilst changes in spreads between sovereign bonds provide some indication of the risk premia between countries, they do not distinguish between the risks associated purely with default (credit risk), or other market factors including liquidity and volatility risks, which are important to international investors. In addition, there are other risks that may explain movements in spreads, including risks that are either idiosyncratic to countries (country risk), or arise from the transmission of shocks across national borders during periods of financial crisis (contagion risk).

The problem of identifying the underlying components of risk is compounded when the risk factors themselves are correlated. For example, a rise in credit risk can impact upon the liquidity of the market resulting in international investors off-loading liquid assets, despite their relatively low default risk (Greenspan 1999). This suggests that at any point in time more than one risk factor is at play and classifying crises in terms of different types of risk, for example the Russian crisis as a credit crisis and the LTCM crisis as a liquidity crisis, may be too simplistic.

There is a growing literature on the impact of risk preferences of investors and consumers on asset market prices. Burger and Warnock (2003) examine credit and liquidity risk for international bond portfolio allocation and find credit risk to be important; also see González-Hermosillo (2008) and González-Hermosillo and Li (2008). Recently, emphasis has shifted to the effects of changes in risk preferences on asset markets. Kumar and Persaud (2002) and the International Monetary Fund (2003) look at measures of risk appetite and particularly relate it to portfolio behavior during periods of financial crises. Bekaert, Engstrom, and Xing (2006) and Bekaert, Engstrom, and Grenadier (2006) find a substantial role for time varying risk aversion in both equities and bonds. Bollerslev, Gibson, and Zhou (2009) estimate time varying volatility risk from option prices for equities.

---

1. See Appendix 6.A for definitions of the variables. For an overview of the Russian, LTCM and Brazilian crises, see Chapter 3, Jorion (2000), Lowenstein (2001), and Goldfajn (2003). For a discussion of the choice of crisis dates, see Appendix 6.B.

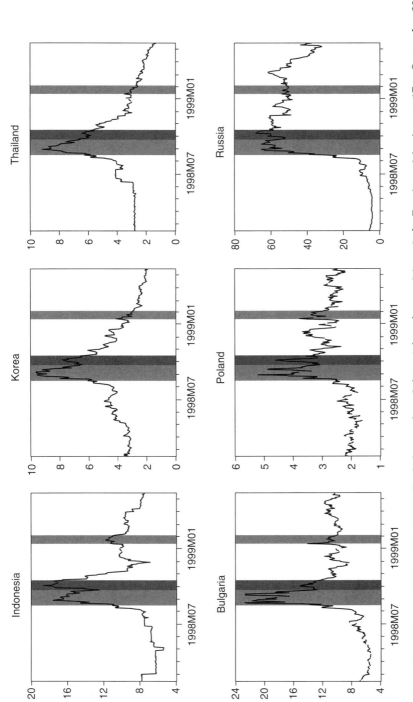

Figure 6.1 February 1998 to May 1999. Shaded areas from left to right refer to crisis periods: Russian crisis, August 17 to September 23, 1998; LTCM crisis, September 23 to October 15, 1998; Brazilian crisis, January 13 to February 2 1999.

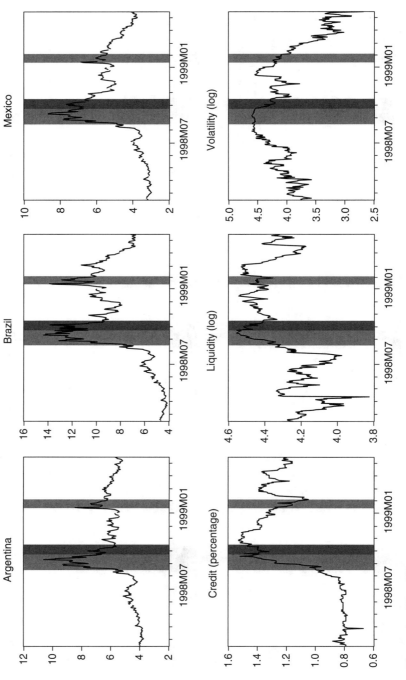

Figure 6.1 (Cont'd)

This chapter decomposes the risk premia of nine emerging market bonds during periods of financial crises in terms of their three broad risk characteristics: global risk (credit, liquidity, volatility), country risk, and contagion risk. The approach is based on developing a model of risk aversion using the stochastic discount factor model, whereby the expected risk premia is expressed as a function of the key characteristics that determine risk; see also Flood and Rose (2004), who adopt a similar modeling framework, and Cochrane and Piazzesi (2005) for an alternative approach using forward rates.

In the empirical application, liquidity and volatility risks are measured using indices compiled by JP Morgan, while credit risk is measured as the spread between U.S. industrial BBB1 10-year yields and the 10-year U.S. Treasury bond. Time series plots of the three global risk variables are given in the bottom three panels of figure 6.1. The country and contagion variables are treated as latent. Country risk is measured as the idiosyncratic shocks from a dynamic model based on a structural vector autoregression (SVAR). Contagion risk is defined as the transmission of shocks from one country to another country during a financial crisis. In keeping with the definition of contagion discussed in Chapter 2, contagion is treated as a short-run phenomenon that dissipates in the long-run. This leads to a set of restrictions that are imposed on the long-run dynamics of the SVAR to identify contagion risk.

An important feature of the model is that it can be used to track the key risk factors underlying changes in the risk premia of bonds over time during the three crises. The empirical analysis is presented in two ways. First, risk premia are decomposed in terms of the quantity and price of risk. The risk quantities are computed directly from the long-run variance-covariance matrix of the SVAR, whilst the risk prices in the crisis periods are implied from the risk quantity estimates and the observed risk premia in each crisis period. These estimates are then compared with the risk price estimates obtained for a noncrisis period. Second, a historical decomposition is performed that separates risk premia into a benchmark spread and the contributions of shocks of risk factor innovations during each financial crisis.

The rest of the chapter proceeds as follows. A theoretical model of risk preferences is developed in Section 6.2.

Estimates of the risk quantities and prices are given in Section 6.3, while Section 6.4 contains the dynamic decompositions of risk using the historical decomposition. Concluding comments are presented in Section 6.5.

6.2 A Model of Risk Premia

This section develops the key theoretical and empirical models of risk used in the empirical analysis to explain the movements in risk premia of the nine countries presented in figure 6.1. The modeling approach consists of using the stochastic discount factor model to price the risks of all assets for the international investor. This has the effect of imposing a set of restrictions on the factor structure of bond spreads, which enables the risk quantities and prices to be identified from the panel of countries; see Piazzesi (2009) for a recent review of factor models of bonds. In specifying the model, a nonparametric approach is adopted to circumvent the need to specify the utility function governing the functional form of the stochastic discount factor.

6.2.1 Model Specification

Consider the following stochastic discount factor model associated with the *jth* portfolio with return $R_{j,t}$, which represents the Euler equation of an intertemporal portfolio model (Campbell, Lo, and McKinley 1997),

$$E_{t-1}\left[M_t\left(1+R_{j,t}\right)\right] = 1, \tag{6.1}$$

where M_t is the stochastic discount factor or pricing kernel which is assumed to be positive, and $E_{t-1}[.]$ is the conditional expectations operator based on information at time $t-1$. Expanding the left-hand side gives

$$E_{t-1}[M_t] + E_{t-1}\left[M_t R_{j,t}\right] = E_{t-1}[M_t] + Cov_{t-1}\left(M_t, R_{j,t}\right)$$
$$+ E_{t-1}[M_t] E_{t-1}\left[R_{j,t}\right]. \tag{6.2}$$

The covariance risk of the portfolio is defined in terms of a set of risk factors ($F_{i,t}$) as follows

$$Cov_{t-1}\left(M_t, R_{j,t}\right) = E_{t-1}[M_t]\sum_{i=1}^{K}\gamma_i E_{t-1}\left[\left(R_{j,t} - E_{t-1}\left[R_{j,t}\right]\right)\right.$$

$$\times \left.\left(F_{i,t} - E_{t-1}\left[F_{i,t}\right]\right)\right], \tag{6.3}$$

where the inclusion of the term $E_{t-1}[M_t]$ acts as a convenient scalar adjustment in deriving the estimating equation. In the empirical analysis $K = 12$, corresponding to three global risk factors (credit, liquidity, and volatility) and nine country risks. Using (6.2) and (6.3) in (6.1) gives

$$E_{t-1}\left[R_{j,t}\right]E_{t-1}[M_t]\sum_{i=1}^{K}\gamma_i E_{t-1}\left[\left(R_{j,t} - E_{t-1}\left[R_{j,t}\right]\right)\right.$$

$$\times \left.\left(F_{i,t} - E_{t-1}\left[F_{i,t}\right]\right)\right] + E_{t-1}[M_t] + E_{t-1}[M_t] = 1. \tag{6.4}$$

For the case where the pricing kernel is defined in terms of the risk free rate ($R_{f,t}$) then (6.1) becomes

$$E_{t-1}\left[M_t\left(1 + R_{f,t}\right)\right] = \left(1 + R_{f,t}\right)E_{t-1}[M_t] = 1, \tag{6.5}$$

in which case

$$E_{t-1}[M_t] = \frac{1}{1 + R_{f,t}}. \tag{6.6}$$

Using this expression in (6.4) gives

$$1 + \sum_{i=1}^{K}\gamma_i E_{t-1}\left[\left(R_{j,t} - E_{t-1}\left[R_{j,t}\right]\right)\left(F_{i,t} - E_{t-1}\left[F_{i,t}\right]\right)\right]$$

$$+ E_{t-1}\left[R_{j,t}\right] = 1, \tag{6.7}$$

or

$$E_{t-1}\left[R_{j,t}\right] - R_{f,t} = \sum_{i=1}^{K}\beta_i E_{t-1}\left[\left(R_{j,t} - E_{t-1}\left[R_{j,t}\right]\right)\right.$$

$$\times \left.\left(F_{i,t} - E_{t-1}\left[F_{i,t}\right]\right)\right], \tag{6.8}$$

where $\beta_i = -\gamma_i$. This equation shows that the expected excess return over a risk-free asset is expressed as a weighted average of the covariances between the innovations in the return on the portfolio and the innovations in the risk factors. The covariances represent the quantity of risk while the weighting parameters, $\beta_i, i = 1, 2, \cdots, K$, are the prices of risk associated with each risk factor in $F_{i,t}$. The prices of risk are a function of, among other things, the risk parameters of the investor's utility function as well as the parameters that summarize the dynamics of the underlying model linking asset returns. In the case of the CCAPM, Campbell (1996) shows that the risk price is equal to the product of the relative risk aversion parameter less unity and the correlation between innovations in asset returns and revisions in expected future market returns. For a risk aversion parameter greater than unity and a positive correlation between the innovations in the return on an asset and revisions in expected future market returns, this results in a positive risk price and implies a positive trade-off between expected excess returns and covariance risk.

To provide a benchmark with which to compare the variation in prices of the risk factors across crises, the unconditional stochastic discount factor model is defined by expressing (6.8) in terms of unconditional expectations

$$E\left[R_{j,t}\right] - R_{f,t} = \sum_{i=1}^{K} \beta_i E\left[\left(R_{j,t} - E\left[R_{j,t}\right]\right)\left(F_{i,t} - E\left[F_{i,t}\right]\right)\right].$$

(6.9)

In the empirical analysis, the unconditional covariance matrix in (6.9) given by $E[(R_{j,t} - E[R_{j,t}])(F_{i,t} - E[F_{i,t}])]$ is identified by imposing long-run restrictions on the dynamics of a SVAR model, which is specified below.

6.2.2 Identifying Risk Quantities

To estimate the long-run risk quantities in (6.9), a 12-variate SVAR model is specified containing the three global risk variables (credit, liquidity, and volatility) and nine emerging markets Indonesia (I), Korea (K), Thailand (T), Bulgaria (BU), Poland (P), Russia (R), Argentina (A), Brazil (B), and Mexico (M). Let the full set of variables at t be represented by the (12×1) vector Z_t, and let the long-run variance-covariance matrix between Z_t and the innovations to the risk factors be represented by

$$E\left[(Z_t - E[Z_t])(F_t - E[F_t])\right] = E\left[(Z_t - E[Z_t])e_t\right] = H, \quad (6.10)$$

where

$$u_t = F_t - E[F_t], \qquad (6.11)$$

are the innovations to the risk factors, and H contains the unknown long-run parameters. The $u_t = \{u_{i,t}, i = 1, 2, \cdots, 12\}$ is assumed to be an independent normal random vector with zero mean and unit covariance matrix

$$u_t \sim N(0, I). \qquad (6.12)$$

The matrix of long-run parameters in (6.10) is defined as

$$H = \begin{bmatrix}
\lambda_c \\
& \lambda_l \\
& & \lambda_v \\
\delta_I & \gamma_I & \rho_I & \phi_I \\
\delta_K & \gamma_K & \rho_K & & \phi_K \\
\delta_T & \gamma_T & \rho_T & & & \phi_T \\
\delta_{BU} & \gamma_{BU} & \rho_{BU} & & & & \phi_{BU} \\
\delta_P & \gamma_P & \rho_P & & & & & \phi_P \\
\delta_R & \gamma_R & \rho_R & & & & & & \phi_R \\
\delta_A & \gamma_A & \rho_A & & & & & & & \phi_A \\
\delta_B & \gamma_B & \rho_B & & & & & & & & \phi_B \\
\delta_M & \gamma_M & \rho_M & & & & & & & & & \phi_M
\end{bmatrix},$$

$$(6.13)$$

where blank cells represent zeros. The long-run global risk parameters for credit, liquidity and volatility are respectively $\lambda_c, \lambda_l, \lambda_v$ This implies that the three global risk factors are assumed to be independent processes determined entirely by their own dynamics in the long run. The parameters $\delta_i s$, measure the long-run effects of a credit innovation on bond spreads (credit risk), the parameters $\gamma_i s$ measure the long-run effects of a liquidity innovation on bond spreads (liquidity risk), and the parameters $\rho_i s$ measure the long-run effects of a volatility innovation on bond spreads (volatility risk).

The effects of country innovations on bond spreads (country risk) is controlled by the ϕ_is parameters.

The long-run risk quantities, $E[(R_{j,t} - E[R_{j,t}])(F_{i,t} - E[F_{i,t}])]$ in (6.9), correspond to the submatrix represented by the last 9 rows and 12 columns of H. The zeros in (6.13) impose the restriction of no contagion risk in the long-run. In the short run however, contagion risk can occur whereby shocks in the risk premia of one country can impact on the bond risk premia of another country. In addition, the three risk indicators are also allowed to be interconnected in the short run as they can be affected by all of the innovations in the model, including idiosyncratic country shocks of the emerging markets as well as shocks related to all risk indicators. To capture these short-run interactions a VAR with p lags is specified as

$$\left(I - A_1 - A_2 L^2 - \ldots - A_p L^p\right) \Delta Z_t = \alpha + v_t, \tag{6.14}$$

where $L^k Z_t = Z_{t-k}$ defines the lag operator, $\Delta = (I - L)$ is the first difference operator, A_k are (12×12) matrices of autoregressive parameters, α is a (12×1) vector of intercept parameters to capture the levels of the variables, and v_t is the VAR disturbance term, which is assumed to be distributed as[2]

$$v_t \sim N\left(0, \Omega\right). \tag{6.15}$$

The specification of the VAR in first differences follows Blanchard and Quah (1989) as the approach to impose the long-run restrictions defined in (6.13).

The short-run dynamics of the variables in the model are identified by the relationship between the VAR disturbance term v_t, and the innovations in the risk factors u_t in (6.11)

$$v_t = Gu_t, \tag{6.16}$$

where from (6.15) and the definition of u_t in (6.12), implies that $\Omega = GG'$, while G is related to H as

$$G = \left(I - A_1 - A_2 - \ldots - A_p\right) H. \tag{6.17}$$

---

2. An extension of the assumption of a constant covariance matrix is to specify a conditional covariance matrix based on a multivariate GARCH model (Bekaert, Harvey, and Ng 2005), or a factor GARCH model as in Chapters 2 and 3.

6.2.3 Estimation

The long-run parameters in (6.13) are estimated by maximum likelihood. Given the assumption of normality for v_t, the log of the likelihood at the *tth* observation is

$$\ln L_t = -\frac{N}{2}\ln(2\pi) - \frac{1}{2}\ln|G'G| - \frac{1}{2}v_t'(G'G)^{-1}v_t, \qquad (6.18)$$

where v_t is the vector of VAR disturbances in (6.14), G is defined by (6.17), and $N = 12$. The log of the likelihood function for a sample of $t = 1, 2, \cdots, T$ observations, is given by

$$\ln L = \sum_{t=1}^{T}\ln L, \qquad (6.19)$$

which is maximized using the procedure MAXLIK in GAUSS, version 5.0. The BFGS iterative gradient algorithm is used with derivatives computed numerically. Estimation is performed in two steps. First, the VAR parameters $\widehat{A}$ are estimated. Second, the long run parameters in H are estimated by maximizing the likelihood function in (6.19), subject to the restriction in (6.17) with A replaced by $\widehat{A}$ from the first step.

6.3 Empirical Estimates of Risk Quantities and Risk Prices in the Long Run

This section presents estimates of the risk quantities and risk prices from daily data on the global risk variables (credit, liquidity, and volatility) and the bond spreads of nine emerging markets across three regions: Asia (Indonesia, Korea, and Thailand), Eastern Europe (Bulgaria, Poland, and Russia), and Latin America (Argentina, Brazil, and Mexico). The sample period begins February 12, 1998, and ends May 17, 1999. The 12-variate VAR in (6.14) is specified with a lag length of $p = 5$, based on the AIC and the likelihood ratio lag structure tests.

6.3.1 Risk Quantities

The long-run parameter estimates of H are reported in table 6.1, with QMLE standard errors given in parentheses. The VAR parameter estimates are not reported. Instead the contribution of these estimates is presented graphically in figures 6.3 and 6.4 below.

The estimates of the long-run risk quantities in (6.9) are given in the second block of table 6.1. All risk quantity parameter estimates are positive showing that a positive innovation to each of the risk factors on average widens bond spreads. Most of the risk quantity estimates are statistically significant, with the main exceptions being the covariances between liquidity

Table 6.1
Long-run parameter estimates of H in (6.1): risk quantity estimates given in the second part of the table. QMLE standard errors are in brackets.

Variables	Risk Factors			
	Credit	*Liquidity*	*Volatility*	*Country*
Credit	0.03			
	(0.00)			
Liquidity		0.03		
		(0.01)		
Volatility			0.06	
			(0.00)	
Risk premia: Asia				
Indonesia	0.13	0.13	0.18	0.83
	(0.05)	(0.06)	(0.05)	(0.07)
Korea	0.01	0.02	0.02	0.15
	(0.01)	(0.01)	(0.09)	(0.01)
Thailand	1.27	0.36	0.37	2.31
	(0.15)	(0.22)	(0.14)	(0.17)
Risk premia: Eastern Europe				
Bulgaria	0.09	0.01	0.08	0.58
	(0.04)	(0.03)	(0.03)	(0.05)
Poland	0.06	0.04	0.06	0.31
	(0.02)	(0.02)	(0.02)	(0.03)
Russia	0.06	0.04	0.07	0.26
	(0.02)	(0.02)	(0.03)	(0.02)
Risk premia: Latin America				
Argentina	0.09	0.06	0.03	0.30
	(0.02)	(0.02)	(0.02)	(0.02)
Brazil	0.13	0.09	0.06	0.39
	(0.02)	(0.02)	(0.02)	(0.02)
Mexico	0.07	0.04	0.03	0.20
	(0.01)	(0.01)	(0.01)	(0.01)

risk innovations and the three European spreads, which are all statistically insignificant.

The country risk quantity estimates dominate the three global risk innovations for all countries. Of the quantity risk estimates associated with the three global risk innovations the relative rankings varies across countries. For the Latin American countries, credit risk dominates liquidity risk , which in turn dominates volatility risk. The credit risk quantity estimate for Thailand dominates the liquidity and volatility estimates, with the results for Indonesia and Thailand mixed. For the Eastern European countries, the credit and volatility quantity estimates are similar in magnitude, while the liquidity estimates tend to be at least 50% smaller.

Another way to compare the relative magnitudes of the size of the quantity risk estimates given in table 6.1 is to decompose the long-run volatility of the risk premia into the contributions of the global risk factors and the country risk components. Using (6.13) and the independence assumption of the innovations u_t, the volatility decomposition for the jth risk premium is given by

$$Var\left(R_{j,t}\right) = \delta_j^2 + \gamma_j^2 + \rho_j^2 + \phi_j^2, \tag{6.20}$$

where δ_j^2 is the contribution of credit risk, γ_j^2 is the contribution of liquidity risk, ρ_j^2 is the contribution of volatility risk, and ϕ_j^2 is the contribution of country risk.

The results of the long-run volatility decomposition in (6.20) are given in table 6.2, where all terms are expressed in percentages. The risk quantity estimates are dominated by the country risk factors, where the estimates range from as low as 53.67% for Russia and as high as 76.80% for Indonesia. The contribution of the three global risk factors to long-run volatility is relatively even for most countries. The contribution of liquidity risk to quantity risk is smallest for the Asian countries, while the contribution of credit risk to quantity risk is smallest for the Latin American countries.

6.3.2 Risk Prices

The estimates of the risk prices of the three global risks and the country risk are now presented for the three crisis periods.

Table 6.2
Long-run volatility decomposition of risk premia into risk factors.
Based on (6.20), expressed in percent.

Country	Credit risk δ_j^2	Liquidity risk γ_j^2	Volatility risk ρ_j^2	Country risk ϕ_j^2
Asia				
Indonesia	10.60	1.39	11.21	76.80
Korea	13.31	8.02	12.44	66.23
Thailand	15.51	9.32	13.53	61.65
Eastern Europe				
Bulgaria	14.42	9.89	10.46	65.23
Poland	11.21	10.64	4.76	73.40
Russia	8.50	8.45	29.38	53.67
Latin America				
Argentina	6.84	13.28	17.54	62.34
Brazil	8.34	13.83	20.00	57.83
Mexico	7.24	11.73	21.67	59.36

The estimates of the risk prices are obtained by computing β_i in (6.9) as (Campbell 1996)

$$\beta = Q^{-}\mu, \tag{6.21}$$

where β is the (9×12) vector containing the risk prices, μ is a (9×1) vector representing the average value of risk premia, and Q^{-} is the (generalized) inverse of the matrix of quantity risks given by the submatrix represented by the last 9 rows and 12 columns of H in (6.13). To track the changes in risk prices during each of the three crises, the estimates of the quantity risk are fixed at their long-run estimates, while μ is estimated using the sample mean of bond spreads in each of the three crisis periods. For comparative purposes the long-run estimates of the risk prices are also computed by choosing μ as the sample mean of the bond spreads for the total sample period.

The estimates of the risk prices are given in table 6.3. The results show that the prices of all three global risk factors increase above their long-run levels during the Russian crisis. A similar result occurs during the LTCM crisis. In the case of the Brazilian crisis, only the price of credit risk shows any substantial increase above its long-run level, while the liquidity and volatility risk prices tend to remain at their respective long-run levels.

Table 6.3

Risk price estimates in the long-run and during crises: Based on (6.21).

Risk Factor Price	Long-run	Crisis		
		Russia	LTCM	Brazil
Global risk				
Credit	17.45	27.94	26.98	22.79
Liquidity	11.63	18.45	16.52	14.52
Volatility	11.60	20.34	18.06	12.83
Country risk: Asia				
Indonesia	11.77	18.54	21.65	13.96
Korea	6.49	14.85	12.12	2.18
Thailand	5.48	15.58	10.66	1.07
Country risk: Eastern Europe				
Bulgaria	4.61	10.65	5.61	4.83
Poland	12.81	16.93	16.82	16.19
Russia	1.52	2.47	5.69	5.47
Country risk: Latin America				
Argentina	9.66	12.81	8.46	12.30
Brazil	9.87	13.14	13.89	16.96
Mexico	13.09	18.39	18.96	16.34

A comparison of the country risk prices during the Russian and LTCM crises reveals that both crises are widespread as all countries, with the exception of Bulgaria, experience increases in the prices of their country risks. This empirical result is also consistent with the results obtained in Chapter 3 on bond markets, Chapter 4 on equity markets, and Chapter 5 on bond and equity markets. Bulgaria experiences an increase in its country risk price during the Russian crisis, but this falls immediately during the LTCM crisis. In contrast, the Brazilian crisis is more localized, with just the Latin American countries experiencing increases in their country risk prices. During this period all Asian country risk prices return to their long-run levels, while the country risk prices in Poland and Russia maintain the levels achieved during the Russian and LTCM crises.

6.4 Historical Decomposition of Risk Premia

In the previous section, the calculations of the risk prices for the three crises are computed relative to the long-run risk quantity estimates. An alternative way of identifying the relative importance of the components of risk during financial crises is to decompose the risk premia of each country at each point in time in terms of the innovations associated with each measure of risk: global factors, country, and contagion. Formally, this is accomplished by using the estimated SVAR to compute a historical decomposition over the crisis periods.

From 6.14, rewrite the VAR in terms of its vector moving average (VMA) representation and use (6.16) to express the model in terms of the risk innovations u_t

$$\Delta Z_t = \left(I - A_1 - A_2 L^2 - \ldots - A_p L^p \right)^{-1} (\alpha + G u_t)$$

$$\Delta Z_t = \psi + \left(I - \Theta_1 - \Theta_2 L^2 - \ldots - \Theta_p L^p \right)^{-1} + G u_t, \qquad (6.22)$$

where Θ are (12×12) matrices of moving average parameters, which are functions of the autoregressive parameters of the VAR, and

$$\psi = \left(I - A_1 - A_2 L^2 - \ldots - A_p L^p \right)^{-1} \alpha,$$

is a (12×1) vector of intercept parameters.[3] To identify the contributions of the innovations of all risk factors during the crisis periods, benchmark spreads for each country risk premium are computed that represent counterfactual estimates of the risk premia if a crisis had not historically occurred. The benchmark spreads are computed as the conditional expectations of the risk premia based on a pre-crisis period. Letting T^* representing the end of the pre-crisis period, from (6.22), the conditional expectation over the crisis period is

$$\Delta Z_{T^*+D|T^*} = \psi + \sum_{i=D}^{\infty} \Theta_i G u_{T^*+D-i}. \qquad (6.23)$$

The forecast error over the crisis period corresponding to the deviations between changes in actual and benchmark

---

3. The matrix polynomial inversion used to generate the vector moving average representation is usually computed numerically; see Hamilton (1994, p.260).

spreads is

$$\Delta Z_{T^*+D} - \Delta Z_{T^*+D|T^*} = \sum_{i=D}^{D-1} \Theta_i Gu_{T^*+D-i}, \qquad (6.24)$$

which combined with (6.23)

$$\Delta Z_{T^*+D} = \left[\psi + \sum_{i=D}^{\infty} \Theta_i Gu_{T^*+D-i} \right] + \sum_{i=0}^{D-1} \Theta_i Gu_{T^*+D-i}, \qquad (6.25)$$

provides the historical decomposition of the change in risk premia over the crisis period in terms of changes in benchmark spreads based on pre-crisis information (first term) and the various innovations to all of the risk variables (second term). The historical decomposition is computed by replacing the unknown parameters and innovations by their estimated values. To express the historical decomposition in terms of the levels of the risk premia, (6.25) is cumulated over the sample.

The historical decompositions are computed with the pre-crisis period ending at $T^* =$ May 30, 1998. This date is several months before the actual disclosure of Russia's default on August 17, 1998, but is chosen to deal with the potential mounting pressure in financial markets that may have occurred before the actual crisis became newsworthy.

6.4.1 Benchmark Spread Estimates

Figure 6.2 compares the observed risk premia with the benchmark spreads for each country over the crisis period. Average estimates over selected periods are also given in table 6.4 for both series. With the exception of the three Asian countries, the benchmark spreads steadily increase over the period of the historical decomposition. For the case of Russia, the benchmark spread deteriorates markedly from around 6.5% on June 1, 1998, to about 35% by May 17, 1999, reflecting the sustained level of risk experienced in the Russian market following the Russian debt default. The benchmark spreads of the Asian countries either tend to be relatively flat over the period (Indonesia) or show a slight fall (Korea and Thailand). This result reflects the recovery from the Asian financial crisis starting in July 1997.

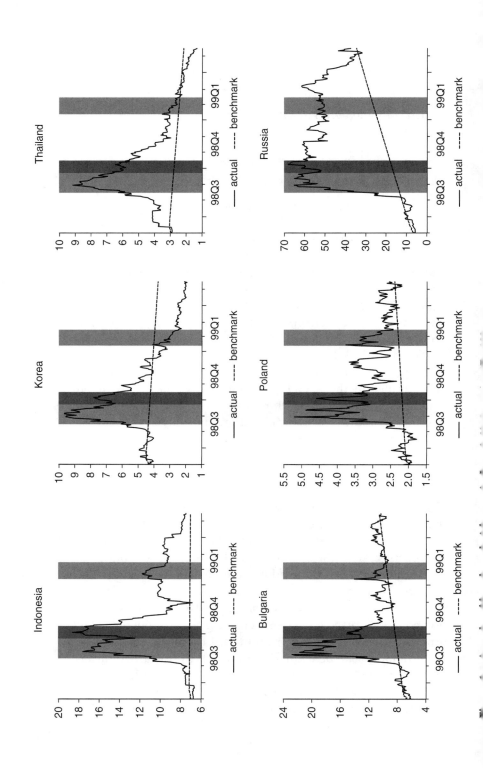

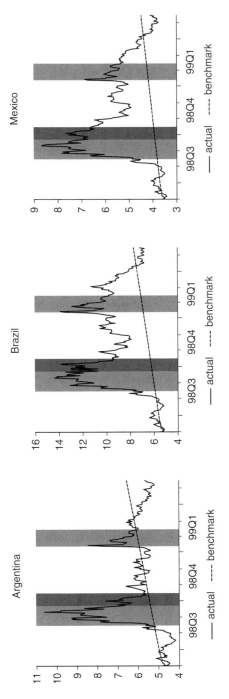

Figure 6.2 (Cont'd)

6.4.2 Global Risk Factor Estimates

The contribution of the innovations of the global risk factors to the bond risk premia of the emerging countries during the financial crisis periods are presented in figure 6.3 with summary estimates given in table 6.4.

Figure 6.3 shows that of the three global risk factors, credit risk has the largest contribution to bond risk premia. This is especially true in Russia and the Latin American countries during the period preceding the Brazilian crisis. The importance of credit risk rises sharply during the Russian crisis for all countries, with the largest effect occurring in Russia where the contribution to Russian bond spreads is about 20%. The effect of credit risk is maintained during the LTCM crisis and approximately for another two months after this crisis. The relative importance of credit risk beginning with the Russian crisis gives credence to the claim that the Russian crisis was a crisis of credit.

The contribution of credit risk to bond risk premia trends downwards for the remainder of the sample period, dipping below trend during the Brazilian crisis. During this crisis all the global risk factors tend to have similar impacts on the bond risk premia. From table 6.4, the average contribution of these factors during the Brazilian crisis is between 0.35% and 0.48% for Argentina, between 0.57% and 0.70% for Brazil, and between 0.26% and 0.36% for Mexico.

Figure 6.3 also shows that the importance of volatility risk to bond risk premia began much earlier than that of the other global risk factors. This rise began closer to the beginning of the historical decomposition period, suggesting early signs of the forthcoming crisis in Russia.

Liquidity risk rose sharply during the Russian crisis for all countries, with the exception of Indonesia. Having obtained a new higher level during the Russian crisis, the liquidity risk factor remains relatively high during the historical decomposition period, and does not substantially decline until after the Brazilian crisis. Liquidity risk is the least likely of the identified risk factors to account for a substantial portion of the decomposition of the risk premia for all but the Latin American countries, where it is often marginally more important than volatility risk.

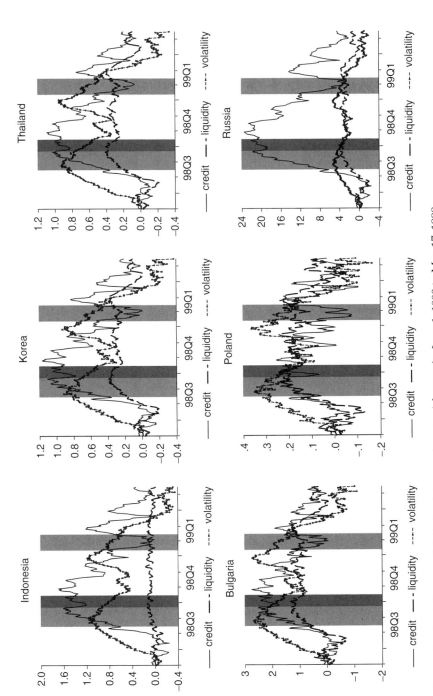

Figure 6.3 Contribution of global risk innovations to risk premia, June 1, 1998 to May 17, 1999.

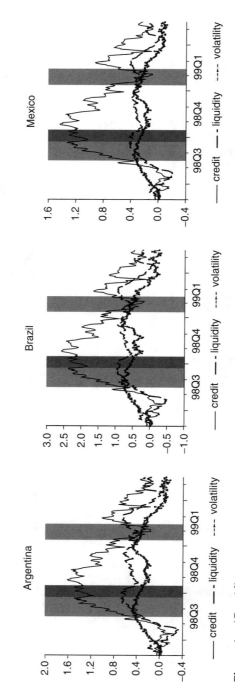

Figure 6.3 (Cont'd)

Table 6.4

Decomposition of risk premia in terms of risk factors (percent. p.a.).

Crisis	Act.	Bench	Cred.	Liq.	Vol.	Ctry	Asia	Eur.	Lat
				Indonesia					
Russian	15.03	7.12	1.21	0.07	1.05	5.71	−0.08	−0.03	−0.02
LTCM	16.56	7.11	1.38	0.10	0.81	7.05	0.09	0.09	−0.08
Brazilian	11.29	7.08	0.32	0.08	0.83	3.07	−0.05	−0.05	0.01
				Korea					
Russian	8.12	4.32	0.82	0.30	0.80	1.83	−0.04	−0.01	0.10
LTCM	7.01	4.25	0.93	0.34	0.61	0.66	0.10	0.07	0.04
Brazilian	3.34	4.01	0.21	0.28	0.63	−1.77	−0.03	−0.02	0.04
				Thailand					
Russian	7.69	2.84	0.75	0.32	0.85	2.90	−0.04	0.02	0.05
LTCM	6.13	2.76	0.92	0.36	0.64	1.31	0.08	0.02	0.04
Brazilian	3.01	2.46	0.27	0.29	0.67	−0.66	−0.04	0.01	0.01
				Bulgaria					
Russian	18.50	8.01	1.85	1.02	2.36	4.87	0.04	−0.04	0.38
LTCM	13.56	8.31	2.12	1.12	1.77	−0.42	0.11	0.21	0.32
Brazilian	11.23	9.41	0.50	0.93	1.84	−1.61	0.14	0.00	0.01
				Poland					
Russian	3.69	2.15	0.18	0.18	0.30	0.77	0.02	0.00	0.09
LTCM	3.57	2.18	0.16	0.20	0.22	0.73	0.03	−0.01	0.06
Brazilian	3.29	2.28	−0.01	0.16	0.23	0.66	−0.01	−0.02	−0.01
				Russia					
Russian	55.19	14.76	15.35	2.92	4.73	18.28	0.14	−0.66	−0.33
LTCM	59.89	17.15	20.21	3.30	3.60	14.40	1.02	0.02	0.19
Brazilian	51.45	25.71	6.96	2.71	3.76	12.75	0.58	−0.53	−0.50
				Argentina					
Russian	8.07	5.30	1.04	0.52	0.43	0.63	0.00	−0.03	0.19
LTCM	6.48	5.45	1.35	0.58	0.34	−1.35	0.13	0.08	−0.09
Brazilian	7.04	6.00	0.44	0.48	0.35	−0.52	0.06	0.00	0.24
				Brazil					
Russian	11.67	6.02	1.71	0.76	0.72	2.35	−0.01	−0.02	0.13
LTCM	11.52	6.22	2.13	0.84	0.54	1.53	0.12	0.01	0.12
Brazilian	11.78	6.94	0.64	0.70	0.57	2.98	0.06	−0.04	−0.08
				Mexico					
Russian	7.06	3.86	0.95	0.33	0.32	1.65	−0.03	0.00	0.00
LTCM	6.97	3.93	1.19	0.37	0.25	1.11	0.07	0.01	0.04
Brazilian	5.95	4.20	0.36	0.30	0.26	0.88	0.02	−0.03	−0.04

6.4.3 Country Risk Factor Estimates

The contribution of innovations to country risk to the risk premia of the nine countries during the financial crisis period are presented in figure 6.4, with summary estimates given in table 6.4. A comparison of the country risk innovations with the actual risk premia in figure 6.4, highlights the importance of idiosyncratic country risks in pricing for all assets. It is interesting to note that the fall in country risk after the Russian crisis reduces spreads for Korea and Thailand, indicating that credit concerns of these two countries become less of an issue compared to the pre-crisis period.

6.4.4 Contagion Risk Factor Estimates

The contributions of contagion risk to the risk premia are summarized in the last three columns of table 6.4, which breakdown the contagion effects originating from each region. A comparison of these estimates with the global risk estimates and country risk estimates shows that contagion has a relatively small effect on risk premia during the three crisis periods. This result is consistent with the early empirical results of Forbes and Rigobon (2002), who found little evidence for the existence of contagion for a broad range of asset markets across a number of financial crises.

6.5 Conclusions

This chapter has identified and quantified the effects of changes in global risks on the risk premia of sovereign bonds issued by emerging markets. Three measures of global risk were used consisting of credit, liquidity, and volatility risk. Additional risks in the form of country and contagion factors were also identified.

The approach consisted of developing a theoretical framework to price risk using the stochastic discount factor model. This yielded a multifactor asset pricing model, which resulted in a set of restrictions being imposed on the long-run dynamics of a SVAR model. The model was applied to analyzing the daily movements in the bond spreads of nine emerging markets from Asia, Eastern Europe, and Latin America, from 1998 to 1999,

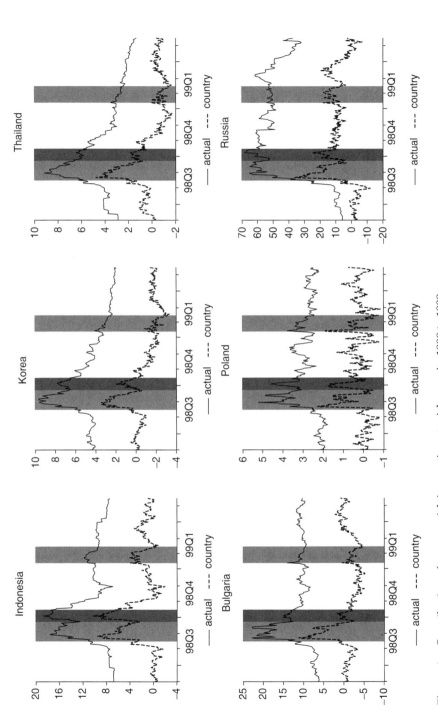

Figure 6.4 Contribution of country risk innovations to risk premia, 1998 to 1999.

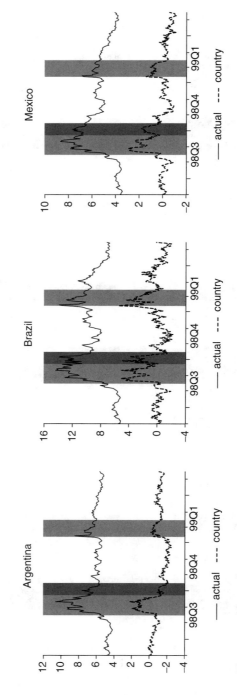

Figure 6.4 (Cont'd)

a period containing the Russian, LTCM, and Brazilian crises. The three global risk variables were based on the JP Morgan indices of risk, while the country and contagion risks were identified and incorporated into the SVAR using long-run restrictions.

The empirical results suggested that different characterizations of global risk patterns were at play during the recent the financial crises analyzed in this chapter. The Russian and LTCM crises were characterized by increases in the price of risk of all three global risk factors. The results of the Brazilian crisis were different however, where the only significant increase in the price of global risk came from credit risk.

All bond markets experienced increases in country risk prices during the Russian crisis, which were sustained during the LTCM crisis, whereas it was just the Latin American and Russian bond markets that incurred increases in the price of country risk during the Brazilian crisis. In contrast, contagion was found to have a smaller effect on bond spreads than the global and country measures of risk during all three financial crises.

Within the set of global risk factors investigated, credit risk was on average the most important contributor to bond spreads over the period investigated. Credit risk was dominant particularly during the Russian crisis, consistent with the view that this period could be viewed as a global credit risk shock. However, the relative importance of credit risk during the Brazilian crisis diminished, where its role was comparable in magnitude to liquidity and volatility risk. Liquidity risk was the least important of the three risk factors.

The results of this chapter are completely consistent with those presented in Chapter 3 for the investigation of the Russian and LTCM crisis periods in bond markets. In Chapter 3, a decomposition of the volatility of the spread between emerging market sovereign bonds and the commensurate U.S. Treasury rate was shown to have a significant but small component due to contagion effects. Most of these effects were under 10%of the volatility observed in the crisis. In Chapter 6, the contagion effects are also small, and in some cases, such as Brazil, smaller than those estimated in Chapter 3. The overall conclusion is the same. However, it should be borne in mind that when the modeling framework was extended to multiple crises with multiple asset markets in Chapter 5, the total effect of contagion on the bond market during the Russian, LTCM, and Brazilian crises was a considerably larger proportion of total volatility, see table 5 of Chapter 5, pointing to the importance of allowing for these extended linkages in assessing contagion. Extending the analysis of Chapter 6 on risk market factors to allow for cross-market linkages is, in the current context relatively difficult, due to data limitations. However, the single market application provides a valuable insight into the time-varying nature of contagion risk and confirms the outcomes from the previous latent factor model frameworks of previous chapters. As with these earlier chapters, the policy implication is that while contagion is a discernible risk factor in financial markets, it is not always the dominant effect during crises, and this should be taken into account in policy design.

6.A Data Definitions and Sources

The sample period is from February 12, 1998, to May 17, 1999, for a total of 328 observations. Data definitions and sources are given in table 6.5.

The risk premia are constructed from a representative long-term emerging bond (rather than Brady bonds) issued in U.S. dollars less a U.S. Treasury bond of comparable country sovereign maturity. Missing observations are replaced with the previous day's observation.

The JP Morgan risk components are expressed as indices. A cumulative distribution function is applied to the raw data, and each observation is then expressed as a percentile of the distribution function such that higher risk is associated with higher percentiles. The indices are the average of these transformed data. See JP Morgan (1999) and JP Morgan Chase Bank (2002).

6.B Crisis Dates

The Russian crisis begins on August 17 corresponding to the announcement of its bond default and ends on September 23, 1998, with the announcement of the orchestrated rescue plan for the hedge fund LTCM, which marks the start of the LTCM crisis. The end of the LTCM crisis corresponds to the

Table 6.5
Data Definitions and Sources.

Variable	Description	Source
Bonds		
Indonesia	Indonesian Yankee bond	US Fed.
Korea	Government of Korea 87/8% 4/2008 bond	US Fed.
Thailand	Kingdom of Thailand Yankee bond	US Fed.
Bulgaria	Bulgarian Discount Stripped Brady bond	US Fed.
Poland	Poland Par Stripped Brady bond	US Fed.
Russia	Government of Russia 9.25% 11/2001 bond	Bloomberg (007149662)
Argentina	Republic of Argentina bond	US Fed.
Brazil	Republic of Brazil bond	US Fed.
Mexico	JP Morgan Eurobond Index Mexico Sovereign bond	US Fed.
Credit	US Industrial BBB1 corporate 10-year bond spread over the US Treasury bond of	Bloomberg (IN10Y3B1)
Liquidity	comparable maturity JP Morgan Chase Bank's (LCVI) liquidity index. 0 = low risk, 100 = high risk, log. Components are: (a) US Treasury yield spreads of benchmark and off-the-run bonds for different maturities; (b) 10-year US swap spreads.	JP Morgan Chase Bank
Volatility	JP Morgan Chase Bank's (LCVI) volatility 0index. = low, 100 = high risk, log. Components are: (a) implied 12-risk, month foreign exchange volatility for six currencies (EUR,JPY, CHF, GBP,CAD, AUD against the USD); (b) implied equity volatility based on option markets on the Chicago Board of Options Exchange; (c) JP Morgan Global Risk Appetite Index (GRAI) based on measures of correlation between the rank of the $ returns of 15 currencies of the past two months, and (d) the rank of risk measured by historical yield.	JP Morgan Chase Bank

inter-FOMC Fed interest rate cut on October 15, 1998, consistent with the findings of the Committee on the Global Financial System, 1999. The Brazilian crisis is dated to begin January 13, 1999, with the effective devaluation of the Real and ends February 2, 1999, to give a crisis duration of two weeks.

7

Conclusions

The existence of contagion has important implications for participants in financial markets and, as seen in the global financial crisis that began in 2007, for all participants in the world economic system. If financial crises spread by well-understood routes between asset markets and countries, then regulating and managing the spread should be a matter for policy design and portfolio management. However, if the links between financial markets are found to change in unpredictable ways during periods of crisis, the task for all stakeholders becomes far more difficult. The phenomenon of contagion is defined as additional linkages that occur during a financial crisis — either in addition to existing links or as a reduction or breakdown of existing links. This book has aimed to throw light on the existence of contagion and, more importantly, to measure and characterize contagion effects during recent financial crises. The ultimate task is to find whether there are any consistencies about contagion across crises that can be used to reduce uncertainty about the spread of financial crises, and to help plan regulatory structures and inform portfolio and financial system management.

As an illustration of the difficulties facing participants in, and regulators of, the financial system, Chapter 2 applied a set of different contagion tests developed in the literature to a common data set pertaining to the crisis beginning in Hong Kong in 1997. The results were a confusing set of mixed outcomes. Some tests found no evidence of contagion at all; others found contagion in almost all combinations of markets. The modelling framework presented in this book showed how to reconcile these different tests and results. Placing the competing tests in a common latent factor modelling framework showed how the different tests used information to detect contagion. It was apparent that even though the tests may use the same data set, they access the information differently, and indeed some tests were found to be biased. This exercise also led to the development of a generalized multivariate form of the popular bivariate Forbes and Rigobon (2002) correlation test.

Having established the latent factor model as an overarching framework for contagion testing in Chapter 2, the next part of the book examined particular crisis incidents in more detail. In particular the suspension of payment of Russian government debt in August 1998 and the near collapse of the U.S.-based hedge fund Long Term Capital Management in September 1998 provided two trigger points for a crisis, that until the recent crisis were the most serious global systemic threat since the collapse of Bretton-Woods. By examining this period in some detail, we both provided some answers to specific questions about that crisis, and provoked some more general questions for the remainder of the book.

At the time of the Russian and LTCM crises a great deal of attention by policy makers was focussed on the seemingly regional nature of crises, and their apparent predominance in developing financial markets. For example, during and after the East Asian financial crisis of 1997–1998 there were calls for an Asian Monetary Union and Asian reserve funds to alleviate future problems in the region. By measuring the extent of contagion in this crisis it became obvious that contagion effects were in fact apparent in all financial markets, including developed markets, a factor which has been borne out in the the crisis that began in 2007. There was also evidence for transmission supported by regional proximity and intertwined banking relationships. In the recent context the role of banking relationships has extended to international linkages, the role of cross jurisdiction supervision, and regulatory structure and new modelling approaches based on network theory.

Examination of the effects of these crises in bond markets in Chapter 3 and equity markets in Chapter 4 showed the substantial difference in crisis transmission in the genres of asset markets. Contagion in bond markets was important in the Russian crisis, while it was equity markets that were affected in the LTCM crisis. The linkages between the different countries examined differed in importance across the two assets classes.

Combining a single model of linkages between different asset markets across a range of geographical locations provided a unique examination of cross-country, cross-asset market linkages in multiple crises, and deepens the existing empirical literature on crises. The latent factor model was shown to relate directly to the theoretical underpinnings of Kodres and Pritsker (2002) — for the first time effectively linking the theoretical and empirical contagion literatures. In such a cross-market, cross-border model, the contagion effects could be refined into three channels: those emanating from shocks associated with a particular asset class (the market channel), those originating with shocks associated with a particular country (country channel), and shocks that were identified with a particular asset in a particular country (idiosyncratic channel). The responses of policy makers to each of these channels should clearly differ. Market-based channels, for example, may point to a need for microstructure reform at an international level, whereas country-specific channels indicate a need for domestic policy reforms. The coherence of the framework was demonstrated by applying the unified model to five separate financial crises covering six countries and two asset markets (bonds and equities) and being able to draw out a number of regularities. The most important of these was that all the channels of contagion identified in the model were present and statistically significant in each and every crisis event examined, but that the relative importance of the contagion links varied over the different crises. This result has very strong implications in that it suggests that information about the types of transmission dominant in a crisis exists in the data and that early recognition of which channel of contagion is dominant will assist in appropriate responses by policy makers, regulators, and investors. It also suggests that policy makers need a strong armory of policy tools to respond to different contagion effects. For example, the banning of short sales in 2008 could be viewed as a response to a market channel contagion effect, while short-term capital controls may be a method of decoupling a country channel.

It is important to retain perspective on the contributions of contagion to overall volatility. Throughout the book the chapters have shown that contagion effects were often dominated by common global effects or country effects. To illustrate the importance of this observation to market participants, Chapter 6 examines the problem from the perspective of risks facing the investor. Risk preference theory was used to decompose returns into risk factors representing credit, liquidity, and volatility risks, country risk, and contagion risk. Returning to the empirical example of the Russian and LTCM crises of Chapters 3 and 4, with the addition of the Brazilian crisis period in 1999, each of the risk factors was shown to be important in explaining the widening of credit spreads in bond markets during this period. However, contagion effects were notably smaller than the combination of the other risk factors.

In summary the work in this book provided empirical support via a broad framework for some general features of the transmission of financial crises. Some of these were clearly evident in the current global financial crisis, but had been at least partially dismissed in prior discussions focussed on pervious crises. Based on the results presented in this book, the summary list of outcomes is given as follows:

1. Contagion, defined as additional linkages, is generally a statistically significant feature of all financial crises and as such warrants the attention of policy makers.

2. Contagion may originate and transmit via a number of different channels: across different assets, across different countries, and from specific assets in a specific country to other specific assets (known respectively as the market channel, country channel, and idiosyncratic channel of contagion). A range of policy tools will be required to combat different channels of contagion effects.

3. Each of the market, country, and idiosyncratic channels of contagion is present and statistically significant in all crises investigated.

4. The weight on each channel of contagion varies by the specific crisis, and hence it seems important for policy

makers to retain a degree of discretion to implement appropriate tools expeditiously as crises unfold.

5. General market conditions often dominated contagion effects: The role of common factors can easily dominate the new channels of contagion, which despite the requirement for discretionary control suggested in point 4, strongly supports the need for a coordinated international approach to monitoring and regulating financial market activity.

6. The risk facing investors is smaller from contagion effects than other aspects of market risk.

7. Contagion effects can be transmitted via banking linkages and other financial networks, strongly supporting the urgency of clarifying and determining forms for dealing with cross-jurisdiction supervision and regulatory structures in a coordinated approach that should be linked to coordinated monitoring as suggested in point 5.

8. Sound economic fundamentals improve the ability of an economy to weather and mitigate contagion.

The work presented here strongly suggests that the evidence for the existence of contagion linkages is present in all crises, but the dominance of one form in a particular crisis can mask the dangers inherent in others. For example, the role of the banking sector in transmitting the Russian crisis was documented, but that did not alert the financial system to the fragility of banking networks in advance of the U.S. subprime crisis sufficiently to promote policy action to correct it.

Although all of the key modern financial crises are to some extent different, they too share fundamental similarities. These differences are largely based on the magnitude of additional linkages and differences in the specific channels for transmission. The framework presented in this book is to quantify these differences. The results strongly support the importance of establishing an international approach to regulation and crisis prevention, while also emphasizing that policy makers and regulators require a number of contingency plans to cover a great number of potential scenarios in crises. Policymakers also require discretion over their actions in order to implement the appropriate plan for crisis management as a crisis unfolds and reveals its particular nature. Regulation to prevent the occurrence of crises is never likely to be fully successful without stifling the creativity of credit creation upon which the current world economy relies or creating new regulatory arbitrage schemes. However, policies and regulation that encourage and promote sound economic fundamentals and sound financial networks will help to reduce the risk of common shocks, which dominate contagion effects in the risks facing the financial system. The important requirement for policy makers with respect to contagion effects is to be able to respond swiftly, with an appropriate plan, to the revealed characteristics of a particular crisis incident. The next step in the agenda to mitigate and manage the effect of contagion is to develop means of recognizing the active links of contagion in a timely and accurate manner, and therefore contain systemic risks.

Bibliography

Allen, F., and D. Gale. 2000. Financial contagion. *Journal of Political Economy* 108: 1–33.

Bae, K.H., G.A. Karolyi, and R.M. Stulz. 2003. A new approach to measuring financial contagion. *Review of Financial Studies* 16: 717–763.

Baig, T., and I. Goldfajn. 1999. Financial market contagion in the Asian Crisis. *International Monetary Fund Staff Papers*, June 46: 167–195.

Baig, T., and I. Goldfajn. 2001. The Russian default and the contagion to Brazil. In *International Financial Contagion*, ed. S. Claessens and K. Forbes, 267–300. Boston: Kluwer Academic Press.

Bayoumi, T., G. Fazio, M. Kumar, and R. MacDonald. 2003. Fatal attraction: A new measure of contagion. IMF Working Paper WP/03/80.

Bekaert, G. and R. Hodrick. 1992. Characterizing predictable components in excess returns on equity and foreign exchange markets. *Journal of Finance* 47: 467–510.

Bekaert, G., E. Engstrom, and S.R. Grenadier. 2006. Stock and bond returns with Moody Investors. NBER Working Paper # W12248.

Bekaert, G., E. Engstrom, and Y. Xing. 2006. Risk, uncertainty and asset prices. NBER Working Paper #W12248.

Bekaert, G., C.R. Harvey, and A. Ng. 2005. Market integration and contagion. *Journal of Business* 78: 39–69.

Blanchard, O. and D. Quah. 1989. The dynamic effects of aggregate demand and supply disturbances. *American Economic Review* 79: 655–673.

Bollerslev, T., R.Y. Chou, and K.F. Kroner. 1992. ARCH modeling in finance: A review of the theory and empirical evidence. *Journal of Econometrics* 52: 5–59.

Bollerslev, T., R.F. Engle, and D.B. Nelson. 1994. ARCH models. In *Handbook of Econometrics*, Vol. 4, ed. R.F. Engle and D. McFadden, Ch. 49. Amsterdam: Elsevier.

Bollerslev, T., M. Gibson, and H. Zhou. 2009. Dynamic estimation of volatility risk and investor risk aversion from option implied and realized volatilities. *Journal of Econometrics*, in press.

Boyer, B.H., M.S. Gibson, and M. Loretan. 1999. Pitfalls in tests for changes in correlations. Federal Reserve Board, International Finance Division, Working Paper 597R.

Boyer, B.H., T. Kumagai, and K. Yuan. 2006. How do crises spread? Evidence from accessible and inaccessible stock indices. *Journal of Finance* 61: 957–1004.

Brunnermeier, M., A. Crockett, C. Goodhart, A. Persaud, and H. Shin. 2009. The fundamental principles of financial regulation. Geneva reports on the world economy, 11, ICMB and CEPR.

Burger, J.D., and F.E. Warnock. 2003. Diversification, original sin, and international bond portfolios. International Finance Discussion Paper 755, Board of Governors of Federal Reserve, USA.

Butler, K.C., and D.C. Joaquin. 2002. Are the gains from international portfolio diversification exaggerated? The influence of downside risk in bear markets? *Journal of International Money and Finance* 21: 981–1011.

Calvo, G.A., and E.G. Mendoza. 2000. Rational contagion and the globalization of securities markets. *Journal of International Economics* 51: 79–113.

Campbell, J. 1996. Understanding risk and return. *Journal of Political Economy* 104: 298–345.

Campbell, J., A.W. Lo, and A.C. MacKinlay. 1997. *The econometrics of financial markets*. Princeton, NJ: Princeton University Press.

Caporale, G.M., A. Cipollini, and N. Spagnolo. 2002. Testing for contagion: A conditional correlation analysis. *Journal of Empirical Finance* 12: 476–489.

Chernov, M.E., A.R. Gallant, E. Ghysels, and G. Tauchen. 2003. Alternative models for stock price dynamics. *Journal of Econometrics* 116: 225–257.

Chue, T.K. 2002. Time varying risk preferences and emerging market covariances. *Journal of International Money and Finance* 21: 1053–1072.

Cifarelli, G., and G. Paladino. 2004. The impact of the Argentine default on volatility co-movements in emerging bond markets. *Emerging Markets Review* 5: 427–446.

Cizeau, P., M. Potters, and J. Bouchard. 2001. Correlation structure of extreme stock returns. *Quantitative Finance* 1: 217–222.

Cochrane, J., and M. Piazzesi. 2005. Bond Risk Premia. *The American Economic Review* 95: 138–160.

Committee on the Global Financial System. 1999. Bank for International Settlements. A review of financial market events in autumn 1998. Basel, Switzerland, October.

Corsetti, G., M. Pericoli, and M. Sbracia. 2001. Correlation analysis of financial contagion: What one should know before running a test. *Yale Economic Growth Center Discussion Paper* No. 822.

Corsetti, G., M. Pericoli, and M. Sbracia. 2005. Some contagion, some interdependence: More pitfalls in tests of financial contagion. *Journal of International Money and Finance* 24: 1177–1199.

Craine, R. and V.L. Martin. 2008. International monetary policy surprise spillovers. *Journal of International Economics* 75: 180–196.

Del Torre, A., E.L. Yeyati, and S. Schmulker. 2003. Living and dying with hard pegs: The rise and fall of Argentina's currency board. *Economia*, Spring, 43–107.

Diebold, F.X., and M. Nerlove. 1989. The dynamics of exchange rate volatility: A multivariate latent-factor ARCH model. *Journal of Applied Econometrics* 4: 1–22.

Dooley, M.P. 2000. A model of crises in emerging markets. *Economic Journal* 110: 256–272.

Dornbusch, R., Y.C. Park, and S. Claessens. 2000. Contagion: Understanding how it spreads. *The World Bank Research Observer* 15: 177–197.

Duffie, D., and K. Singleton. 1993. Simulated moments estimator of Markov models of asset prices. *Econometrica* 61: 929–962.

Dumas, B., and B. Solnik. 1995. The world price of foreign exchange risk. *Journal of Finance* 50: 445–479.

Dungey, M., and V.L. Martin. 2004. A multifactor model of exchange rates with unanticipated shocks: Measuring contagion in the East Asian currency crisis. *Journal of Emerging Markets Finance* 3: 305–330.

Dungey, M., and V.L. Martin. 2007. Unravelling financial market linkages during crises. *Journal of Applied Econometrics* 22: 89–119.

Dungey, M., and D. Zhumabekova. 2001. Testing for contagion using correlations: Some words of caution. Federal Reserve Bank of San Francisco, Pacific Basin Working Paper PB01–09.

Dungey, M., R.A. Fry, and V.L. Martin. 2003. Equity transmission mechanisms from Asia to Australia: Interdependence or contagion? *Australian Journal of Management* 28: 157–182.

Dungey, M., R.A. Fry, B. González-Hermosillo, and V.L. Martin. 2002a. The transmission of contagion in developed and developing international bond markets. In *Risk Measurement and Systemic Risk*, ed. Committee on the Global Financial System, 61–74. Third Joint Central Bank Research Conference.

Dungey, M., R.A. Fry, B. González-Hermosillo, and V.L. Martin. 2002b. International Contagion effects from the Russian crisis and the LTCM near collapse. IMF Working Paper WP/02/74.

Dungey, M., R.A. Fry, B. González-Hermosillo, and V.L. Martin. 2003a. Characterizing global investors' risk appetite for emerging market debt during financial crises. IMF Working Paper WP/03/251.

Dungey, M., R.A. Fry, B. González-Hermosillo, and V.L. Martin. 2003b. Unanticipated shocks and systemic influences: The impact of contagion in global equity markets in 1998. IMF Working Paper WP/03/84.

Dungey, M., R.A. Fry, B. González-Hermosillo, and V.L. Martin. 2005a. A comparison of alternative tests of contagion with applications. In *Identifying International Financial Contagion: Progress and Challenges*, ed. M. Dungey and D. Tambakis. New York: Oxford University Press.

Dungey, M., R.A. Fry, B. González-Hermosillo, and V.L. Martin. 2005b. Empirical modelling of contagion: A review of methodologies. *Quantitative Finance* 5: 9–24.

Dungey, M., R.A. Fry, B. González-Hermosillo, and V.L. Martin. 2006. Contagion in international bond markets during the Russian and LTCM crises. *Journal of Financial Stability* 2: 1–27.

Dungey, M., R.A. Fry, B. González-Hermosillo, and V.L. Martin. 2007. Contagion in global equity markets in 1998: The effects of the Russian and LTCM crises. *North American Journal of Economics and Finance* 18: 155–174.

Dungey, M., V.L Martin, and A.R. Pagan. 2000. A Multivariate latent factor decomposition of international bond yield spreads. *Journal of Applied Econometrics* 15: 697–715.

Dungey, M., G. Milunovich, and S. Thorp. 2009. Unobservable shocks as carriers of contagion: A dynamic analysis using identified structural GARCH. *Journal of Banking and Finance*: in press.

Dungey, M., R.A. Fry, B. González-Hermosillo, V.L. Martin and C. Tang. 2010. Are financial crises alike? From the 1998 Russian/LTCM crisis to the 2007 subprime debacle and liquidity crisis. IMF Working Paper No. 10/14.

Durbin, J.M. 1954. Errors in Variables. *Review of the International Statistical Institute* 22: 23–32.

Edwards, S. 2000. Interest rates, contagion and capital controls. NBER Working Paper 7801.

Ehrmann, M., M. Fratzscher, and R. Rigobon. 2005. Stocks, bonds, money markets and exchange rates: Measuring international financial transmission. ECB Working Paper 452.

Eichengreen, B., A.K. Rose, and C. Wyplosz. 1995. Exchange market mayhem: The antecedents and aftermath of speculative attacks. *Economic Policy* 21: 249–312.

Eichengreen, B., A.K. Rose, and C. Wyplosz. 1996. Contagious currency crises. NBER Working Paper 5681.

Ellis, L. and E. Lewis. 2000. The response of financial markets in Australia and New Zealand to news about the Asian crisis. Paper presented at the BIS Conference on International Financial Markets and the Implications for Monetary and Financial Stability, Basle, October 25–26 , 1999, Vol. 8.

EMTA Survey. 2007. Emerging markets debt trading. August. Published by the Emerging Markets Traders Association, http://www.emta.org/.

Engle R.F. 2009. *Anticipating correlations*. Princeton, NJ: Princeton University Press.

Engle, R.F. and K.F. Kroner. 1995. Multivariate simultaneous generalized ARCH. *Econometric Theory* 11: 122–150.

Engle R.F., T. Ito, and W. Lin. 1990. Meteor showers or heat waves? Heteroskedastic Intra-Daily Volatility in the Foreign Exchange Market. *Econometrica* 58: 525–542.

Favero, C.A. and F. Giavazzi. 2002. Is the international propagation of financial shocks non-linear? Evidence from the ERM. *Journal of International Economics* 57: 231–246.

Fiorentini, G., E. Sentana, and N. Shephard. 2004. Likelihood-based estimation of latent generalized ARCH structures. *Econometrica* 72: 1481–1517.

Fitch Ratings. 2007a. Russian bank liquidity: CBR support is positive, but more may be needed. October.

Fitch Ratings. 2007b. Russian federation special report – premium. October.

Flood, R. and N. Marion. 1999. Perspectives on the recent currency crisis literature. *International Journal of Finance and Economics* 4: 1–26.

Flood, R.P. and A.K. Rose. 2004. Equity integration in times of crisis. In *Market discipline across countries and industries*, ed. C. Borio, W.C. Hunter, G.G. Kaufman, and K. Tsatsaronis, 211–224. Boston: The MIT Press.

Forbes, K. and R. Rigobon. 2001. Measuring contagion, conceptual and empirical issues. In *International Financial Contagion*, ed. S. Claessens and K. Forbes. Boston: Kluwer Academic Publishers.

Forbes, K. and R. Rigobon. 2002. No contagion, Only interdependence: Measuring stock market co-movements. *Journal of Finance* 57: 2223–2261.

Gallant, A.R. and G. Tauchen. 1996. Which moments to match? *Econometric Theory*, October, 12: 657–681.

Glick, R. and A.K. Rose. 1999. Contagion and trade: Why are currency crises regional? *Journal of International Money and Finance* 18: 603–617.

Goldfajn, I. 2003. The swings of capital flows and the Brazilian crisis. In *International capital flows in calm and turbulent times: The need for new international architecture*, ed. S. Griffith-Jones, R. Gottschalk, and J. Cailloux, 267–290. Ann Arbor: Michigan University Press.

Goldstein, M. 1998. The Asian financial crisis: Causes, cures and systemic implications. Policy Analysis in International Economics 55, Washington DC: Institute for International Economics.

Goldstein, M., G.L. Kaminsky, and C.M. Reinhart. 2000. *Assessing financial vulnerability: An early warning system for emerging markets*. Washington DC: Institute for International Economics.

González-Hermosillo, B. 2008. The role of international investors' risk appetite in global financial market crises: 1998–2007. IMF Working Paper WP/08/85.

González-Hermosillo, B. and J. Li. 2008. A banking firm model: The role of market, liquidity and credit risks. In *Computational methods in financial engineering*, ed. E.J. Kontoghiorghers, B. Rustem, and P. Winker, 259–272, Berlin Heidelberg: Springer Press.

Goodhart, C. and L. Dai. 2003. *Intervention to save Hong Kong: Counter-Speculation in financial markets*. Oxford: Oxford University Press.

Gourieroux, C. and A. Monfort. 1994. Simulation based econometric methods, CORE Discussion paper.

Gourieroux, C., A. Monfort, and E. Renault. 1993. Indirect inference. *Journal of Applied Econometrics* 8, 85–118.

Granger, C., B. Huang, and C. Yang. 2000. A bivariate causality between stock prices and exchange rates: Evidence from recent Asian flu. *The Quarterly Review of Economics and Finance* 40: 337–354.

Greenspan, A. 1999. Risk, liquidity and the economic outlook. *Business Economics*, January: 20–24.

Gregory, A.W. and D.G. Watts. 1995. Sources of variation in international real interest rates. *Canadian Journal of Economics* 28: S120–S140.

Grubel, H.G. and R. Fadner. 1971. The interdependence of international equity markets. *Journal of Finance* 26: 89–94.

Hamilton, J. 1994. *Time series analysis*. Princeton, NJ: Princeton University Press.

Hartmann, P., S. Straetmans, and C.G. de Vries. 2004. Asset market linkages in crisis periods. *Review of Economics and Statistics* 86: 313–326.

Hernandez, L. and R. Valdes. 2001. What drives contagion: Trade, neighborhood, or financial links? *International Review of Financial Analysis* 10: 203–218.

International Monetary Fund. 2003. *Global financial stability report*. Washington DC: International Monetary Fund.

International Monetary Fund. 2005. *Global markets monitor*. Global Markets Analysis Division, Monetary and Capital Markets Department, May 27.

International Monetary Fund. 2007. *Global financial stability report*. Washington DC: International Monetary Fund.

JP Morgan. 1999. Introducing our new liquidity and credit premia update. *Global FX and Precious Metals Research*, New York, August 25.

JP Morgan. 2004. Emerging markets bond index plus (EMBI+) rules and methodology, December.

JP Morgan Chase Bank. 2002. Using equities to trade FX: Introducing the LCVI. *Global Foreign Exchange Research*, New York, October 1.

Jeanne, O., and P. Masson. 2000. Currency crises, sunspots and Markov-switching regimes. *Journal of International Economics* 50: 327–350.

Jorion, P. 2000. Risk management lessons from Long Term Capital Management. *European Financial Management* 6: 277–300.

Kaminsky, G.L. 2006. Currency crises: Are they all the same? *Journal of International Money and Finance* 25: 503–527.

Kaminsky, G.L. and C.M. Reinhart. 2000. On crises, contagion and confusion. *Journal of International Economics* 51: 145–168.

Kaminsky, G.L. and C.M. Reinhart. 2002. Financial markets in times of stress. *Journal of Development Economics* 69: 451–470.

Kaminsky, G.L. and C.M. Reinhart. 2003. The center and the periphery: The globalization of financial turmoil. NBER Working Paper 9479.

Kaminsky, G.L. and S.L. Schmukler. 1999. What triggers market jitters? A chronicle of the Asian crisis. *Journal of International Money and Finance* 18: 537–560.

Karolyi, A. and R. Stulz. 1996. Why do markets move together? An investigation of U.S.-Japan stock return comovements. *Journal of Finance* 51: 951–986.

Kendall, M. and A. Stuart. 1969. *The advanced theory of statistics, Vol. 1.* London: Charles Griffin and Co.

Kendall, M. and A. Stuart. 1973. *The advanced theory of statistics, Vol. 2.* London: Charles Griffin and Co.

Kharas, H., B. Pintos, and S. Ulatov. 2001. An analysis of Russia's 1998 meltdown: Fundamentals and market signals. *Brookings Papers on Economic Activity* 1: 1–68.

King, M. and S. Wadhwani. 1990. Transmission of volatility between stock markets. *Review of Financial Studies* 3: 5–33.

King, M., E. Sentana, and S. Wadhwani. 1994. Volatility and links between national stock markets. *Econometrica* 62: 901–933.

Kiyotaki, N. and J. Moore. 2002. Balance-sheet contagion. *American Economic Review Papers and Proceedings* 92: 46–50.

Kodres, L.E. and M. Pritsker. 2002. A rational expectations model of financial contagion. *Journal of Finance* 57: 768–799.

Kose, A.M., C. Otrok, and C.H. Whiteman. 2003. International Business Cycles: World, region and country-specific factors. *American Economic Review*, September, 93: 1216–1239.

Krueger, A. 2002. Crisis prevention and resolution: Lessons from Argentina. Presented at conference on The Argentina crisis, July, Cambridge. http://www.imf.org/external/np/speeches/2002/071702.htm.

Kruger, M., P.N. Osakwe, and J. Page. 1998. Fundamentals, contagion and currency crises: An empirical analysis. Bank of Canada Working Paper 98–10.

Krugman, P. 1998. What happened to Asia? Mimeo, Massachusetts Institute of Technology.

Kumar, M. and A. Persaud. 2002. Pure contagion and investors' Shifting risk appetite: Analytical issues and empirical evidence. *International Finance* 5: 401–436.

Kyle, A. and W. Xiong 2001. Contagion as a wealth effect. *Journal of Finance* 56: 1401–1440.

Loisel, O. and P. Martin. 2001. Coordination, cooperation, contagion and currency crises. *Journal of International Economics*, April, 53: 399–419.

Longin, F. and B. Solnik. 1995. Is the correlation in international equity returns constant: 1960–1990? *Journal of International Money and Finance* 14: 3–26.

Loretan, M. and W. English. 2000. Evaluating correlation break-downs during periods of market volatility. Board of Governs of the Federal Reserve System, International Finance Discussion Paper No. 658.

Lowell, J., C.R. Neu, and D. Tong. 1998. Financial crises and contagion in emerging market countries. RAND, MR-962.

Lowenstein, R. 2001. *When genius failed. The rise and fall of Long Term Capital Management*. London: Fourth Estate.

Mahieu, R. and P. Schotman. 1994. Neglected common factors in exchange rate volatility. *Journal of Empirical Finance* 1: 279–311.

Malliaroupulos, D. 1997. A multivariate GARCH model of risk premia in foreign exchange markets. *Economic Modelling* 14: 61–79.

Masson, P. 1999a. Contagion: Macroeconomic models with multiple equilibria. *Journal of International Money and Finance* 18: 587–602.

Masson, P. 1999b. Contagion: Monsoonal effects, spillovers, and jumps between multiple equilibria, In *The Asian financial crises: Causes, contagion and consequences*, ed. P.R. Agenor, M. Miller, D. Vines, and A. Weber, 265–283. Cambridge: Cambridge University Press.

Masson, P. 1999c, Multiple equilibria, contagion and the emerging market crises. IMF Working Paper WP/99/164.

Mody, A. and M.P. Taylor. 2003. Common vulnerabilities. CEPR Discussion Paper 3759.

Nelson, C.R. and R. Startz. 1990. The distribution of the instrumental variables estimator and its t-ratio when the instrument is a poor one. *Journal of Business* 63: S125–S140.

Ng, V.K., R.F. Engle, and M. Rothschild. 1992. A multi-dynamic factor model for stock returns. *Journal of Econometrics*, April–May, 52: 245–266.

Pavlova, A. and R. Rigobon. 2007. Asset prices and exchange rates. *Review of Financial Studies* 20: 1139–1180.

Pericoli, M. and M. Sbracia. 2003. A primer on financial contagion. *Journal of Economic Surveys* 17: 571–608.

Pesaran, H. and A. Pick. 2007. Econometric issues in the analysis of contagion. *Journal of Economic Dynamics and Control* 31: 1245–1277.

Piazzesi, M. 2009. Affine term structure models. In *Handbook of Financial Econometrics Vol. 1*, ed. Y. Ait-Sahalia and P.L. Hansen, Ch. 12. North Holland.

Pritsker, M. 2001. The channels for financial contagion. In *International Financial Contagion*, ed. S. Claessens and K. Forbes. New York: Kluwer Academic Publishers.

Radelet, S. and Sachs, J. 1998. The East Asian Financial Crisis: Diagnosis, Remedies, Prospects. *Brookings Papers on Economic Activity* 1: 1–74.

Reside Jr., R.E. and M.S. Gochoco-Bautista. 1999. Contagion and the Asian currency crisis. *The Manchester School* 67: 460–474.

Rigobon, R. 2002. The curse of non-investment grade countries. *Journal of Development Economics* 69: 423–449.

Rigobon, R. 2003a. Identification through heteroskedasticity. *Review of Economics and Statistics* 85: 777–792.

Rigobon, R. 2003b. On the measurement of the international propagation of shocks: Is the transmission stable? *Journal of International Economics* 61: 261–283.

Rigobon, R. and B. Sack. 2004. Measuring the reaction of monetary policy to the stock market. *Quarterly Journal of Economics* 118: 639–669.

Sachs, J., A. Tornell, and A. Velasco. 1996. Financial crises in emerging markets: The lessons from 1995. Brookings Papers on Economic Activity 1: 146–215.

Sentana, E. and G. Fiorentini. 2001. Identification, estimation and testing of conditionally heteroskedastic factor models. *Journal of Econometrics* 102: 143–164.

Sharpe, W. 1964. Capital asset prices: A theory of market equilibrium under conditions of risk. *Journal of Finance* 19: 425–442.

Shirref, D. 1998. The eve of destruction. *Euromoney*, November, 355: 34.

Solnik, B.H. 1974. The international pricing of risk: An empirical investigation of the world capital market structure. *Journal of Finance* 29: 365–378.

Steinherr, A. 2006. Russian banking since the crisis of 1998. *Economic Change and Restructuring* 39: 235–259.

Stock, J.H., J.H. Wright, and M. Yogo. 2002. A survey of weak instruments and weak identification in generalized method of moments. *Journal of Business and Economic Statistics* 20: 518–529.

Toyoda, T. and K. Ohtani. 1986. Testing equality between sets of coefficients after a preliminary test for equality of disturbance variances in two linear regressions. *Journal of Econometrics* 31: 67–80.

Upper, C. 2001. How safe is the "Safe haven"? Financial market liquidity during the 1998 turbulences. *Bank for International Settlement Papers* 2: 241–266.

Upper, C. and T. Werner. 2002. How resilient are financial markets to stress? Bund futures and bonds during the 1998 turbulence. *Bank for International Settlement Papers* 12: 110–123.

Van Rijckeghem, C.V. and B. Weder. 2001. Sources of contagion: Is it finance or trade? *Journal of International Economics* 54: 293–300.

Van Rijckeghem, C.V. and B. Weder. 2003. Spillovers through banking centers: A panel data analysis of bank flows. *Journal of International Money and Finance* 22: 483–509.

Wald, A. 1940. The fitting of straight lines if both variables are subject to error. *Annals of Mathematical Statistics* 11: 284–300.

Wirjanto, T.S. 1999. Empirical indicators of currency crises in East Asia. *Pacific Economic Review*, June, 4: 165–183.

Yuan, K. 2005. Asymmetric price movements and borrowing constraints: A rational expectations equilibrium model of crises, contagion and confusion. *Journal of Finance* 60: 379–411.

Index

Figures and tables are indicated by f and t following page numbers